C000076439

Described by Sir Francis Drake as "the fairest Cape in all the circumference of the earth", the southwestern tip of South Africa has attracted seafarers since the 16th century. Today few people fail to recognize the iconic images of cloud drifting across the flat-top of Table Mountain, whales leaping dramatically out of the Atlantic Ocean, animals wandering across acacia-studded plains, or sweeping wild beaches backed by towering mountains and verdant forests. South Africa is also home to a fascinating mix of cultures and its history is compelling too, from the early hunter-gatherers to the arrival of the Europeans, the Boer War and the more recent breakdown of Apartheid. This is reflected in colonial architecture, lively townships, moving memorials and contemporary museums.

Cape Town, one of the world's favourite cities, features historic monuments, the botanical gardens of Kirstenbosch, the famous Constantia wine estates, and has some of the best eating and shopping opportunities on the African continent.

Beyond Cape Town, the Winelands' old towns of Stellenbosch, Franschhoek and Paarl nestle in a range of low mountains and scenic valleys covered by the vineyards of historic wine estates which have been cultivating grapes for some 300 years.

The southern coast claims to have the best land-based whale watching in the world; in season, sightings are almost guaranteed from the clifftops in Hermanus, while further south the waters around Gansbaai are home to seals, penguins and great white sharks.

To the east, the famous Garden Route is a 200-km stretch of rugged coast backed by mountains, with long stretches of sand, nature reserves, leafy forests and seaside towns. The larger resorts are highly developed for tourism while other areas offer stunning uncrowded beaches, pretty wildernesses and wonderful hikes, and there are various attractions hugging the N2 coast road to distract the motorist.

Planning your trip

Best time to visit Cape Town and the Garden Route

South Africa's Western Cape has a moderate Mediterranean-type climate with long sunny days for most of the year. During summer, from mid-October to mid-February, daytime temperatures seldom dip below 25°C and it rarely gets hotter than 30°C. At this time of year the coast around Cape Town and the Garden Route is at its best, and in the evening there are lingering sunsets over the ocean when the sun sets as late as 2100. However, January and February are the season for a southeasterly wind, which many Capetonians refer to as the 'Cape Doctor' as it blows the pollution off the city. It can get fairly strong and is irritating, so if you're heading to the coast consider the most sheltered beaches.

It is still warm enough to consider a beach holiday until about Easter and during the autumn months of March to June the Winelands look their best as the vines turn an array of gold and brown colours. Most of the rain falls in the winter months of July and August and there are often very heavy storms. It can get cold at night in Cape Town when temperatures rarely top 15°C on a sunny day and fall to around 7°C at night and the interior mountains sometimes get frosts and snowfalls. However, winter is the best time for hiking, avoiding the summer's high temperatures and frequent thunderstorms, and July to November are the best months for whale watching. Nowhere in South Africa is more spectacular than the Western Cape during the spring months of September and October when the grey winter is forgotten and the landscape is covered in an iridescent carpet of wild flowers.

December and January, followed by Easter, are by far the busiest periods for South African domestic tourism in the region. Despite being cooler, July and August are also popular with overseas visitors as they coincide with the European school holidays. Be sure to book your car hire and accommodation well in advance during these times. For further advice on when to go to South Africa, visit www.weathersa.co.za.

Getting to Cape Town and the Garden Route

The three main international airports in **South Africa** are: **OR Tambo International Airport** in Johannesburg, **Cape Town International Airport** in Cape Town, page 21, and **King Shaka International Airport** in Durban. Johannesburg is the regional hub with numerous daily flights to and from Europe, North America, Asia and Australia. Although most flights arrive in Johannesburg, a fair number of international carriers also fly directly to Cape Town, and a couple directly to Durban.

With a huge choice of routes and flights, you need to book well in advance for the best fares, especially over the Christmas and New Year period which is the peak summer holiday season in South Africa.

For live flight information visit the Airport Company of South Africa's website, www.acsa.co.za, T0867-277888, or send an SMS to T38648 with the flight number, in reply to which you'll receive up-to-date flight details.

Jet lag is not an issue if flying from Europe to South Africa as there is only a minimal time difference.

Don't miss...

1 **Table Mountain** Ride the dizzying cable car or hike to the stunning table-top, page 28.
2 **V&A Waterfront** Cape Town's original Victorian harbour is buzzing with entertainment, page 42.
3 **Robben Island** A fascinating and moving museum synonymous with Nelson Mandela, page 46.
4 **Kirstenbosch National Botanical Garden** South Africa's oldest and most beautiful formal gardens, page 49.
5 **The Cape Peninsula** Dramatic mountain scenery, pretty fishing villages and penguins, page 71.
6 **Atlantic Seaboard** Dazzling beaches, palm-fringed promenades and swish restaurants, page 72.
7 **Winelands** World-class wines and gourmet food in historical Cape Dutch estates, page 91.
8 **Whale Coast** Land-based whale watching from an exhilarating coastline, page 118.
9 **Garden Route** A journey past beaches, forests, lagoons and seaside towns, page 131.

Numbers relate to the map on page 4.

Transport in Cape Town and the Garden Route

South Africa has an efficient transport network linking its towns and cities, making travelling the considerable distances a straightforward experience. Affordable domestic flights link the cities, a sophisticated army of private coaches criss-crosses the country, and the train system, although painfully slow, offers another way of getting from A to B. City transport is limited, though, and South Africa's cities generally lack safe and reliable urban public transport. This is improving all the time, however, and new transport systems are being developed at a rapid pace, while existing ones are being upgraded. Nevertheless, having your own transport on a visit to South Africa remains the most flexible option.

Air
There are numerous daily flights linking the cities, and Johannesburg and Durban are no more than two hours' flying time to Cape Town. There are also flights from Johannesburg to George on the Garden Route and Port Elizabeth in the Eastern Cape, the nearest airport to the eastern end of the Garden Route.

Airlines By booking early online, good deals can be found with all the airlines. You can either book directly or through the national booking agency Computicket; online at www.computicket.com, or in South Africa, at any of their kiosks in the shopping malls or any branch of Checkers and Shoprite supermarkets.
   British Airways Comair, T011-441 8600, www.britishairways.com, has daily flights between Johannesburg, Cape Town, Durban, Nelspruit and Port Elizabeth, as well as regional flights between Johannesburg and Mauritius, Windhoek, Livingstone, Victoria Falls and Harare.

Kulula, T0861-585 852 (in South Africa), T011-921 0111 (from overseas), www.kulula.com, also owned by British Airways, is a no-frills airline with daily services between Cape Town, Durban, Johannesburg, Port Elizabeth, Nelspruit, East London and George. They also fly to Mauritius, Maputo, Windhoek, Victoria Falls, Livingstone and Harare on a code-share agreement with BA.

Mango, T0861-162 646 (in South Africa), T011-359 1222 (from overseas), www.flymango.com, another no-frills operator, has daily flights between Johannesburg, Cape Town, Durban, George and Bloemfontein.

South African Airways (**SAA**), T0861-359 722 (in South Africa), T011-978 1111 (from overseas), www.flysaa.com, cover all the country's major centres and have flights to most southern African cities, in conjunction with both their subsidiaries **SA Airlink** and **SA Express**.

Rail

Most of the major cities are linked by rail and, while this is a comfortable and relaxing way to travel, it is very slow. The trains are run by **Shosholoza Meyl**, part of the national network **Spoornet**, T0860-008 888 (in South Africa), T011-774 4555 (from overseas), www.shosholozameyl.co.za. There are services between Johannesburg and Cape Town (27 hours) and Johannesburg and Port Elizabeth (20 hours); timetables and fares can be found on the website. All the trains travel overnight, so they arrive at some stations en route at inconvenient times, but they have dining cars and sleeping carriages with coupés that sleep two or four people.

Spoornet also operate a more upmarket service, the **Premier Classe**, T011-774 5247, www.premierclasse.co.za, between Johannesburg and Cape Town (25 hours), twice a week. A lot nicer than the regular train, the two-bed coupés have extras like dressing gowns, toiletries and 'room service', and there's a good restaurant car serving breakfast, high tea and dinner; fares include all meals. The train has an additional 'spa-car' for pampering, and vehicles can be taken on the trains, which gives the option of taking the train in one direction and driving in the other.

Luxury trains If the journey is more important than the destination, then old-fashioned luxury trains operate much like five-star hotels on wheels. The **Blue Train**, T021-334 8459, www.bluetrain.co.za, is considered to be southern Africa's premier luxury train. The wood-panelled coaches feature luxury coupés with en suite bathrooms, elegant lounge cars and fine dining in the restaurant car. It runs between Johannesburg and Cape Town and takes one day and one night. **Rovos Rail**, T012-315 8242, www.rovos.co.za, is a similar luxury train that runs between Tshwane (Pretoria) and Cape Town. Check out the websites for schedules and prices.

Road

Bus and coach Baz Bus: The Baz Bus (T021-439 2323, www.bazbus.com), a hop-on, hop-off bus that collects and drops off passengers at their chosen backpacker hostel, remains one of the most popular ways of seeing the country on a budget. There are a few exceptions such as Hermanus, where the bus will drop you off at the closest point on the main road, and the hostels will then meet you for an extra charge. The Baz Bus route is **Cape Town–Durban** along the coast, and **Durban–Tshwane (Pretoria)** via the Drakensberg. Tickets are priced per segment, for example from Cape Town to Port Elizabeth, and you can hop on and off as many times as you like in the given segment, but must not backtrack. Visit the website for the full timetable.

Intercity coaches: **Greyhound**, T083-915 9000 (in South Africa), T011-276 8550 (from overseas), www.greyhound.co.za; **Intercape**, T0861-287 287 (in South Africa), T012-380 4400 (from overseas), www.intercape.co.za; and **Translux**, T0861-589 282 (in South Africa), T011-774 3333 (from overseas), www.translux.co.za, are the three major long-distance bus companies that run between towns and popular destinations, and to some cities in South Africa's neighbouring countries. All bus tickets can be booked directly with the companies or through the national booking agency, **Computicket**; online at www.computicket.com, or at any of their kiosks in the shopping malls or any branch of Checkers and Shoprite supermarkets in South Africa. The coaches are air conditioned and have a toilet; some sell refreshments and show videos. They will stop at least every three to four hours to change drivers and give the passengers a chance to stretch their legs. Note that long-distance buses are more than twice as fast as the trains.

Car Hiring a car for part, or all, of your journey is undoubtedly the best way to see South Africa; you get to travel at your own leisurely pace and explore more out-of-the-way regions without being tied to a tour or a timetable. Driving isn't challenging; the roads are generally in excellent condition and, away from the major urban centres, there is little traffic. Fuel is available 24 hours a day at the fuel stations in the cities and along the national highways. Driving is on the left side of the road and speed limits are 60 kph in built-up areas, 80 kph on minor roads and 120 kph on highways.

There is a range of vehicles to choose from, from basic hatchbacks and saloon cars, to camper vans and fully equipped 4WD vehicles. Costs for car hire vary considerably and depend on days of the week, season, type of vehicle and terms (insurance, excess, mileage, etc). A compact car starts from as little as R200-250 per day; a fully equipped 4WD or camper van with tents and equipment from R800-1300 per day.

The minimum age to rent a car is usually 23. A driver's licence (with a translation if it's not in English) and a credit card are essential. Tourist offices usually recommend large international organizations such as **Avis** or **Budget**, but there are a number of reliable local companies and it is worth asking at hotels for recommended local car hire companies. Most of the large companies have kiosks at the airport and partner with the airlines, so it's also possible to book a car online with your flight. For car hire companies see Cape Town Transport, page 69.

In the event of an accident, call your car hire company's emergency number. For emergency breakdown and traffic update information contact the **Automobile Association of South Africa**, T083-84322, www.aa.co.za.

Hitchhiking This is not common in South Africa and is not recommended as it can be very dangerous. Women should never hitch, under any circumstances, even in a group. If you have to hitch, say if your vehicle has broken down, be very wary of who you are accepting a lift from, and a car with a family or couple is usually the best option.

Taxi Except in the major cities there are few taxi ranks in South African towns so it's generally a better idea to order a taxi in advance. Any hotel or restaurant will make a booking for you. Taxis are metered and charge around R11-14 per kilometre. Groups should request a larger vehicle if available as these can carry up to seven people. Some can also accommodate wheelchairs.

Minibus taxi: The majority of South Africa's population travel by minibus taxis and, in many areas, including inner cities, they are the only way of getting around. However, the accident rate of such vehicles is notoriously high, with speeding, overcrowding and lack of maintenance being the main causes. There is also the problem of possible robbery, especially at the taxi ranks, so many visitors and locals are wary of using them.

Nevertheless, minibus taxis remain the cheapest and most extensive form of transport in the country. Many routes have experienced little or no crime, but you should exercise extreme caution and always ask people in the know before using them. In central Cape Town minibus taxis provide an efficient (and relatively safe) means of transport into the city centre from places such as Observatory, Camps Bay, Sea Point, Rondebosch and Claremont.

Where to stay in Cape Town and the Garden Route

South Africa offers a wide variety of accommodation from top-of-the-range five-star hotels, game lodges and tented camps that charge R3000-8000 or more per couple per day, to mid-range safari lodges and hotels with air-conditioned double rooms for R1500-3000, to guesthouse or B&Bs that charge R500-1500 and dormitory beds or camping for under R200 a day. Generally, there are reasonable discounts for children and most places offer family accommodation. Comprehensive accommodation information can be found on the regional tourism websites listed in each area. All accommodation in South Africa is graded a star value by the **Tourism Grading Council of South Africa**, www.tourismgrading.co.za, and the website has comprehensive lists in all categories. There are numerous resources for independently booking accommodation in South Africa; exploring the websites of **AA Travel Guides**, www.aatravel.co.za, **SA-Venues**, www.sa-venues.com, and **Sleeping Out**, www.sleeping-out.co.za, is a good start.

Hotels There are some delightful family-run and country hotels, boutique hotels with stylish interiors in the cities and towns and, for those who enjoy the anonymity of a large hotel, chains like **Sun International**, **Protea** and **City Lodge**. Many of the more upmarket hotels offer additional facilities like spas, golf courses and fine restaurants, which are almost always open to non-guests. Every small town has at least one hotel of two- or three-star standard, and although some tend to be aimed at local business travellers and may be characterless buildings with restaurants serving bland food, they nevertheless represent good value.

Guesthouses Guesthouses can offer some of the most characterful accommodation in South Africa, with interesting places springing up in both cities and small towns. Standards obviously vary enormously; much of what you'll get has to do with the character of the owners and the location of the homes. Some are simple practical overnight rooms, while at the more luxurious end, rooms may be in historic homes filled with antiques. For listings look at the websites of the **Guest House Association of Southern Africa**, www.ghasa.co.za, or the **Portfolio Collection**, www.portfoliocollection.com.

Backpacker hostels Apart from camping, backpacker hostels are the cheapest form of accommodation, and a bed in a dormitory will cost as little as R120 a night. Some also have budget double rooms with or without bathrooms, while others have space to pitch a tent in the garden. You can usually expect a self-catering kitchen, hot showers, a TV/DVD room and internet access. Many hostels also have bars and offer meals or nightly braais, plus a garden and a swimming pool. Most hostels are a good source of travel information and many act as booking agents for bus companies, budget safari tours and car hire. The

Price codes

Where to stay

$$$$	over US$365	**$$$**	US$180-365
$$	US$75-180	**$**	under US$75

Prices refer to the cost of a double room with breakfast, not including service charge or other meals unless otherwise stated. See page 15 for exchange rates.

Restaurants

$$$ over US$40	**$$** US$20-40	**$** under US$20

Prices refer to the cost of a two-course meal for one person including a soft drink, beer or glass of wine.

Baz Bus (see page 8) caters for backpackers and links most hostels along the coast between Cape Town and Durban. **Coast to Coast**, www.coastingafrica.com, publishes a free annual backpackers' accommodation guide and is available in all the hostels.

Camping and caravan parks Every town has a municipal campsite, many of which also have simple self-catering chalets.

As camping is very popular with South Africans, sites tend to have very good facilities, although they may be fully booked months in advance, especially during the school holidays. Even the most basic site will have a clean washblock with hot water, electric points, lighting and braai facilities. Some sites also have kitchen blocks. At the most popular tourist spots, campsites are more like holiday resorts with shops, swimming pools and a restaurant; these can get very busy and are best avoided in peak season.

Camping equipment is widely available in South Africa if you don't want to bring your own. Lightweight tents, sleeping bags, ground mats, gas lights, stoves and cooking equipment, etc, can be bought at good prices in all the major cities, and some car hire companies rent out equipment. **Cape Union Mart**, www.capeunionmart.co.za, is a quality outdoor adventure shop for gear, as well as outdoor clothing, and branches can be found in the larger shopping malls across the country.

Self-catering Self-catering chalets, cottages or apartments are particularly popular with South African holidaymakers. The choice is enormous, especially along the coast, and accommodation in national parks and nature reserves is generally self-catering. The quality and facilities vary, from basic rondavels with bunks, to chalets with a couple of bedrooms and fully equipped kitchens. They can be excellent value and the cost could be as little as R100-200 per person per day and are ideal for families or a group of friends on a budget.

National parks across South Africa are under the jurisdiction of **South African National Parks** (**SANParks**), central reservations T012-428 9111, www.sanparks.org, which also has a drop-in office at the tourist office on the corner of Burg and Castle streets in central Cape Town, T021-487 6800. The smaller nature and game reserves in the Western Cape are managed by **Cape Nature**, T021-659 3500, www.capenature.co.za. Both offer online reservations and are good sources of information.

Food and drink in Cape Town and the Garden Route

South African food tends to be fairly regional, although a ubiquitous love of meat unites the country. In and around Cape Town visitors will find many restaurants offering Cape Malay cuisine, a blend of sweet and spicy curries and meat dishes cooked with dried fruit. Seafood along the coast is excellent and usually very good value. Portuguese influences, thanks to neighbouring Mozambique, are strong – spicy peri-peri chicken or Mozambiquan prawns are widespread. Meat, however, is universal and, as well as quality steak and Karoo lamb, South Africa offers plenty of opportunities to try an assortment of game such as popular ostrich or springbok. One of the first local terms you are likely to learn will be braai, which quite simply means barbecue. The braai is incredibly popular, part of the South African way of life, and every campsite, back garden and picnic spot has one. Given the excellent range of meat available, learning how to cook good food on a braai is an art that needs to be mastered quickly, especially if you are self-catering. A local meat product which travellers invariably come across is biltong – a heavily salted and spiced sun-dried meat, usually made from beef but sometimes from game.

Supermarkets have a similar selection of groceries to that found in Europe. There are several large supermarket chains and the larger ones also feature extensive counters for takeaway hot meals, pizzas and sandwiches (in some, even sushi). The region's numerous farmers' markets and roadside *padstalls*, are great for picking up tasty home-made goodies, organic vegetables, wine and olives.

Drink

South Africa is a major player in the international market and produces a wide range of excellent wines. The Winelands in the Western Cape have the best-known labels (see pages 91-116) but there are a number of other wine regions dotted around the country. South Africa also produces a range of good beer. Major names include Black Label, Castle and Amstel. Bitter is harder to come by, although a good local variety is brewed at Mitchell's Brewery in Knysna and can be found at outlets in Cape Town and along the Garden Route.

No liquor may be sold on Sundays (and public holidays) except in licensed bars and restaurants. The standard shop selling alcohol is known as a bottle store, usually open Monday-Friday 0800-1800, Saturday 0830-1400 (some may stay open until 1600). Supermarkets do not sell beer or spirits, stop selling wine at 2000, and don't sell alcohol on Sundays.

Soft drinks Tap water in South Africa is safe to drink. Bottled mineral water and a good range of fruit juices are available at most outlets – the Ceres and Liquifruit brands are the best. Another popular drink is Rooibos (or red bush) tea – a caffeine-free tea with a smoky flavour, usually served with sugar or honey, that is grown in the Cederberg Mountains in the Western Cape.

South African dishes

Bobotie A Cape Malay dish similar to shepherd's pie but with a savoury custard topping instead of mashed potatoes, and the mince stew is mixed with fruit. Some consider it as South Africa's national dish.

Boerewors A coarse, thick sausage made from beef or game meat and usually cooked in a spiral on the braai. The word is a combination of 'farmer' and 'sausage' in Afrikaans.

Bredie The Afrikaans word for 'stew' this is usually made with mutton, cinnamon, chilli and cloves and is cooked for a very long time and is traditionally served with saffron rice.

Waterblommetjie bredieis Meat cooked with the flower of the Cape pondweed (tastes a bit like green beans).

Cape brandy pudding Also known as tipsy tart, this warming winter pudding was probably concocted soon after brandy was distilled in the Cape in 1672. Dates and nuts are added to this syrupy dish.

Frikkadels Beef or lamb meatballs, usually made with nutmeg and coriander and baked or deep fried.

Koeksisters A popular sweet snack, which is (sometimes) plaited, made of deep-fried sugary dough and then coated in honey and cinnamon.

Malva pudding A traditional caramelized dessert made with apricot jam and sponge and usually served with custard. Many restaurants have this on the menu, and a twist is to soak the sponge in dessert wine.

Melktart A variation of a baked custard tart, with a biscuit shell and dusted with cinnamon. Popular at braais (after all the meat) and often served in cafés.

Potbrood A traditional yeasty bread cooked with honey in a cast-iron covered pot over the coals. Another accompaniment to a braai.

Potjiekos Stews cooked over coals in three-legged cast-iron pots of the same name, and thought to originate from the Voortrekkers who hooked the pots under their wagons and then heated them up again over the fire at night after adding ingredients collected during the day.

Restaurants

South Africa has an excellent variety of restaurants that represent every kind of international cuisine as well as a good choice of quality South African dishes. A great starting point for choosing a restaurant is the *Eat Out* website, www.eatout.co.za, which features South Africa's best selection of restaurants, or you can buy the latest edition of their magazine, available at CNA and Exclusive Books. *Dining Out*, www.dining-out.co.za. is another excellent resource that provides hundreds of reviews and contact details for restaurants throughout the country.

Essentials A-Z

Accident and emergency
Police, T10111; Medical, T10177;
Fire, T10111. All emergencies from
a cell phone, T112.

Electricity
Voltage 220/230 volts AC at 50 Hz. Most
plugs and appliances are 3-point round-pin
(1 10-mm and 2 8-mm prongs). Hotels
usually have 2-pin sockets for razors
and chargers.

Embassies and consulates
For embassies and consulates of South
Africa, see www.embassiesabroad.com.

Health
See your GP or travel clinic at least 6 weeks
before departure for general advice on travel
risks and vaccinations. Make sure you have
sufficient medical travel insurance, get a
dental check, know your own blood group
and, if you suffer a long-term condition such
as diabetes, epilepsy or a serious allergy,
obtain a Medic Alert bracelet/necklace
(www.medicalert.co.uk). If you wear
glasses, take a copy of your prescription.

Vaccinations
Confirm your primary courses and boosters
are up to date. Courses or boosters usually
advised: diphtheria; tetanus; poliomyelitis;
hepatitis A. Vaccines sometimes advised:
tuberculosis; hepatitis B; rabies; cholera;
typhoid. The final decision, however, should
be based on a consultation with your doctor
or travel clinic. A yellow fever certificate
is required if over 1 year old and entering
from an infected area. If you don't have one,
you'll be required to get one at the airport.
Specialist advice should be taken on the
best anti-malarials to use.

Health risks
Diarrhoea Symptoms should be relatively
short lived but if they persist beyond
2 weeks specialist medical attention should
be sought. Also seek medical help if there is
blood in the stools and/or fever. Adults can
use an antidiarrhoeal medication to control
the symptoms but only for up to 24 hrs. In
addition keep well hydrated by drinking
plenty of fluids and eat bland foods. Oral
rehydration sachets taken after each loose
stool are a useful way to keep well hydrated.
These should always be used when treating
children and the elderly.

The standard advice to prevent problems
is to be careful with water and ice for
drinking. If you have any doubts then boil
the water or filter and treat it. Food can
also transmit disease. Be wary of salads, re-
heated foods or food that has been left out
in the sun having been cooked earlier in the
day. There is a simple adage that says 'wash
it, peel it, boil it or forget it'. Also be wary of
unpasteurized dairy products as these can
transmit a range of diseases. On the positive
side, very few people experience stomach
problems in South Africa.

HIV/AIDS Southern Africa has one of the
highest rates of HIV and AIDS in the world.
Visitors should be aware of the dangers of
infection and take the necessary precautions
with sex, needles, medical treatment and in
the case of a blood tranfusion.

Malaria South Africa only has a very
low seasonal (Oct-May) risk of malaria in
the extreme east of the country along the
Mozambique border. This includes part of
Kruger National Park, so if you are travelling
there from the Western Cape, consult
your doctor or travel clinic about taking
anti-malarials and ensure you finish the
recommended course.

Sun Protect yourself adequately against the sun. Apply a high-factor sunscreen (greater than SPF15) and also make sure it screens against UVB. Prevent heat exhaustion and heatstroke by drinking enough fluids throughout the day. Use rehydration salts mixed with water to replenish fluids and salts and find somewhere cool and shady to recover. If you suspect heatstroke rather than heat exhaustion, you need to cool the body down quickly (cold showers are particularly effective).

If you get sick

There are plenty of private hospitals in South Africa, which have 24-hr emergency departments and pharmacies, run by **Medi-Clinic** (www.mediclinic.co.za) or **Netcare** (www.netcare.co.za). It is essential to have travel insurance as hospital bills need to be paid at the time of admittance, so keep all paperwork to make a claim. If you need to have a vaccination or buy malaria prophylactics while in South Africa, visit one of the Netcare Travel Clinics in Cape Town, www.travelclinic.co.za.

Holidays

South African school holidays are mid-Dec to mid-Jan; mid-Apr to early May; early Aug to early Sep. During these times the price of accommodation in Cape Town and along the Garden Route is often higher and most of the popular destinations are fully booked. The government lists the exact dates for the school calendar on their website: www.gov.za. When a public holiday falls on a Sun, the following Mon becomes a holiday. Most businesses will close but shopping malls and large supermarkets in city centres remain open (public holidays are some of their busiest days). All tourist attractions are open on public holidays.

1 Jan New Year's Day
21 Mar Human Rights' Day
Mar/Apr Good Fri; Family Day (Mon following Easter Sun)
27 Apr Freedom Day
1 May Workers' Day
16 Jun Youth Day
9 Aug National Women's Day
24 Sep Heritage Day (also National Braai Day)
16 Dec Day of Reconciliation
25 Dec Christmas Day
26 Dec Day of Goodwill

Money → *US$1 = R10.8; £1 = R17.8; €1 = R14.8 (Jan 2014).*

Currency

The South African currency is the **rand** (R) which is divided into 100 **cents** (c). Notes are in 200, 100, 50, 20 and 10 rand, and coins are in 5, 2, 1 rand and 50, 20 and 10 cents. You can carry your funds in traveller's cheques (TCs), currency cards, credit cards, rand, US dollars, euros or pounds sterling.

Changing money

South Africa's main banks are **ABSA**, **First National**, **Nedbank** and **Standard Bank**. All have foreign exchange services. You can also change money at **Master Currency**, www.mastercurrency.co.za, which has branches at the main airports and large shopping malls in the cities. **American Express Foreign Exchange Service**, www.americanexpress.co.za, has offices in the larger cities and offers a poste restante service to card holders. Larger hotels offer exchange facilities, but these often charge exorbitant fees.

Currency cards

If you don't want to carry lots of cash, prepaid currency cards allow you to preload money from your bank account, fixed at the day's exchange rate. They look like a credit or debit card and are issued by specialist money changing companies, such as Travelex and Caxton FX. You can top up and check your balance by phone, online and sometimes by text.

Credit and debit cards
Lost or stolen cards American Express, T0800-110929; Diners Club, T0800-112017; **MasterCard**, T0800-990418; **Visa**, T0800-990475.

You can get all the way around South Africa with a credit or debit card. Not only are they a convenient method of covering major expenses but they offer some of the most competitive exchange rates when withdrawing cash from ATMs, and you can only hire a car with a credit (not debit) card. The chip and pin system is common, though not yet universal in South Africa. ATMs are everywhere: Plus, Cirrus, Visa, MasterCard, American Express and Diners Club are all accepted. The amount you can withdraw varies between systems and cards, but you should be able to take out at least R2000 a day. Note that theft during or immediately after a withdrawal is not unknown, so never accept a stranger's help at an ATM and avoid using street-side ATMs. Instead, go into a bank or shopping mall, where guards are often on duty.

Cost of travelling
South Africa is fairly good value for money for tourists spending US dollars, pounds sterling or euro. If you are travelling independently and propose to hire a car, you will need to budget R250-500 per day, depending on the season and type of vehicle. If this is shared among a group of 4 it's the most affordable way to get around. The cost of fuel is about two-thirds of what Europeans are used to, but distances travelled can be considerable so longer holidays will run up a hefty fuel bill.

Accommodation will represent your other principal daily expense. In first-rate 5-star hotels, luxury lodges or tented camps expect to pay in excess of R3000-5000 per night for a double, rising to R8000-10,000 in the most exclusive establishments. If staying in mid-range hotels and lodges, expect to pay in the region of R1500-3000, and in B&Bs and guesthouses, budget R500-1500 per couple per night. By staying in self-catering accommodation, camping or staying in backpacker dorms, you can bring this down to R150-300 on average per person per night. See also page 10.

Food and drink are fairly good value in South Africa and a 2-course evening meal with wine in a reasonable restaurant will cost under R300 for 2 people, and you can be pretty assured of good food and large portions. For the budget traveller there are plenty of fast-food outlets, and almost every supermarket has a superb deli counter serving hot and cold meals. Food in supermarkets is considerably cheaper than, say, in Europe, especially meat and fresh fruit and vegetables, and a bottle of wine and beer are an affordable R40 and R15 respectively. See also Food and drink, page 12.

Safety
Dangers facing tourists are on the whole limited to mugging or, on occasion, carjacking. You should be aware that your assailant may well be armed and any form of resistance could be fatal. South Africa has had more than its fair share of well-publicized crime problems but, despite the statistics, much of the serious, violent crime is gang-based and occurs in areas that tourists are unlikely to visit. The crime rate in the districts where most of the hotels, hostels, nightlife and shops are located has dropped significantly in recent decades, due mainly to an increase in security measures, and you should experience few problems in these areas. Nevertheless, listen to advice from locals about which areas to avoid, and as the likelihood of being mugged increases sharply after dark, take a taxi directly to and from your destination. Avoid driving after dark, and if you are going to be travelling alone in a car, it's a good idea to take a mobile phone in case of break down.

Tax

Tourists can reclaim the 14% VAT on purchases bought in South Africa whose total value exceeds R250. You can do this when departing, at the VAT reclaim desks at airports in Johannesburg, Cape Town and Durban or at border posts. For more information visit www.taxrefunds.co.za.

Telephone → *Country code: +27; international direct dialling code 00; directory enquires T1023; international enquires T1025.* You must dial the full 3-digit regional code for every number in South Africa, even when you are calling from within that region.

The telephone service is very efficient. Card and coin phones are widespread and work well. Cards are available in supermarkets, some pharmacies and Telkom vending machines. Even in remote national parks there are usually card phones from which one can dial direct to anywhere in the world. Note that hotels usually double rates.

Mobile phones

Overseas visitors should be able to use their mobiles on international roaming. Alternatively, you can buy a local SIM card and start-up pack from any of the phone shops and at the 3 international airports, which also offer phone and SIM hire.

Time

South Africa has only 1 time zone: GMT +2 hrs.

Tipping

Waiters, hotel porters, chambermaids and tour guides should be tipped 10-15%. When leaving tips make sure it goes to the intended person. It is common practice to tip petrol pump attendants, depending on their service – around R5 for a fill up, oil and water check and comprehensive windscreen clean. It is also customary to tip car guards R2-5 if parking on the street. They are usually identified by a work vest or badge. On safari you are expected to tip guides. If in any doubt, ask the company that you booked with for advice on how much to tip.

Tourist information

South African Tourism (SATOUR), T011-895 3000, www.southafrica.net, has a very useful website with information on special interest travel, maps, latest travel news, airlines, accommodation and national parks. The website is published in 15 languages and each version provides specific information for people coming from specific countries. SATOUR also has offices around the world. Regional and local tourism authorities are some of the best sources of information once in the country; even the smallest town will have a tourist office with details of local sights and accommodation. Local tourist offices are listed under individual towns.

Visas and immigration

Most nationalities, including EU nationals and citizens from the USA, Canada, Australia and New Zealand, don't need visas to enter South Africa. On arrival, visitors from these countries are granted a 90-day **visitors' permit**. You must have a valid return ticket or voucher for onward travel and at least 2 empty pages in your passport to get a permit. It is possible to apply for an extension to the permit at the office of the **Department of Home Affairs**, T021-462 4970 (Cape Town), www.home-affairs. gov.za. This can take up to 10 days and costs R425. You will need to produce documentation to show when you are leaving the country, as well as proof of funds such as a credit card.

Citizens of countries other than those listed above should consult the South African embassy or consulate in their country for information on visa requirements. See www.home-affairs.gov.za, to find the nearest office.

Weights and measures

The metric system is used in South Africa.

Contents

Footprint features

Cape Town & Winelands

Cape Town

South Africa's 'Mother City', dominated by Table Mountain and surrounded by the wild Atlantic, has unquestionably one of the most beautiful city backdrops in the world. Despite being a considerable urban hub, its surroundings are surprisingly untamed, characterized by a mountainous spine stretching between two seaboards and edged by rugged coast and dramatic beaches. Central Cape Town with its grandiose colonial buildings and beautiful public gardens crammed up against modern skyscrapers lies in the steep-sided bowl created by Table Mountain. Atmospheric Victorian suburbs stretch around the lower slopes, while the Atlantic Seaboard with its promenade and dense crop of holiday flats and the popular V&A Waterfront development hug the coast. Further out on False Bay are the Cape Flats, their sprawling townships a lasting testimony of the Apartheid era.

Cape Town's population is the most cosmopolitan in the country, with a mix of cultures, ethnicities and religions that drive the very pulse of the city. The mishmash of people, including white descendants of Dutch and British settlers, a black African population and the distinctive 'Cape Coloured' community, results in a vibrant cultural scene.

It is this mixture of environments and communities that makes Cape Town such an instantly likeable and captivating city. Few places in the world can offer mountain hiking, lazing on a beach, tasting world-class wines and drinking beer in a township shebeen all in one day. Put simply, it is a city worth crossing the world for.

Arriving in Cape Town

Getting there

Cape Town International Airport ① *airport enquiries, T021-937 1200, flight information T0867-277888, www.acsa.co.za*, is 22 km east of the city centre on the N2, or, out of rush hour, a 20-minute drive.

The airport has a full range of facilities, and domestic and international arrivals and departures are linked by one long terminal and a retail mall. Wi-Fi is available in all public areas. Within international arrivals, **Cape Town Tourism** ① *T021 934 1949, www.capetown. travel, Mon-Fri 0600-2100, Sat-Sun 0800-2000*, can arrange accommodation and has a number of maps and leaflets to give out. The **Master Currency** exchange counters remain open for international arrivals and there are ATMs throughout the airport. You can hire mobile phones and buy local SIM cards at **Vodacom's Vodashop** ① *www.vodacom.com, open 0500-2400*, or from **MTN's Fone 4 Hire** ① *www.mtnsp.co.za, open 0500-2400*, which both have desks at international and domestic arrivals.

All the car hire outlets can be found across the road from the Transport Plaza (the concourse outside the terminal building) and are accessed by pedestrian subways. Several shuttle services run from kiosks in the international and domestic arrivals halls and drop off at hotels and guesthouses in central Cape Town. They charge around R180 per person plus R30 for each additional person from the same group. Alternatively you can pre-book one through your hotel, guesthouse or backpacker hostel, or directly through **Citi Hopper** ① *T021-936 3469, www.citihopper.co.za*, **Cape Town Shuttles** ① *T021-556 5606, www.capetownshuttles.co.za*, **Citi Shuttles** ① *T021-559 5467, www.citishuttles.co.za*, or **The Backpacker Bus** ① *T021-439 7600, www.backpackerbus.co.za*. Taxis running between the airport and city centre should have a special airport licence and they must use their meter by law. **Touch Down Taxis** ① *T021-919 4659*, is the authorized airport taxi company and again kiosks are in the arrivals halls; expect to pay around R280-350 to the city centre, depending on traffic.

The MyCiTi Bus ① *T0800-65 64 63, www. myciti.org.za*, airport service runs between the airport bus station, which is located on the Transport Plaza immediately outside the arrivals halls, and the Civic Centre on Hertzog Boulevard near the railway station in central Cape Town. Many of these airport services then carry on to/from the V&A Waterfront (check the front of the bus), and the bus stop there is outside the Victoria Wharf shopping mall on Breakwater Boulevard. At the Civic Centre, there are MyCiTi buses to other destinations (see page 22), regular taxis for onward journeys and a drop-and-go facility for private vehicles. The buses depart every

1 Cape Town orientation

➡ **Cape Town maps**
1 Cape Town orientation, page 21
2 Cape Town Centre, page 31
3 Gardens & Tamboerskloof, page 33
4 De Waterkant, V&A Waterfront & Green Point, page 42
5 V&A (Victoria & Alfred) Waterfront, page 44

Cape Town's public transport

Public transport in Cape Town has been revolutionized in the last few years, and is now well organized and very efficient. For all public transport enquiries call the 24-hour, toll-free **Transport Information Call Centre** (T0800-65 64 63), which offers assistance for MyCiTi (including the airport bus) and Golden Arrow bus services, Metrorail services, and can help with the location of minibus and regular taxi rank locations.

MyCiTi buses (T0800-65 64 63, www.myciti.org.za) are part of the city's new **Integrated Rapid Transport (IRT)** system and the main terminus where all services start and finish and where passengers change between routes is at the bus station at the Civic Centre on Hertzog Boulevard in the city centre. Buses operate roughly every 10-20 minutes, 0630-2200. Each MyCiTi station and bus has been designed for wheelchair users and bicycles can be accommodated. Services from the Civic Centre include a non-stop bus to and from the airport (see page 21); to the Gardens Centre via Long Street and Orange Street, which returns via Loop Street; to the V&A Waterfront via Green Point (some buses continue on as far as Hout Bay via Sea Point and Camps Bay, while there's another service directly from the Civic Centre through Green Point, Sea Point and Camps Bay to Hout Bay); and the West Coast suburbs to the bus station at Table View, from where there are feeder services as far as Blouberg. Further phases continue to be developed.

Fares start from R5.20 for a short journey, but are a couple of rand more during peak hours (Monday-Friday 0630-0830 and 1600-1800). Passengers need a **myconnect** card loaded with money, except for children under four years old and less than 1 m tall who travel free. Cards are 'tapped' in and out on the bus so the fare is calculated and they can be bought and loaded at the Civic Centre (and other main stations) or from some local convenience shops such as 7-Eleven or Spar (look for the 'Top Up Here' signs). The deposit for a card is R25 which is refundable from any station kiosk when you've finished with it.

20-30 minutes (depending on the time of day) between 0445 and 2220 from the airport, and 0420 and 2140 from the Civic Centre, and outside peak traffic hours take around 30 minutes (45-55 minutes in morning and evening rush hours). Tickets are available at kiosks in the stations; R61.50 during peak hours (0600-0830, 1600-1800); R59.80 at all other times; children under 4 years or under 1 m tall are free (all MyCiTi Bus services operate this child policy). Timetables and fares can be found on the website. The main **railway station** is in the centre of town and is also the terminus for the mainline long-distance bus companies, **Greyhound**, **Intercape** and **Translux**.

Getting around

Most of Cape Town's oldest buildings, museums, galleries and the commercial centre are concentrated in a relatively small area and are easily explored on foot. However, to explore more of the city, and to visit Table Mountain, the suburbs or the beaches, there are several public transport options (see box, above), and taxis are affordable, particularly if you use **Rikki**'s shared taxis (see page 70). There are also a number of day tours to join and, for the greatest flexibility, it's always a good idea to rent a car.

Golden Arrow buses (T0800-65 64 63, www.gabs.co.za) follow all the major routes across Cape Town's metropolitan area at regular intervals and bus stops are clearly marked. Timetables and fares are published on the website (though few services run after 2100), and a short journey costs around R6 (children 5-11 half price; under 5s free) and payment is made on board. The central bus station is on Strand Street across the road from the railway station and next to the Grand Parade.

Minibus taxis also serve all areas of the city on fixed routes, and leave from the minibus terminal accessed from the top floor of the railway station on Adderley Street. They can also be flagged down from the street. Most trips cost around R6, and stop running at around 1900. Minibus taxis are generally safe to use, although you'd be advised to avoid looking like a tourist and leave all valuables at home. The most popular route for visitors are the minibuses from Cape Town along the Atlantic Seaboard as far as Camps Bay; these usually leave every few minutes from the corner of Strand Street and Plein Street.

Metrorail (T0800-65 63 64, www. capemetrorail.co.za) operates suburban trains across the Cape Town Metropolitan region as far as Bellville in the northern suburbs, Paarl in the Winelands, Strand on False Bay, and Simon's Town on the Cape Peninsula. Tickets cost from around R8 (children 5-11 half price; under 5s free) for a short journey; fares and timetables are published on the website. These trains generally run from 0530 to 2000 and are fine to use in rush hour (0700-0800 and 1600-1800), but are best avoided at quieter times due to safety issues; also avoid the routes to the east, which pass through the Cape Flats. Of these routes, the Cape Town–Simon's Town route is recommended for visitors as the scenic line goes through the towns on the False Bay coast; the **Southern Line** initiative is a hop-on hop-off rail ticket designed for tourists (see page 77). Metrorail also put on special trains for certain events – rugby matches at Newlands, for example.

Alternatively, **Sightseeing Cape Town** ① *T021-511 6000, www.citysightseeing.co.za, daily from 0830*, is a red, double-decker, open-top, hop-on hop-off bus that follows a 2¼-hour route around the city. There are two routes; the Red Route has 13 stops and a bus comes by every 15 minutes, while the Blue Route has 13 stops and buses come by every 35 minutes. Audio-commentary is available in eight languages and there's a special kids' channel. The main ticket kiosk is outside the Two Oceans Aquarium on Dock Road at the V&A Waterfront, however, you can buy tickets on the bus or online (for a discount) and join anywhere on the routes. It's ideal if you don't want to drive, and stops include the Lower Cableway Station, Camps Bay, Kirstenbosch, all the city centre museums, and as far south as Hout Bay on the peninsula. A one-day ticket costs R150, children (5-15) R70, under 5s free, and a two-day ticket is R250/R150. The buses are wheelchair friendly.

Orientation

To get the best idea of Cape Town's layout, head to the top of Table Mountain. From its summit, the city stretches below in a horseshoe formed by the mountains: Table Mountain is in the centre, with Devil's Peak to the east and Lion's Head and Signal Hill to the west. Straight ahead lies the City Bowl, the central business district backed by leafy suburbs. This is also the site of Cape Town's historical heart and where all the major museums, historical buildings and sights are. Further down is the V&A Waterfront, a slick development of shopping malls and restaurants. Following the coast around to the west, you come to the modern residential districts of Green Point and Sea Point, which are dominated by the enormous Cape Town Stadium, which was built for the 2010 FIFA World Cup™. In the opposite direction the southern suburbs stretch west and south, dipping from the mountain's slopes, and here, under a blanket of trees, are Cape Town's largest mansions as well as the beautiful Kirstenbosch National Botanical Garden.

Tourist information

Cape Town Tourism ① *The Pinnacle, corner of Burg and Castle streets, T021-487 6800, www. capetown.travel, Oct-Mar Mon-Fri 0800-1900, Sat 0830-1400, Sun 0900-1300, closes 1 hr earlier in winter (Apr-Sep)*, the official city tourist office, can help with bookings and tours throughout the Western Cape. It is an excellent source of information and a good first stop in the city. In addition to providing practical information about Cape Town, it can help with accommodation bookings and has plenty of information on nightlife and events. It is also home to **Western Cape Tourism** (same contact details) and there is a desk for **South Africa National Parks (SANParks)** ① *www.sanparks.co.za*, where you can make reservations for the parks. There's also a café, gift shop and free Wi-Fi. There are 12 other branches/desks around Cape Town including at the Table Mountain Lower Cableway and Kirstenbosch National Botanical Garden.

If you are planning a trip to Namibia, it is well worth picking up maps and brochures at the **Namibian Tourist Office** ① *underneath Cape Town Tourism, in the Pinnacle, T021-422 3298, www.namibiatourism.com.na, Mon-Fri 0800-1700*. There's also a Namibia Wildlife Resorts desk where you can pre-book accommodation in Namibia's national parks (see Footprint *Namibia Handbook*).

Background

First people

The first evidence of human inhabitants in the Cape has been dated back to nearly 30,000 years ago. Rock art found in the area was created by nomadic San people (also known as Bushmen), a hunter-gatherer group which roamed across much of southern Africa. Some San groups survive today, mostly in Namibia and Botswana, despite continuing persecution. The original San were replaced about two thousand years ago by Khoi groups, a semi-nomadic people who settled in the Cape with herds of sheep and cattle.

First landing

António de Saldanha, a Portuguese admiral who lost his way going east, landed in Table Bay in 1503. They called the bay Aguada da Saldanha (it was renamed Table Bay in 1601 by **Joris van Spilbergen**). Saldanha and a party of the crew went ashore in search of drinking water. They followed a stream to the base of Table Mountain and then proceeded to climb to the top. From here Saldanha was able to get a clear view of the surrounding coastline and the confusion caused by the peninsula. On their return they found the crew unsuccessfully trying to barter with local indigenous Khoi for livestock. The trade quickly developed into a row which ended in bloodshed. There was another battle between the Portuguese and the Khoi in March 1510. On this occasion the Khoi had struck back after children and cattle were stolen by the sailors. Seventy-five Portuguese were killed, including **Dom Francisco**

de Almeida, who had just finished five years as the first Portuguese Viceroy to India. Few Portuguese ships landed in Table Bay after this.

The Dutch and the VOC

By the end of the 16th century British and Dutch mariners had caught up with the Portuguese and they quickly came to appreciate the importance of the Cape as a base for restocking ships with drinking water and fresh supplies as they made their long journeys to the East. Indeed, seafarers found that they were able to exchange scraps of metal for provisions to supply a whole fleet.

The first moves to settle in the Cape were made by the Dutch, and on 6 April 1652 **Jan Van Riebeeck** landed in Table Bay. His ships carried wood for building and some small cannons, the first building to be erected being a small fort at the mouth of the Fresh River. The site of the original fort is where Grand Parade in the centre of Cape Town is today. Van Riebeeck was in charge of the supply station that belonged to the Dutch East India Company (Vereenigde Oost-Indische Compagnie or VOC). After the fort was built, gardens for fruit and vegetables were laid out and pastures for cattle acquired. As the settlement slowly grew, the Khoi people were driven back into the interior. Surprisingly, the early settlers were forbidden from enslaving the Khoi; instead, slaves were imported by the VOC from Indonesia and West Africa. Although many died, these slaves were the origin of the Cape Malay community.

In 1662 Jan van Riebeeck was transferred to India. Because of rivalries in Europe, the VOC was worried about enemy ships visiting the Cape, so work started on a new stone fort in 1666. Over the next 13 years several governors came and went. During this time the French and British went to war with Holland, but the British and the Dutch East India companies joined in a treaty of friendship in March 1674, and then in July of the same year a ship arrived with the news that the British and Dutch had made peace. In October 1679 one of the most energetic governors arrived in the Cape, **Simon van der Stel**. For the next 20 years van der Stel devoted his energies to creating a new Holland in southern Africa. During his period as Governor, van der Stel paid particular attention to the growth and development of Cape Town and the surrounding farmlands. The company garden was replanted, nursery plots were created and new experimental plants were collected from around the world. North of the gardens he built a large hospital and a lodge to house VOC slaves. New streets were laid out which were straight and wide with plenty of shade. New buildings in the town were covered in white limewash, producing a smart and prosperous appearance. In 1685, in appreciation for his work, he was granted an estate by the VOC, which he named **Constantia**. During his life he used the estate as an experimental agricultural farm and to grow oak trees which were then planted throughout the Cape.

One of his more significant contributions was the founding of the settlement at Stellenbosch. He directed the design and construction of many of the town's public buildings, and then introduced a number of the crops to be grown on the new farms. For many years he experimented with vines in an effort to produce wines as good as those in Europe. He was particularly pleased when in 1688 French Protestant Huguenot refugees arrived in the Cape. He saw to it that they were all settled on excellent farmlands in what became to be known as **Franschhoek** (French glen), the upper valley of the Berg River. In 1693 he had the foresight to appoint the town's first engineer to tackle problems of a clean water supply and the removal of rubbish. Van der Stel died in June 1712 at Constantia.

Under the British

The next period of Cape Town's history was closely related to events in Europe, particularly the French Revolution. The ideas put forward by the Revolution of Liberty, Fraternity and Equality were not welcome in colonies such as the Cape. The Dutch East India Company was seen to be a corrupt organization and a supporter of the aristocracy. When the French invaded Holland, the British decided to seize the Cape to stop it from falling into French hands. After the Battle of Muizenberg in 1795, Britain took over the Cape from the representatives of the Dutch East India Company, which was bankrupt. In the Treaty of Amiens (1803) the Cape was restored to the Batavian Republic of the Netherlands. In 1806 the British took control again at the resumption of the Anglo-French wars.

When the British took over power it was inevitable that they inherited many of the problems associated with the colony. The principal issue was how to manage European settlement. The Dutch East India Company had only encouraged settlement as a cheap and efficient means of supplying their base in Cape Town. Thereafter they were only interested in controlling the Indian Ocean and supplying ships. By the time the British arrived, the Dutch settler farmers (the Boer) had become so successful that they were producing a surplus. The only problem was high production costs due to a shortage of labour. To alleviate the situation, a policy of importing slaves was implemented. This in turn led to decreased work opportunities for the settler families. Gradually the mood changed and the Boer looked to the interior for land and work. They were not impressed by the British administration and in 1836 the Great Trek was under way.

The growth of the city and the port

Industrialization in Europe brought great change, especially when the first steamship, the *Enterprise*, arrived in Table Bay in October 1825. After considerable delay and continual loss of life and cargoes, work began on two basins and breakwater piers. The first truckload of construction rocks was tipped by Prince Alfred, the 16-year-old son of Queen Victoria, on 17 September 1860. The Alfred Basin was completed in 1870 and a dry dock was added in 1881.

No sooner had the first basin been completed than diamonds and gold were discovered in South Africa. Over the next 40 years Cape Town and the docks were to change beyond recognition. In 1900 work began on a new breakwater which would protect an area of 27 km. After five years' work the **Victoria Basin** was opened. This new basin was able to shelter the new generation of ships using Table Bay but was unable to cope with the increase in numbers during the **Anglo-Boer War**. A third basin was created to the east of Victoria Basin in 1932 and for a while this seemed to have solved the problem, but fate was against Cape Town. In January 1936 the largest ship to visit South Africa docked with ease at B berth in the new basin. The boat, which was being used to help promote tourism in South Africa, was filled with wealthy and famous visitors. The morning on which she was due to sail, a strong southeasterly wind blew up and pressed the liner so firmly against the quay that she couldn't sail. In one morning all of the new basin's weaknesses had been exposed.

The next phase of growth was an ambitious one, and it was only completed in 1945. The project involved the dredging of Table Bay and the reclaiming of land. The spoil from the dredging provided 140 sq km of landfill, known as Foreshore. This new land extends from the present-day railway station to **Duncan Dock**. As you walk or drive around Cape Town today, remember that just over 50 years ago the sea came up to the main railway station.

Desmond Tutu

Desmond Tutu was a stalwart opponent of Apartheid and, like Nelson Mandela, became an influential and respected figure far beyond the borders of South Africa. His powerful oration and his simple but brave defiance of the Apartheid state impressed the world, and won him the Nobel Peace Prize in 1984. He was born in Klerksdorp in 1931 and, after being educated in church schools in Johannesburg and at university in England, he rose through the ranks to become secretary general of the South African Council of Churches from the 1970s. He first caught the international headlines with his call for the international community to stop buying South African goods, which lead to economic sanctions from 1985 to pressurize the government towards reform.

Tutu's opposition to Apartheid was vigorous and unequivocal, and he was outspoken both in South Africa and abroad. As a result, the government twice revoked his passport and he was jailed briefly in 1980 after a protest march. However, it was thought by many that Tutu's increasing international reputation and his rigorous advocacy of non-violence protected him from harsher penalties. He became the first black Anglican Archbishop of Cape Town from 1986 until 1996, and it was from this position that he consistently advocated reconciliation between the parties as Apartheid began to be dismantled.

After Apartheid, Tutu chaired the hearings of the Truth and Reconciliation Commission in 1996, and argued forcibly that the policy of granting amnesty to all who admitted their crimes was an important step in healing the nation's scars. Since then, Tutu has used his voice in the fight against AIDS, poverty and racism in South Africa, and in international conflict resolution. Nelson Mandela once said of him, "sometimes strident, often tender, never afraid and seldom without humour, Desmond Tutu's voice will always be the voice of the voiceless".

Impact of the Apartheid years

The descendants of the large and diverse slave population have given Cape Town a particularly cosmopolitan atmosphere. Unfortunately, Apartheid urban planning meant that many of the more vibrant areas of the city in the earlier part of this century were destroyed. The most notorious case is that of District Six, a racially mixed, low income housing area on the edge of the City Bowl. The Apartheid government could not tolerate such an area, especially so close to the centre of the city, and the residents, most of whom were classified as 'coloured', were moved out to the soulless townships of the Cape Flats, such as Mitchell's Plain. The area was bulldozed but few new developments have taken place on the site: this accounts for the large areas of open ground in the area between the City Bowl and the suburb of Woodstock. Happily, the government recently handed over the first pocket of re-developed land to a small group of ex-residents of District Six and their descendants. What the area will become remains to be seen – the issue remains controversial as many ex-residents feel the open, barren land should remain as a poignant testimony to the forced removals.

Other reminders of the cosmopolitan history of Cape Town can be experienced in the area to the west of Buitengracht Street. This district, known as **Bo-Kaap**, is still home to a small Islamic (Cape Malay) community that somehow managed to survive the onslaught of Apartheid urban planning. The coloured population of Cape Town has historically outweighed both the white and African populations, hence the widespread use of Afrikaans in the city. This balance was maintained by Apartheid policies that prevented Africans from migrating into the Western Cape from the Eastern Cape and elsewhere. This policy was not, however, able to withstand the pressure of the poor rural Africans' desire to find opportunities in the urban economy. Over the past couple of decades there has been an enormous growth in the African population of Cape Town. Many of these new migrants have been forced to settle in squatter areas, such as the notorious Crossroads Camp next to the N2 highway. During the Apartheid era these squatter camps were frequently bulldozed and the residents evicted but as soon as they were cleared they sprang up again. Crossroads was a hotbed of resistance to the Apartheid state and much of the Cape Flats area existed in a state of near civil war throughout much of the 1980s.

Today, Cape Town remains the most cosmopolitan city in South Africa. The official colour barriers have long since disappeared and residential boundaries are shifting. The economic balance, too, is beginning to change: and the black and coloured middle class has strengthened considerably. There are still pockets of low-income housing, notably the sprawling townships on the Cape Flats, but large areas in the northern suburbs have expanded into middle-income districts, and the Atlantic seaboard and southern suburbs continue to boast some of the most exclusive and expensive real estate on the African continent.

Table Mountain National Park → *For listings, see pages 51-70.*

① *www.sanparks.co.za. The most popular ascent of the mountain directly above the City Bowl is described below; other parts of the park are covered later in the chapter.*

Cape Town is defined, first and foremost, by Table Mountain. Rising a sheer 1073 m from the coastal plain, it dominates almost every view of the city, its sharp slopes and level top making it one of the world's best-known city backdrops. For centuries, it was the first sight of Cape Town afforded to seafarers, its looming presence visible for hundreds of kilometres. Certainly, its size continues to astonish visitors today, but it is the mountain's wilderness, bang in the middle of a bustling conurbation, that makes the biggest impression. Table Mountain sustains over 1400 species of flora, as well as baboons, dassies (large rodents) and countless birds. The Table Mountain National Park encompasses the entire peninsula stretching from here to Cape Point. Between September and March you have the additional pleasure of seeing the mountain covered in wild flowers. The most common vegetation is fynbos, of which there is an extraordinary variety, but you'll also see proteas plus the rare silver tree, *Leucadendron argenteum*.

Aerial Cableway

① *Tafelberg Rd, information line T021-424 8181, www.tablemountain.net; the first car up is at 0800, the last car down varies from 1800 to 2130 depending on the time of year, both the information line and the website has up-to-the-minute details of times and, given Cape Town's unpredictable weather, will tell you if the cableway is open or not (always check before going up to the Lower Cableway Station). Return ticket R205, children (4-18) R100, one-way ticket R105, children (4-18) R52.50, under 4s free. Also check the website for special offers; 2 for the price of 1 on summer evenings to watch the sunset for example. Tickets bought online or at the Cape Town Tourism offices (not a bad idea to avoid lengthy queues at the ticket office at the Lower Cableway Station in summer) are valid for 14 days. The cableway is closed for annual maintenance for 2 weeks end Jul/beginning Aug (check the website for exact dates). There are* a number of options of getting to the lower cableway station; you can drive and parking is along Tafelberg Rd on either side of the station, go by taxi and once you come back down there is a taxi rank at the station, by Rikki Taxi and there is a free Rikki phone at the station, by the Cape Town City Sightseeing bus, or by regular Golden Arrow bus from the city centre to Camps Bay and get off at Kloof Nek, from where it is a 1.5-km walk up Tafelberg Rd to the station.

The dizzying trip to the top in the Aerial Cableway is one of Cape Town's highlights. The first cableway was built in 1929, and since then has had three upgrades, the latest being in 1997. It's estimated to have carried up some 20 million people to date. There are two cars, each carrying up to 65 passengers, and as you ride up the floor rotates, allowing a full 360° view. Journey time is just under five minutes. In the base of each car is a water tank that can carry up to 4000 litres of fresh water to the top. There is the Table Mountain Café at the top station, which also has a deli for takeaway sandwiches, cheese and sushi platters and other light meals. To conserve water, they use compostable plates and containers. An extensive network of paths has been laid out from the top station, allowing walks of various lengths, leading to different lookout points with stunning views of the City Bowl, Cape Flats, Robben Island and back along the peninsula. There are also free guided walks daily at 1000 and 1200.

Hiking

The entire area is a nature reserve, and the mountain is protected as a national monument. There are numerous paths climbing to the top. The most popular route starts 1.5 km beyond the Lower Cableway Station and follows a course up Platteklip Gorge; there's another path from Kirstenbosch National Botanical Garden. Both take about two to three hours to the top, although they are both fairly tough and should not be taken lightly. Given Table Mountain's size and location, conditions can change alarmingly quickly. The weather may seem clear and calm when you set out, but fog (the famous 'Table Cloth' which flows from the top) and rain can descend without warning. Numerous people have been caught out and the mountain has claimed its fair share of lives.

Before venturing out, make sure you have suitable clothing, food and water. Take warm clothes, a windbreaker, a waterproof jacket, a hat, sunscreen, sunglasses, plenty of water (2 litres per person) and energy foods. Never climb alone and inform someone of which route you're taking and what time you should be back. Also be aware that if the weather is too unfavourable for the cableway to be open, you can't rely on it being open to take you back down, so allow enough daylight hours to make the descent on foot.

For those wanting to spend more time on the mountain, there is the 75-km overnight – **Hoerikwaggo Trail** (meaning 'sea mountain' in Khoi). The five-day trek involves sleeping in tented camps dotted along the top of the mountain. It starts at Cape Point and then follows the spine of the peninsula to finish at the Lower Cableway Station after descending Platteklip Gorge. For full details, contact SANParks (see Tourist information, page 24).

Signal Hill

Signal Hill's summit offers spectacular views of the city, the Twelve Apostles (the mountainous spine stretching south from Table Mountain) and the ocean. It is possible to drive to the 350-m summit, which means that it can get pretty busy with tour groups around sunset. Nevertheless, watching the sun dip into the Atlantic from this viewpoint with a cold sundowner in hand is a highlight of a visit to Cape Town. Avoid being there after dark, as there have been reports of muggings, although the presence of security officers has now reduced this considerably. From the town centre, follow signs for the Lower Cableway Station and take a right at Kloof Nek opposite the turning for the cableway station. On the lower slopes of Signal Hill, above and accessed from Wale Street in Bo-Kaap, is the Noon Day Gun which is fired electronically at noon every day, except Sunday. Originally at the castle and fired to announce the arrival of ships, the two cannon were moved to Signal Hill in 1902 as time-keeping instruments. The view from here takes in the high-rises in the commercial area of the City Bowl, and the harbour and V&A Waterfront. There's a small café.

Lion's Head

Halfway along the road up Signal Hill you pass Lion's Head, a popular hiking spot. The signposted climb to the 669-m peak is fairly challenging and takes about two to three hours. The path spirals around the head to reach a part with chains that help climbers over a particularly rocky section; the 360° views from the top are incredible. In the 17th century the peak was known as Leeuwen Kop (Lion's Head) by the Dutch, and Signal Hill was known as Leeuwen Staart (Lion's Tail), as the shape resembles a crouching lion.

City Bowl → *For listings, see pages 51-70.*

From the Table Mountain Lower Cableway Station, you look out over the central residential suburbs of Tamboerskloof (Drummers' Ravine), Gardens, Oranjezicht (Orange View) and Vredehoek (Peaceful Corner), and beyond here lie the high-rise blocks of the business district. Together these form the City Bowl, a term inspired by the surrounding mountains. Closest to the mountain is **Oranjezicht**, a quiet district that was, up until 1900 the area was a farm of the same name. On the boundary with Gardens are the **De Waal Park** and **Molteno Reservoir**, originally built as a main storage facility for the city in 1881, which now provides a peaceful wooded spot from where you can enjoy a view of the city.

There is nothing peaceful about **Vredehoek** today, as the De Waal Drive (M3) brings rush hour traffic into the top end of town from the southern suburbs and beyond. Most of the area has been given over to ugly high-rise apartments, though the residents benefit from some excellent views. This was the area in which many Jewish immigrants from Eastern Europe settled, and have to a large part remained.

Gardens is a lively neighbourhood with a choice of quality restaurants and comfortable guesthouses. Cape Town's best-known hotel, the **Mount Nelson**, is situated here in its own landscaped gardens. The grand gateway to the hotel was built in 1924 to welcome the Prince of Wales.

From here the land slopes gently towards the harbour and the V&A Waterfront, with the commercial heart of the city laid out in between. This was the area where the Dutch East India Company first created fruit and vegetable gardens to supply the ships' crews who suffered greatly from scurvy. Across Orange Street from the entrance to the Mount Nelson Hotel is the top end of **Government Avenue**, a delightful pedestrian route past Company's Garden and many of the city's main museums. Originally sheltered by lemon trees, it is now lined with oaks and myrtle hedges, and is one of Cape Town's most popular walks.

South Africa Museum and Planetarium

ⓘ *25 Queen Victoria St, at the top end of Company's Garden, T021-481 3800, www.iziko.org. za, 1000-1700, R30, children (6-18) R15, family of 4 ticket R75, under 5s free.*
This, the city's most established museum, specializes in natural history, ethnography and archaeology, and is a good place to take children. There are extensive displays of the flora

2 Cape Town centre

To Cape Town International
Convention Centre (CTICC) & Docks

To N1 & N2

To 2

Artscape

To Helen Suzman Blvd and V&A Waterfront

To Green Point, Sea Point & De Waterkant

To N2 & Woodstock

Hertzog
MyCiTi Hertzog
Bus
Civic Centre

Hans Strijdom
Long
Bree
Buitengracht

Prestwich

Tulbagh Square
Riebeeck Statue

Thibault Square
UK High Commission

Taxis
Greyhound, Intercape & Translux
Minibus Taxi Rank

Somerset
Riebeeck
Fugard Theatre
Waterkant

Railway Station

Gold of Africa Museum
Hertz

Koopmans-De Wet House

Minibuses to the Atlantic Seaboard Strand

Golden Arrow

Castle of Good Hope

To N2 & Woodstock

Strand

Heritage Square
Signal Hill Winery
Hout Berg
Shortmarket St

Castle St
Burg
St George's Mall

Pan African Market
Old Town House

Greenmarket Square

Grand Parade

Darling

BO-KAAP

Christiaan Barnard Memorial Hospital

Church
Church St Antiques Market
St George's Cathedral

Metropolitan Methodist Church
Groote Kerk

Longmarket St
City Hall

Old Drill Hall & Cape Town Central Library Caledon

Longmarket St

Church Square

District Six Museum

Bo-Kaap Museum

Bree
Wale
Dorp

Slave Church Museum

Slave Lodge

Houses of Parliament

Barrack

Leeuwen

South African Public Library

Commercial

Upper Pepper
Pepper
Bloem

Loop
Long
Keerom
Queen Victoria St

Company's Garden

Parliament
St Johns
Hope

Roeland

Rust en Vreugd

Buiten

Select Books

Orphan

St Martin

National Gallery

Buitensingel

South African Museum & Planetarium

Paddock

Jewish Museum & Holocaust Centre

Vrede

Bryant
Jordaan

Whitford
Klook St
Orange
Government Av

Carisbrook

Bertram House

Dunkley Square

Hatfield

To Lower Cableway Station for Table Mountain

To De Waal Drive, M3 & Southern Suburbs

➜ Cape Town maps

1 Cape Town orientation, page 21

2 Cape Town Centre, page 31

3 Gardens & Tamboerskloof, page 33

4 De Waterkant, V&A Waterfront & Green Point, page 42

5 V&A (Victoria & Alfred) Waterfront, page 44

200 metres
200 yards

Where to stay

15 on Orange **3** *E2*
The Backpack **1** *E1*
Cape Diamond **18** *C2*
Cape Heritage **8** *B1*
Cape Town Lodge **6** *C1*
Daddy Long Legs **16** *C1*

Grand Daddy **12** *B1*
Hilton Cape Town **7** *C1*
Inn on the Square **9** *B2*
Long St Backpackers **11** *D2*
Protea Hotel Fire & Ice! **4** *E1*
Taj Cape Town **10** *C2*
Urban Chic **19** *D1*
Westin Cape Town **2** *A1*

Restaurants 🍴

95 Keerom **4** *D2*
Africa Café **1** *C1*
Biesmiellah **9** *C1*

Bukhara **8** *C2*
Café Mozart **11** *C2*
Dias Tavern **10** *C3*
Eastern Food Bazaar **15** *C2*
Keenwä **23** *A1*
Mama Africa **5** *D1*
Marco's African Place **6** *B1*
Mr Pickwicks **7** *D1*
Royale Eatery **12** *D2*
Savoy Cabbage **2** *B1*

Bars & clubs 🍸

Assembly **20** *C3*

Bang Bang Club **21** *B1*
Chrome **14** *D1*
Jo'burg **17** *D1*
Mercury Live & Lounge **22** *D3*
Zula **19** *D1*

and fauna of southern Africa, including the popular Whale Well and interactive Shark World area, but the highlight is the 'IQe – the Power of Rock Art' exhibition. The displays of ancient San rock art have been in the museum for almost 100 years but, following a process of consultation and dialogue with Khoi-San communities, they have been re-interpreted in a far more sensitive and illuminating manner. The exhibits focus on the significance and symbolism of San rock art, with some fascinating examples including the beautifully preserved Linton panel, which depicts the trance experiences of shamans. Other themes explored include rainmaking and the significance of animal imagery; the eland, for example, appears more often than any other animal in San rock art, and it holds a central role in all major rituals, from teenage initiation to marriage and rainmaking. The whole exhibition, although short, is beautifully arranged and accompanied by the sound of San singing, a disjointed and haunting sound.

Nearby are the ethnographic galleries, offering interesting displays on the San, Khoi and Xhosa, among others, as well as the original Lydenburg Heads. There is also a small display of pieces recovered from Great Zimbabwe that illustrate its importance as a trade centre – there are beads from Cambay, India, Chinese Celadon ware, 13th-century Persian pottery and Syrian glass from the 14th century. The Stone Bones is an exhibition about the fossilized skeletons found in the Karoo, which date back 250 million years – predating dinosaurs. There are life-sized reproductions of the reptile-like creatures, including walk-around dioramas and examples of the actual fossils. Every year in spring the museum hosts the excellent BBC Wildlife Photographer of the Year exhibition. Contact the museum for exact dates.

Next door, at the **Planetarium** ① *T021-481 3900, www.iziko.org.za, 1000-1700, show times vary depending on what's on; check the website, R40, children (under 18) R20*, presentations change every few months, but usually a view of the current night sky is shown and visitors receive a star map to find the constellations and planets that are visible each month. Shows last an hour and are fascinating. Children (aged 5-10) will enjoy the Davy the Dragon show, which sends Davy off into space to learn how to be the best flying dragon ever.

Bertram House

① *Corner of Government Av and Orange St, T021-424 9381, www.iziko.org.za, Mon-Fri 1000-1700, R20, children (6-18) R10, under 5s free.*

This early 19th-century red-brick Georgian House has a distinctly English feel to it. The building houses a collection of porcelain, jewellery, silver and English furniture, the majority of which was bequeathed by Ann Lidderdale. Winifred Ann Lidderdale was an important civic figure in Cape Town in the 1950s. After her marriage to Henry Maxwell Lidderdale, she lived in England and the USA, but in 1951 the couple returned to Cape Town for their retirement. It was her desire to establish a house museum to commemorate the British contribution to life at the Cape. Downstairs the two drawing rooms contain all the trappings of a bygone elegant age – card tables, a Hepplewhite settee, a square piano and a fine harp. Three rooms have wallpaper from London, a very expensive luxury for the period.

Jewish Museum

① *88 Hatfield St, T021-465 1546, www.sajewishmuseum.co.za, Sun-Thu 1000-1700, Fri 1000-1400, closed on Jewish and public holidays, R40, under 16s free.*

Inside this excellent, contemporary museum is a rich and rare collection of items depicting the history of the Cape Town Hebrew Congregation and other congregations in the Cape Province. The history of the community is interesting in itself: in 1841 a congregation of 17 men assembled for the first time in Cape Town to celebrate Yom Kippur. At the meeting they set about the task of raising funds to build a synagogue, and in 1862 the foundation stone was laid for the first synagogue in southern Africa. The following year the building was completed and furnished – quite a feat for such a small community at the time. On display upstairs are bronze Sabbath oil lamps, *Chanukkah* lamps, *Bessamin* spice containers, *Torah* scrolls, *Kiddush* cups and candlesticks. There is a beautiful stained-glass window depicting the Ten Commandments in Hebrew. From here a glass corridor leads you to a newer section of the museum that is devoted to the history of Jewish immigration to the Cape, mainly from Lithuania. A lot of thought has been put into the displays, which include photographs, immigration certificates, videos and a full reconstruction of a Lithuanian *shtetl*, or village. There are special displays outlining the stories of famous Jewish South Africans, including Helen Suzman and Isie Maisels. The museum complex also houses a library, café and bookshop.

3 Gardens & Tamboerskloof

➡ **Cape Town maps**
1 Cape Town orientation, page 21
2 Cape Town Centre, page 31
3 Gardens & Tamboerskloof, page 33
4 De Waterkant, V&A Waterfront & Green Point, page 42
5 V&A (Victoria & Alfred) Waterfront, page 44

Where to stay 🛏
15 on Orange **5**
Ashanti Lodge **2**
Cape Cadogan **4**
Cape Milner **8**
Kensington Place **12**
Leeuwenvoet House **13**
Mount Nelson **15**
Parker Cottage **17**
The Backpack **3**
Zebra Crossing Backpackers **21**

Restaurants 🍴
Arnold's **1**
Aubergine **7**
Chef Pon's Asian Kitchen **8**
Manna Epicure **2**
Miller's Thumb **3**
Saigon **4**
Societi Bistro **6**
Vida e Caffè **9**
Yindee's **11**

Bars & clubs 🍸
Rafiki's **5**
Rick's Café Américain **10**

Holocaust Centre

ⓘ *88 Hatfield St, T021-462 5553, www.ctholocaust.co.za, Sun-Thu 1000-1700, Fri 1000-1400, entry by donation.*

An intelligent and shocking examination of the Holocaust can be found next door at this modern museum. Exhibits follow a historical route, starting with a look at anti-Semitism in Europe in previous centuries, and then leading to the rise of Nazism in Germany, the creation of ghettos, death camps and the Final Solution, and liberation at the end of the war. Video footage, photography, examples of Nazi propaganda and personal accounts of the Holocaust produce a vividly haunting and shocking display. The exhibits cleverly acknowledge South Africa's emergence from Apartheid and draw parallels between both injustices, as well as looking at the link between South Africa's Greyshirts (who were later assimilated into the National Party) and the Nazis. The local context is highlighted further at the end of the exhibition, with video accounts of Jews who survived the Holocaust and moved to Cape Town.

National Gallery

ⓘ *Government Av, T021-467 4660, www.iziko.org.za, 1000-1700, R30, children (6-18) R15, family of 4 ticket R75, under 5s free.*

The National Gallery houses a permanent collection but also hosts some excellent temporary exhibitions that include the best of the country's contemporary art. The original collection was bequeathed to the nation in 1871 by Thomas Butterworth Bailey, and features a collection of 18th- and 19th-century British sporting scenes, portraits and Dutch paintings. Far more interesting are the changing exhibitions of contemporary South African art and photography. Check the website to see what's on. There's a good souvenir shop on site.

Rust en Vreugd

ⓘ *78 Buitenkant St, T021-467 7205, www.iziko.org.za, Mon-Fri 1000-1700, R20, children (6-18) R10, family of 4 ticket R50, under 5s free.*

A few hundred metres east of the National Gallery, hidden behind a high whitewashed wall, is this 18th-century mansion. Today it houses six galleries displaying a collection of watercolours, engravings and lithographs depicting the history of the Cape. Of particular note are Schouten's watercolour of Van Riebeeck's earth fort (1658), watercolours by Thomas Baines (a British artist who travelled extensively in South Africa and Australia) of climbing Table Mountain, lithographs by Angas of Khoi and Zulus, and a collection of cartoons by Cruikshank depicting the first British settlers arriving in the Cape.

Company's Garden

ⓘ *T021-400 2521, daily 0700-1900, closes 1800 Jun-Aug, café 0900-1700.*

Running alongside Government Avenue are the peaceful Company's Garden, situated on the site of Jan van Riebeeck's original vegetable garden, which was created in 1652 to grow produce for settlers and ships bound for the East. Cape Town's earliest records show that the garden was originally divided into rectangular fields protected by high trimmed myrtle windbreaks, and watered via a system of open irrigation furrows fed by mountain streams. The design was typical Dutch agricultural practice of the time, apart from the furrows, which had been adapted to suit the region's weather. It is now a small botanical garden, with lawns, a variety of labelled trees, ponds filled with Japanese koi and a small aviary. It's a popular spot with office workers at lunchtime. The grey squirrels living amongst the oak trees were introduced by Cecil Rhodes from America. There are also a couple of statues here: opposite the South African Public Library at the lower end of the garden, is the oldest statue in Cape Town, that of Sir George Grey, governor of the Cape from 1854 to 1862. Close by is a statue of Cecil Rhodes, pointing northwards in a rather unfortunate flat-handed gesture, with an inscription reading, "Your hinterland is there", a reminder of his ambition to paint the map pink from the Cape to Cairo. There is a café in the garden, serving drinks and snacks beneath the trees; best known for its scones, jam and cream. Quite uniquely, the whole garden is now a free Wi-Fi hotspot, which is sponsored by Cape Town's city council. More than 70 historic trees have been labelled with a code to scan with smartphones to get more information about the tree and the gardens in general.

South African Public Library

ⓘ *5 Queen Victoria St, behind St George's Cathedral, T021-424 6320, www.nlsa.ac.za, Mon-Fri 0900-1700, free.*

Adjoining the garden is the South African Public Library, which opened in 1818. It is the country's oldest national reference library and was one of the first free libraries in the world. Today it houses an important collection of books covering South Africa's history. The building also has a bookshop and Wi-Fi access.

Houses of Parliament

ⓘ *Entry via Parliament St gate, T021-403 2266, www.parliament.gov.za, public gallery tickets available during parliamentary sessions Jan-Jun, overseas visitors must present their passports, phone ahead for tours of the chambers and Constitutional Assembly.*

On the other side of the avenue are the Houses of Parliament. The building was completed in 1885, and when the Union was formed in 1910 it became the seat for the national parliament. In front of the building is a marble statue of Queen Victoria, erected by public subscription in honour of her Golden Jubilee. It was unveiled in 1890.

St George's Cathedral

ⓘ *5 Wale St, T021-424 7360, www.sgcathedral.co.za, Mon-Fri 0800-1600 and during services in the evenings and at weekends.*

The last building on Government Avenue and on the corner of Wale Street is St George's Cathedral, best known for being Archbishop Desmond Tutu's territory from 1986 until 1996 (see box, page 27). It is from here that he led over 30,000 people to City Hall to mark the end of Apartheid, and where he coined the now universal phrase 'Rainbow Nation'. The building was designed by Sir Herbert Baker in the early 20th century. Inside, some of the early memorial tablets have been preserved, while over the top of the stairs leading to the crypt is a memorial to Lady D'Urban, wife of Sir Benjamin D'Urban, the Governor of the Cape from 1834 to 1838. Under the archway between the choir and St John's Chapel is a bronze recumbent statue of Archbishop West Jones, the second Archbishop of Cape Town (1874-1908). The Great North Window is a fine piece of stained glass depicting the pioneers of the Anglican church. The Cathedral's choir is superb and they regularly perform at evensong.

Slave Lodge

ⓘ *T021-460 8242, www.iziko.org.za, Mon-Sat 1000-1700, R30, children (6-18) R15, family of 4 ticket R75, under 5s free.*

On the corner of Adderley and Wale streets is Slave Lodge, the second oldest building in Cape Town. The building has had a varied history, but its most significant role was as a slave lodge for the VOC (see page 25) – between 1679 and 1811 the building housed up to 1000 slaves. Local indigenous groups were protected by the VOC from being enslaved; most slaves were consequently imported from Madagascar, India and Indonesia, creating the most culturally varied slave society in the world. Conditions at the lodge were appalling and up to 20% of the slaves died every year.

It has now been developed into a museum chartering the history of the building and slavery in South Africa. At the entrance to the exhibition is a slick cinema room, with two TVs showing a 15-minute film on the history of slavery in the Cape, highlighting the rules under which slaves lived, the conditions in which they were imported and sold, and the fundamental role slavery played in the success of Cape Town. Beyond here, the museum has a series of displays, including a model of a slave ship and images and sounds of what life was like in the lodge. The top floor houses a muddle of British and VOC weapons, household goods, furniture and money, as well as relics from Japan and ancient Rome, Greece and Egypt.

Groote Kerk
ⓘ T021-422 0569, www.grootekerk.org.za, 1000-1900, free guided tours available.
Nearby is one of Cape Town's older corners, **Church Square**, site of the Groote Kerk. Up until 1834 the square was used as a venue for the auctioning of slaves from the Slave Lodge, which faced onto the square. All transactions took place under a tree – a concrete plaque marks the old tree's position.

The Groote Kerk was the first church of the Dutch Reformed faith to be built in South Africa (building started in 1678 and it was consecrated in 1704). The present church, built between 1836 and 1841, is a somewhat dull, grey building designed and constructed by Hermann Schutte after a fire had destroyed most of the original. Many of the old gravestones were built into the base of the church walls, the most elaborate of which is the tombstone of Baron van Rheede van Oudtshoorn. Inside, more early tombstones and family vaults are set into the floor, while on the walls are the coats of arms of early Cape families. Note the locked pews, which were rented out to wealthy families in the 19th century. Two of the Cape's early governors are buried here – Simon van der Stel (1679-1699) and Ryk Tulbagh (1751-1771).

District Six Museum
ⓘ 25A Buitenkant St, T021-466 7200, www.districtsix.co.za, Mon 0900-1400, Tue-Sat 0900-1600, R30, R45 guided tour, children (under 16) R5, café and bookshop.
Housed in an old Methodist Church, this is one of Cape Town's most powerful museums and gives a fascinating glimpse of the inanity of Apartheid. District Six was once the vibrant, cosmopolitan heart of Cape Town, a largely coloured inner-city suburb renowned for its jazz scene. In February 1966, PW Botha, then Minister of Community Development, formally proclaimed District Six a 'white' group area. Over the next 15 years, an estimated 60,000 people were given notice to leave their homes and were moved to the new townships on the Cape Flats. The area was razed, and to this day remains largely undeveloped. Over the years there has been much talk about relocating some of those who were originally displaced to new housing in the area, but as yet there has been no progress.

The museum contains a lively collection of photographs, articles and personal accounts depicting life before and after the removals. There are usually a couple of musicians at the back, tinkering away at their guitars and tin pipes and adding immeasurably to the atmosphere of the place. Highlights include a large map covering most of the ground floor on which ex-residents have been encouraged to mark their homes and local sights. The **Namecloth** is particularly poignant: a 1.5-m-wide length of cloth has been provided for ex-residents to write down their comments, part of which hangs by the entrance. It has grown to over 1 km, and features some moving thoughts. A display in the back room looks at the forced removals from the Kirstenbosch area.

City Hall and Grand Parade

From Adderley Street, a short walk down Darling Street will take you to the City Hall and the Grand Parade. The latter is the largest open space in central Cape Town and was originally known as Wapen Plein (Square of Arms), which was the site of Jan van Riebeck's original fort in the 1650s before the castle was built and the square was used for garrison parades. In 1994, after his release from prison, Nelson Mandela made his first speech from City Hall to over 250,000 people. More recently it was used as the city's principal fan park during the 2010 FIFA World Cup™. The neoclassical City Hall, built to celebrate Queen Victoria's golden jubilee and built of honey-coloured Bath stone imported from England, overlooks the parade. Its clock tower is a half-size replica of Big Ben in London. In 1979 the municipal government moved to a new Civic Centre on the Foreshore, a dominant tower block which straddles Hertzog Boulevard. The hall is now a function venue and is regularly used by the Cape Town Philharmonic Orchestra (see page 62) because of its fine 3165-pipe organ. Its specifications were drawn up by Sir George Martin, organist of St Paul's Cathedral in London at the time. Adjacent to City Hall on the corner of Darling and Parade streets is the Old Drill Hall, which was originally built in 1884 as an indoor venue for garrisons during bad weather as an alternative to the Grand Parade. It has been remodelled a number of times since then and now houses the **Cape Town Central Library** ① *T021-444 0209, Mon-Thu 0900-2000, Fri 0900-1800, Sat 0900-1600.*

Castle of Good Hope

① *Buitenkant St, entry from the Grand Parade side, T021-481 7223, www.castleofgoodhope. co.za, www.iziko.org.za, 0900-1600, R30, children (5-16) R15, under 5s free, reduced rates on Sun. Free guided tours Mon-Sat 1100, 1200 and 1400. Expect to have any bags checked since the castle is still used as the regional offices for the National Defence Force.*

Beyond the Grand Parade, on Darling Street, is the main entrance of South Africa's oldest colonial building, the Castle of Good Hope. Work was started in 1666 by Commander Zacharias Wagenaer and completed in 1679. Its original purpose was for the Dutch East India Company to defend the Cape from rival European powers, and today it is an imposing sight, albeit a rather gloomy one. Under the British, the castle served as government headquarters and since 1917 it has been the headquarters of the South African Defence Force, Western Cape.

Today the castle is home to three museums. The **William Fehr Collection** is one of South Africa's finest displays of furnishings reflecting the social and political history of the Cape. There are landscapes by John Thomas Baines and William Huggins, 17th-century Japanese porcelain and 18th-century Indonesian furniture. Upstairs is an absurdly huge dining table which seats 104, in a room still used for state dinners.

To the left of the William Fehr Collection is the **Secunde's House**. The Secunde was second in charge of the settlement at the Cape, responsible for administrative duties for the Dutch East India Company. None of the three rooms contains original furniture from the castle, but they do recreate the conditions under which an official for the Dutch East

India Company would have lived in the 17th, 18th and early 19th centuries. The third museum is the **Military Museum**, a rather indifferent collection depicting the conflicts of early settlers. More absorbing are the regimental displays of uniforms and medals.

The free guided tours are informative and fun, although a little short. Tour highlights include the torture chambers, cells, views from the battlements and Dolphin Court, where Lady Anne Barnard was supposedly seen bathing in the nude by the sentries. While waiting for a tour you can enjoy coffee and cakes at a small café, or explore van der Stel's restored wine cellars, where you can taste and buy wines. There is full ceremonial changing of the guard at noon, which coincides with the firing of the Noon Gun from Signal Hill.

Adderley Street and Heerengracht

Adderley Street is one of the city's busiest shopping areas, and is sadly marred by a number of 1960s and 1970s eyesores, but it does still boast some impressive bank buildings. On the corner of Darling Street is the **Standard Bank Building** (1880), a grand structure built shortly after the diamond wealth from Kimberley began to reach Cape Town. Diagonally across is the equally impressive **Barclays Bank Building** (1933), a fine Ceres sandstone building which was the last major work by Sir Herbert Baker in South Africa. At the corner of Adderley Street and Strand Street stands a modern shopping mall complex, the **Golden Acre**. On the lower level of the complex the remains of an aqueduct and a reservoir dating from 1663 can be viewed.

Continuing down towards the docks, Adderley Street passes Cape Town Railway Station and becomes Heerengracht. At the junction with Hans Strijdom Street is a large roundabout with a central fountain and a bronze statue of Jan van Riebeeck, given to the city by Cecil Rhodes in 1899. At the bottom end of Heerengracht on the foreshore are statues of Bartholomew Dias and Maria van Riebeeck, donated respectively by the Portuguese and Dutch governments in 1952 for Cape Town's tercentenary celebrations. The palm trees here once graced a marine promenade in this area, a further indication of how much additional land has been reclaimed from Table Bay over the years. At the end of Heerengracht, on the corner of Coen Steytler Street, is the Cape Town International Convention Centre (CTICC). This is a much-used venue with several exhibition spaces that regularly holds events for the public such as the Design Indaba, Cape Town Book Fair, Decorex and the Cape Town International Jazz Festival. Check press for details or visit www.cticc.co.za.

Greenmarket Square

A couple of blocks south of the junction of Strand Street and St George's Mall, a pedestrianized road lined with shops and cafés, is Greenmarket Square, the old heart of Cape Town and the second oldest square in the city. It has long been a meeting place, and during the 19th century it became a vegetable market. In 1834 it took on the significant role of being the site where the declaration of the freeing of all slaves was made. Today it remains a popular meeting place, with a busy market (Monday to Saturday) selling African crafts and jewellery.

Dominating one side is the **Inn on the Square** hotel (see Where to stay, page 52), housed in what was once the headquarters of Shell Oil – note the shell motifs on its exterior. It was erected in two stages, in 1929 and 1941, and was modeled on Shell Mex House on the Thames Embankment in London. Diagonally opposite is the **Old Town House** ① *T021-481 3933, www.iziko.org.za, Mon-Sat 1000-1700, R20, children (6-18) R10, family of 4 ticket R50, under 5s free* (1751), originally built to house the town guard. It became the first town hall in 1840 when Cape Town became a municipality. Much of the exterior remains unchanged, and with its decorative plaster mouldings and fine curved fanlights, it is one of the best preserved Cape baroque exteriors in the city. The first electric light in Cape Town was switched on in the Old House on 13 April 1895. Today the white double-storeyed building houses the Michaelis Collection of Flemish and Dutch paintings. At the entrance to the house is a circle set into the floor which marks the spot from which all distances to and from Cape Town are measured.

Koopmans-De Wet House
ⓘ 35 Strand St, T021-481 3935, www.iziko.org.za, Mon-Fri 1000-1700, R20, children (6-18) R10, family of 4 ticket R50, under 5s free.
Just off St George's Mall, is the delightfully peaceful Koopmans-De Wet House. The house is named in memory of Marie Koopmans-De Wet, a prominent figure in cultured Cape Society who lived here between 1834 and 1906. The inside has been restored to reflect the period of her grandparents who lived here in the late 18th century. All of the pieces are numbered and a small catalogue gives a brief description. Though not too cluttered, there is a fascinating collection of furnishings which gives the house a special tranquil feel. Look out for the early map of the Cape coastline at the head of the stairs, dating from 1730 – Saldanha Bay and Cape Agulhas are clearly visible. At the back of the house is a shaded courtyard and the original stables with the slave quarters above.

Gold of Africa Museum
ⓘ 96 Strand St, T021-405 1540, www.goldofafrica.com, Mon-Sat 0930-1700, R40, children (4-16), under 4s free, R25, guided tours R70/50.
A few blocks west of Koopmans-De Wit House is the **Lutheran Church**, and next door is the **Martin Melck House**, now home to the Gold of Africa Museum. It's is also referred to as the of Africa Barbier-Mueller Museum after the museum in Geneva, Switzerland where many of the exhibits have come from. Originally the house served as a clandestine Lutheran church, as in the 18th century the Dutch authorities refused to tolerate any churches other than those belonging to the Dutch Reformed Church. The present museum celebrates the art of African goldsmithing and houses a slick display of 19th- and 20th-century gold artworks from West Africa including Mali, Ghana and Senegal, while one room is dedicated to southern Africa. Elaborate pieces include jewellery, masks, hair ornaments and statuettes and the giant gold earrings (big enough to fit around a waist) are perhaps the most astonishing. It's an absorbing collection, given the amount of valuable precious metals on display. Upstairs is a workshop where you can watch goldsmiths at work and in the leafy courtyard is a restaurant. Phone first for guided tours including the one-hour **Pangolin Tour** at 1800 after the museum has closed, when the lights are dimmed to showcase the glittering booty at its best advantage. A glass of wine sprinkled with gold leaf is included.

Long Street
Stretching for more than 20 blocks in the CBD, Long Street is one of the trendiest and most energetic streets in Cape Town and it gets particularly lively at night. Lined with street cafés, fashionable shops, bars, clubs and backpacker hostels, it has a distinctly youthful feel about it, although a clutch of new boutique hotels, posh apartment complexes and upmarket restaurants are injecting the area with a new sophisticated edge. Long Street is also home to some fine old city buildings. One of Cape Town's late Victorian gems is at No 117, now an antiques shop. On the outside is an unusual

cylindrical turret with curved windows; inside is a fine cast-iron spiral staircase leading to a balustraded gallery.

The **Slave Church Museum** ① *No 40, T021-423 6755, Mon-Fri 0900-1600, by donation*, is the oldest mission church in South Africa, built between 1802 and 1804 as the mother church for missionary work carried out in rural areas by the South African Missionary Society. It was used for religious and literacy instruction of slaves in Cape Town. Inside are displays of missionary work throughout the Cape, and behind the pulpit are displays showing early cash accounts and receipts for transactions such as the transfer of slaves.

Heritage Square

Two blocks north of Long Street, the entrance is on Shortmarket Street, is this renovated block of 17th- and 18th-century townhouses, which is home to a clutch of excellent restaurants including the **Africa Café** (see Restaurants, page 56) and the **Cape Heritage Hotel** (see Where to stay, page 51). In the centre is a cobbled courtyard holding the Cape's oldest living grape vine, which was planted in 1781. **Signal Hill Winery** ① *100 Shortmarket St, T021-424 5820, www.winery.co.za, Mon-Fri 1100-1700, Sat 1200-1600*, has alfresco tables in the courtyard for wine tasting accompanied by light snacks.

Bo-Kaap and the Bo-Kaap Museum

About 600 m west along Wale Street is Bo-Kaap, Cape Town's historical Islamic quarter and one of the city's most interesting residential areas. It was developed in the 1760s and today feels a world away from the nearby CBD. Here the streets are cobbled and tightly woven across the slopes of Signal Hill, and the closely packed houses are painted in bright hues of lime, pink and blue. The name means 'upper Cape' and it developed as a working-class district for freed slaves, who were mostly imported by the Dutch from Malaysia, Indonesia and other parts of Asia. Today's Cape Malay community in Bo-Kaap are the descendents of these. It was this community who also introduced Islam to South Africa and the Owal Mosque on Dorp Street, built in 1794, is the oldest mosque in the country and there are nine other mosques in the district. The air here rings with muezzin calls before the five daily prayers. Opposite the museum on Wale Street, **Atlas Trading** is a shop worth stopping by to see the shelves stacked with relishes and pickles and at the back the wooden boxes of spices used in Cape Malay cooking. You can do a great half-day tour of Bo-Kaap with **Andulela Experience** (see page 68), which includes a walkabout, a visit to the museum and a cookery class and lunch in a local family's home. To the west, Bo-Kaap blends into the trendy new shopping and nightlife area of De Waterkant (see over)

The **Bo-Kaap Museum** ① *71 Wale St, T021-481 3938, www.iziko.org.za, Mon-Sat 1000-1700, R20, children (6-18) R10, family of 4 ticket R50, under 5s free*, housed in an attractive 18th-century house, is dedicated to the Cape's Malay community and contains the furnishings of a wealthy 19th-century Muslim family. There are antique furnishings and Islamic heirlooms such as an old Koran and *tasbeh* beads set in front of the mihrab alcove, while the back room has displays dedicated to the input that slaves had in the economy and development of Cape Town. The photos are the most interesting articles, giving a fascinating glimpse of life in the Bo-Kaap in the early 20th century. The house itself is one of the oldest buildings in Cape Town surviving in its original form. It was built by Jan de Waal for artisans in 1763 and it was here that Abu Bakr Effendi started the first Arabic school and wrote important articles on Islamic law. He originally came to Cape Town as a guest of the British government to try and settle religious differences amongst the Cape Muslims.

De Waterkant, Green Point and Sea Point → *For listings, see pages 51-70.*

These suburbs are the closest residential areas to the city. De Waterkant – once a run-down area of flaking bungalows – is now Cape Town's most fashionable district, with beautifully restored Victorian and Georgian homes painted in bright hues crammed into a tight cobbled grid of streets, climbing up towards Signal Hill. This is not only the city's main gay area, but has an excellent choice of nightlife, super-trendy restaurants, bars and boutiques. Most of these are in the **Cape Quarter** ① *T021-421 1111, www.capequarter. co.za,* a shopping/dining complex with two charming outside piazzas surrounded by restaurants with central water features and trees with twinkly lights. Recently extended, this now covers several large blocks between Waterkant Street and Somerset Road, and the Victorian façades on Somerset Road have been incorporated into the complex. The origins of the district come from when the first merchant, a Michiel Christiaan Vos, developed the land for commercial use in 1817. Vos Lane still exists (and now serves as the main entrance to the Cape Quarter), as does Hudson and Dixon streets, also named after early merchants.

About 500 m beyond, along Somerset Road, is the start of Green Point, where there is a large roundabout with a turning northeast to the V&A Waterfront. From here, Somerset Road turns into Main Road and then runs through Green Point and the length of Sea Point. Both are upmarket suburbs of high-rise apartment blocks on the side of Signal Hill with ocean views and all the conveniences along Main Road, such as shopping malls and restaurants. Flanking the roundabout is the unmissable new Cape Town Stadium, built for the 2010 FIFA Football World Cup™ at a cost of US$600 million. At 52 m high and surrounded by 60 ha of parkland, it accommodates 55,000 seated spectators (although nearer 65,000 when standing on the pitch is included, as attested to during the 2013 Justin Bieber Believe Tour™). When a sports event or concert is on, Cape Town City Council widely publishes information locally about road closures, parking and special public transport.

To the west of the stadium, the main entrance gates to the Green Point Urban Park (0700-1900; free) is off Helen Suzman Boulevard or opposite the lighthouse on Beach Road, although there are also several others around its perimeter. Another legacy of the development for the 2010 FIFA Football World Cup™, it's a series of perfectly manicured lawns and beds planted with indigenous flowers and trees, and it shares ponds and water features with the neighbouring Metropolitan Golf Club (see page 66). Interestingly, the whole of this green area in Green Point was vested land that was granted to the Cape Town City Council in 1923 by the Union Government as 'commonage' for general public recreation and sports fields.

Running parallel to Main Road is Beach Road which winds its way from the V&A Waterfront and around Mouille Point, where there is another smart row of apartment blocks and the 20-m-tall red and white candy-striped **Green Point Lighthouse**. This is the oldest working lighthouse on the South African coast, built by Herman Schutte (a German builder) in 1824, and electrified in 1929. The pleasant Sea Point Promenade follows the length of Beach Road from Mouille Point to Bantry Bay, a distance of about 5 km. It's intercepted by short stretches of beach and has an adjoining strip of park where there are attractions for children such as a mini-train, maze, mini-golf and playgrounds. Primarily it's a place where local people jog, rollerblade or walk their dogs and there are good views of Table Bay and some surf spots below the promenade wall. The beach is unsafe for swimming, but there are a couple of rock pools and an excellent open-air swimming pool (see page 68).

ⓘ *Information desks on Dock Rd next to the Ferryman's Pub and on the lower floor of Victoria Wharf, 0900-2100, information line T021-408 7600, www.waterfront.co.za, shops open 0900-2100, restaurants and other attractions vary; details of all amenities can be found on the website.*

The V&A (Victoria and Alfred) Waterfront, Cape Town's original Victorian harbour and the city's most popular attraction, receives in excess of 10 million visitors a year. The whole area was completely restored in the early 1990s, and today it is a lively district packed with restaurants, bars and shops, and there is a whole host of things to see and do. Original buildings stand shoulder to shoulder with mock-Victorian shopping malls, museums and cinemas, all crowding along a waterside walkway with Table Mountain towering beyond. Despite being geared towards tourists it remains a working harbour, which provides much of the area's real charm. To explore the harbour and beyond, there are boat companies

④ De Waterkant, V&A Waterfront & Green Point

500 metres	De Waterkant Village	Village Lodge **5**	La Petite Tarte **3**
500 yards	& Charles Hotel **3**	Westin Cape Town **10**	Mano's **9**
	Graeme **9**		Wafu & Wakame **10**
Where to stay 🛏	Radisson BLU Hotel	**Restaurants** 🍴	
Big Blue Backpackers	Waterfront **6**	Giovanni's **2**	**Bars & clubs** 🍸
Lodge **7**	Sunflower Stop **1**	Grand Café & Beach **4**	Buena Vista Social Café **12**
Cape Royale **8**			

along Quay 5 in front of Victoria Wharf offering all manner of boat cruises, from short half-hour harbour tours to two-hour sails to Camps Bay by schooner.

The choice of shops, restaurants and entertainment is unrivalled. When the main mall **Victoria Wharf** opened, it was similar to any other South African shopping mall and featured the usual chain stores. Over the years and with growing popularity the quality of shops has shifted upmarket. The majority now sell clothes, souvenirs, jewellery and specialist items, with luxury brands such as Gucci, Jimmy Choo and Burberry. There are more than 80 restaurants. However, the location and popularity come at a price, and the cost of a meal here is considerably more than elsewhere in Cape Town.

Arriving at the Victoria and Alfred Waterfront

Getting there To get here there is a MyCiTi bus service that runs from the Civic Centre on Herzog Boulevard near the railway station in the city centre or there's a Golden Arrow bus service that runs along Beach Road in Sea Point and Green Point to the V&A. City Sightseeing has its ticket office outside the Two Oceans Aquarium on Dock Road. If you're driving there are several multi-storey car parks. The one underneath Victoria Wharf is the most expensive – put it this way, if you went to see a movie, it would cost more to park than the price of a movie ticket. The other car parks are half the price.

Background

The V&A Waterfront derives its name from the two harbour basins around which it is developed. Construction began in 1860, when Prince Alfred, Queen Victoria's second son, tipped the first load of stone to start the building of the breakwater for Cape Town's harbour. Alfred Basin could not handle the increased shipping volumes and subsequently a larger basin, the Victoria Basin, was built. A number of original buildings remain around the basins and are an interesting diversion from the razzmatazz of the shops and restaurants.

Clock Tower

At the narrow entrance to the Alfred Basin, on the Berties Landing side, is the original Clock Tower, built in 1882 to house the port captain's office. This is in the form of a red octagonal Gothic-style tower and stands just in front of the **Clock Tower Centre**, a modern mall with a collection of shops, offices and restaurants. The Clock Tower Centre houses the Nelson Mandela

Victoria Basin

South Arm

Port

4

Duncan Rd

Customs Gate

Flyover

10

Cape Town International Convention Centre (CTICC)

Long St

Coen Steytler Av

2

To Airport & Winelands

➡ **Cape Town maps**
1 Cape Town orientation, page 21
2 Cape Town Centre, page 31
3 Gardens & Tamboerskloof, page 33
4 De Waterkant, V&A Waterfront & Green Point, page 42
5 V&A (Victoria & Alfred) Waterfront, page 44

Café Manhattan **11**
Crew Bar **5**
Fireman's Arms **6**
Slug & Lettuce **13**
Tobago's **14**

Gateway to Robben Island, from where you catch the main ferry to the island (see page 46). Just next to the Clock Tower Centre, is the small **Chavonnes Battery Museum** ① *T021-416 6230, www.chavonnesmuseum.co.za, 0900-1600, R25, children (10-18) R10,*

⑤ V&A (Victoria & Alfred) Waterfront

▲ To Robben Island (11.4 km)

To Helipad

Granger Bay

3

Jetty 2

Victoria Basin

Quay 6

Collier Jetty

1
2
Victoria Wharf
3

Buses to City Centre, Green Point & Sea Point

Jetty 1

8 Boat & helicopter operators & Table Bay Diving
6

Penny Ferry

Nelson Mandela Gateway

Clock Tower

Nu Metro Cinema & Red Shed Craft Workshop

Maritime Centre

Quay 5

T Jetty

Swing Bridge

Clock Tower Square

Clock Tower Centre
5

11 V&A Waterfront Amphitheatre

Quay 4
7
Pierhead

Port Captain's Building

Market Plaza
Union Castle Building
Cape Wheel
12
10
Vaughan Johnson's Wines

Alfred Mall
4

Chavonnes Battery Museum

Nobel Square

Time Ball Tower
5

Alfred Basin

Somerset
Cape Medical Museum

Bascule Bridge
2 **13**

Craft Market

Robinson Graving Dock

Portswood Square
Cape Town Sightseeing

Two Oceans Aquarium

Fort Wynyard

1

6

➡ **Cape Town maps**
1 Cape Town orientation, page 21
2 Cape Town Centre, page 31
3 Gardens & Tamboerskloof, page 33
4 De Waterkant, V&A Waterfront & Green Point, page 42
5 V&A (Victoria & Alfred) Waterfront, page 44

To Mouille Point, Sea Point
To Cape Town Stadium & Green Point

400 metres
400 yards

To Helen Suzman Boulevard & Green Point
4

To Docks & City Centre
To City Centre
To Docks Entrance & City Centre
To Green Point & Sea Point
To City Centre
Helen Suzman Blvd

Where to stay 🛏
Cape Grace **2**
One & Only **6**
Protea Hotel
  Breakwater
  Lodge **1**
Queen Victoria
  & Dock House **5**

Radisson BLU Hotel
  Waterfront **8**
The Table Bay **3**
Victoria & Alfred **4**

Restaurants 🍴
Baia **1**
Balducci's **2**

Bascule Whiskey, Wine
  & Cocktail Bar **13**
Belthazar **3**
Cape Town Fish Market **11**
Den Anker **4**
Emily's **5**
Quay Four **7**
San Marco **8**

Wang Thai **6**

Bars & clubs 🍸
Ferryman's Tavern **12**
Mitchell's Scottish
  Ale House **10**

which lies underneath a modern office building and displays relics of a fortified structure built by the Marquais of Chavonnes of the Dutch East India Company in 1726. Built in an arc shape, it once held a battery of 16 cannons ready to fire out to sea over a 180° angle. It remained in service until 1860 when the construction of Alfred Basin began and some of the demolished walls were used to fortify the new docks. Parts of the remaining walls can be seen, there are exhibits about Cape Town's history as a military outpost, and visitors can help load an 18-pound cannon. This side of the Waterfront is connected to the bulk of the area by a swing bridge, which swings open every 10 minutes to allow boats to pass underneath.

Union Castle Building

Walking across the swing bridge (look out for the Cape fur seals on a landing to your right as you cross), you come to the stocky square building known as **Union Castle Building** (1919), designed by the firm of architects owned by Sir Herbert Baker. The Union Steamship Company and the Castle Line both ran monthly mail ships between Britain and South Africa in the late 19th century. In 1900 they amalgamated and from then on mail was delivered every week. The last Union Castle ship to sail to England with the mail was the *Windsor Castle* in 1977. This is now home to the **Maritime Centre** ⓘ *T021-405 2880, www.iziko.org.za, 1000-1700, R20, children (6-18) R10, family of 4 ticket R50, under 5s free*, a collection of model ships and objects associated with the era of mail ships. It also holds an archive of over 20,000 photographs of ships that visited Cape Town from the 1920s to the 1960s.

Opposite the Union Castle Building is the **Victoria & Alfred Hotel**. Now a luxury four-star hotel and shopping mall, the building was originally a coal store before being converted into Union Castle's warehouse and customs baggage store.

To the south of the hotel is **Nobel Square** ⓘ *www.nobelsquare.com*, which was opened on 16 December 2006, the Day of Reconciliation, and pays tribute to four of South Africa's Nobel Peace Prize laureates – the late Nkosi Albert Luthuli (1961), Archbishop Desmond Tutu (1984) and FW de Klerk and Nelson Mandela who jointly won it in 1993. Slightly larger than life-size statues of the four formidable men stand next to each other with a backdrop of Table Mountain and, in front of the sculpture, the Laureates' preferred quotations engraved in their chosen language. In the middle of the square, the Peace and Democracy sculpture – a narrative work of a jumble of people and faces on top of each other – represents the contribution made by women and children to the attainment of peace in South Africa.

Market Square

Beyond the Union Castle Building and Quay 4 is Market Square, an open plaza-like area in front of one of the main entrances to Victoria Wharf. It's a popular spot for buskers and is lined with restaurants and pubs with alfresco tables, as well as the main food court of Victoria Wharf that has numerous takeaway counters and a communal seating area. The attractions here include the **V&A Waterfront Amphitheatre** ⓘ *daily at 1700 in summer, and weekends at 1600 in winter, check the programme on the website*, an outdoor semi-circle of brick steps overlooking a stage where there are free concerts and children's entertainment, and the **Cape Wheel** ⓘ *T021-418 2502, www.capewheel.co.za, Sun, Wed-Thu 1200-1800, Fri-Sat 1200-2000, R80, children (4-12) R40, family of 4 ticket R210, under 4s free*, an observation wheel and a mini-replica of the London Eye. It has 30 air-conditioned cars, two of which can accommodate wheelchairs, and the ride takes about 15 minutes to an optimum height of 40 m. It offers superb views of the V&A, Table Mountain, Cape Town Stadium and Robben Island.

Time Ball Tower
Heading south, on the other side of Dock Road above the car park, is the 1894 Time Ball Tower; its purpose was to act as an accurate reference for ships' navigators who set their clocks as the ball on the roof fell. Correct time was vital for navigators to be able to determine precise longitude.

Two Oceans Aquarium
① *Entrance is on Dock Rd, by the Waterfront Craft Market, T021-418 3823, www.aquarium. co.za, 0930-1800, R118, children (4-13) R58 (14-17) R92, under 4s free.*
Focusing on the unique Cape marine environment created by the merging of the Atlantic and Indian Ocean, this aquarium is the top attraction on the Waterfront. The display begins with a walk through the Indian Ocean, where you'll follow a route past tanks filled with a multitude of colourful fish, turtles, seahorses and octopuses. Highlights include giant spider crabs and phosphorescent jellyfish floating in a mesmerizing circular current. Then you walk past touch pools, where children can pick up spiky starfish and slimy sea slugs. Free puppet shows and face painting keep children busy at the **Alpha Activity Centre** in the basement. The main wall here looks out into the water of the actual harbour, and you can watch Cape fur seals dart and dive before the glass. The seals are fed at 1100 and 1400. Upstairs is a vast tank holding the Kelp Forest, an extraordinary tangle of giant kelp that sways drunkenly in the artificial tides. The highlight is the Predators exhibit, a circular tank complete with glass tunnel, holding ragged-tooth sharks, eagle rays, turtles and some impressively large hunting fish. There are daily feeds at 1500 and, with an Open Water diving certificate, you can arrange to dive with the sharks for R655.

Robben Island → *For listings, see pages 51-70.*

Tours to the island are run by the **Robben Island Museum** ① *T021-413 4220, www.robben-island.org.za.* The Nelson Mandela Gateway at the Clock Tower Centre is the embarkation and disembarkation point for tours. The Gateway also houses a shop, the ticket office and a small **museum** ① *open 0730-2100*, with photographic and interactive displays on Apartheid and the rise of African nationalism. An air-conditioned catamaran completes the half-hour journey to the island. Tickets cost R230, children (under 18) R120. Tours begin with a 45-minute drive around the key sites, including Sobukwe's house, the lime quarry where Mandela was forced to work, the leper cemetery and the houses of former warders. Tours around the Maximum Security Prison are conducted by ex-political prisoners whenever possible, who paint a vivid picture of prison life here. Departures are daily at 0900, 1100, 1300 and 1500, and the whole excursion lasts 3½ hours. You must remain with your guide throughout the tour. Be sure to book a day ahead (or several days in peak season) as tickets sell out quickly, and always phone ahead to see if the ferry is running in bad weather. Do not drink any tap water on the island.

Lying 12 km off Green Point's shores, Robben Island is best known as the notorious prison that held many of the ANC's most prominent members, including Nelson Mandela and Walter Sisulu. It was originally named by the Dutch, after the term for seals, 'rob' – actually a misnomer as none are found here. The island's history of occupation started in 1806, when John Murray was granted permission by the British to conduct whaling from the island. During this period the authorities started to use the island as a dumping ground for common convicts; these were brought back to the mainland in 1843, and their accommodation was deemed suitable only for lepers and the mentally ill. These were in turn moved to the mainland between 1913 and 1931, and the island entered a new era as a military base during the Second World War. In 1960 the military passed control of the island over to the Department of Prisons, and it remained a prison until 1996. On 1 December 1999 the island was declared a World Heritage Site by UNESCO.

Robben Island's effectiveness as a prison did not rest simply with the fact that escape was virtually impossible. The authorities anticipated that the idea of 'out of sight, out of mind' would be particularly applicable here, and to a certain extent they were correct. Certainly, its isolation did much to break the spirit of political prisoners, not least Robert Sobukwe's. Sobukwe, the leader of the Pan African Congress, was kept in solitary confinement for nine years. Other political prisoners were spared that at least, although in 1971 they were separated from common law prisoners, as they were deemed a 'bad' influence. Conditions were harsh, with forced hard labour and routine beatings. Much of the daily running of the maximum security prison was designed to reinforce racial divisions: all the wardens, and none of the prisoners, were white; black prisoners, unlike those deemed coloured, had to wear short trousers and were given smaller food rations. Contact with the outside world was virtually non-existent – visitors had to apply for permission six months in advance and were allowed to stay for just half an hour. Newspapers were banned and letters were limited to one every six months.

Yet despite these measures, the B-Section, which housed Mandela and other major political prisoners, became the international focus of the fight against Apartheid. The last political prisoners left the island in 1991.

Southern suburbs → For listings, see pages 51-70.

Primarily encompassing the more affluent residential areas of Cape Town, the suburbs, stretching southeast from the centre, are an interesting diversion to the usual tourist spots. Although a car is the best way to visit them, it's possible to reach all by train – the Metrorail service between the city centre and Simon's Town runs through the suburbs and there is the option of buying a hop-on hop-off ticket on this line as part of the Southern Line initiative (see page 77), but to get to the sights away from the railway line you'll need a car or the City Sightseeing bus (page 23) stops at some.

Woodstock and Observatory

The first suburb, less than 3 km from the city centre, is **Woodstock**, a mixed commercial and residential area, and historically a working-class coloured district. Today it is somewhat run down, although the back streets are an attractive mesh of Victorian bungalows, some of which have been taken over by fashionable bars and restaurants, and both Main and Albert roads are dotted with junk and decor shops. Woodstock's most popular attraction is the **Old Biscuit Mill** ① *373-375 Albert Rd, T021-447 8194, www.theoldbiscuitmill.co.za, Mon-Sat 1000-1700*, a converted mill and now home to a variety of 'lifestyle' shops – furniture, interior design and art galleries – and restaurants. The overwhelming reason to come to Woodstock is the **Neighbourgoods Market** ① *T021-448 1438, www.neighbourgoodsmarket.co.za, Sat 0900-1400*, held at the Old Biscuit Mill on a Saturday morning. The stalls sell organic vegetables, home-made bread, pastries, cupcakes, chutneys, jams, goat's cheese, chocolate and many more delicious goodies. You can also get food such as Indian curries, Mexican wraps, Greek kebabs, sushi and pizza, accompanied by a glass of fizz or a bloody Mary, and sit on sociable trestle tables or hay bales to eat.

After Woodstock, **Observatory** is an appealing area of tightly packed houses, narrow streets and, being close to the university, student hangouts. The observatory after which the suburb is named is where Station Road intersects Liesbeeck Parkway. Aside from making astronomical observations the observatory is responsible for accurate standard time in South Africa, and has a seismograph which records earthquakes around the world. Observatory is also where you'll find the **Groot Schuur Hospital**, the site of the world's first heart transplant performed by Professor Christiaan Barnard. The **Heart of Cape Town Museum** ① *Groot Schuur Hospital, Main Rd, Observatory, T021-404 1967, www.heartofcapetown.co.za, 2-hr guided tours run daily at 0900, 1100, 1300 and 1500 and must be pre-booked, R200, children (10-16) R100, under 10 free,* explains the story and has a number of rooms including the two adjoining theatres that were used for the transplant, which took place in 1967. The informative tours go a long way to recreate the tension of the night of 2 December, and the eerie waxwork figures of Barnard and his team are brought to life with a soundtrack of clinking scalpels.

Mowbray, Rosebank and Rondebosch
The next suburbs of Mowbray, Rosebank and Rondebosch lie just below the **University of Cape Town (UTC)**. Again, they are popular with students and have a good selection of restaurants and shops. **Mowbray** was originally known as Driekoppen, or three heads, after the murder by three slaves of a European foreman and his wife in 1724. On their capture they were beheaded and their heads impaled on stakes at the farm entrance to act as a deterrent. **Rondebosch**, is well known for being associated with education, and aside from the university, several important schools were founded in the district. The area was also important from a practical point of view: in 1656 Van Riebeeck realized that Company's Garden was exposed to a damaging southeast wind. His first choice of a more sheltered spot was Rondebosch. This proved a success and a grain storage barn was built. Early accounts describe the area as wild country, with the farmers frequently losing livestock to hyenas, lions and leopards – an image that is hard to imagine as you sit in the evening rush hour on Rhodes Drive. Also in Rondebosch is the **Groot Schuur Estate**, the President's official residence and the original residence of the Cape Governor over 200 years ago.

Irma Stern Museum
① *Cecil Rd, Rosebank, T021-685 5686, www.irmastern.co.za, Tue-Sat 1000-1700, R10, children (under 16) R5.*
Irma Stern was one of South Africa's pioneering artists and her lovely house displays a mixture of her own works, a collection of artefacts from across Africa and some fine pieces of antique furniture from overseas, including 17th-century Spanish chairs, 19th-century German oak furniture and Swiss *mardi gras* masks. Her portraits are particularly poignant and those of her close friends are superb, while her religious art is rather more disturbing. Stern's studio, complete with paint brushes and palettes, has been left as it was when she died.

Rhodes Memorial
① *Cearly signposted off Rhodes Dr (M3), by the Rondesbosch turning, T021-689 9151, www.rhodesmemorial.co.za, Nov-Apr 0700-1900, May-Oct 0800-1800.*

The imposing granite memorial to Cecil John Rhodes (Cape Prime Minister from 1890 to 1896) was designed by Francis Masey and Sir Herbert Baker. Four bronze lions flank a wide flight of steps which lead up to a Greek Temple. The temple houses an immense bronze head of Rhodes, wrought by JM Swan. Above the head are the words "slave to the spirit and life work of Cecil John Rhodes who loved and served South Africa". At the base of the steps (one for each year of his short 49-year life) is an immense bronze mounted figure of *Physical Energy* given to South Africa by GF Watts, a well-regarded sculptor of the time; the original stands in Hyde Park, London. Other than the memorial, the great attraction here is the magnificent view of the Cape Flats and the southern suburbs. Behind the memorial are a number of popular trails leading up the slopes of Devil's Peak. Also tucked away here is an excellent little tea house (0900-1700) set in a garden of blue hydrangeas that serves breakfasts, light meals and excellent cheesecake and cream teas. Bookings (T021-689 9151) are advised for brunch on summer weekends.

South of Rondesbosch

By this point the southern suburbs have reached right around Devil's Peak and the shadowy mountains now dominating the views represent an unfamiliar view of Table Mountain. The suburb of **Newlands** backs right up to the slopes of the mountain and is probably best known for being the home to Western Province Rugby Union and the beautiful Newlands cricket Test Ground, now known as Sahara Park. There are several good hotels and guesthouses in the area.

Newlands ① *Boundary Rd, a few minutes' walk from Newlands Station, T021-659 6700, www.newlandstours.co.za, pre-booked tours run Mon-Fri 0900-1700, from R55, children (under 16) R40.* The first official rugby match at Newlands was played in 1890 and the stadium was a venue for 1995 World Cup matches. The first recorded cricket match in Africa took place between officers in the British army in Cape Town in 1808, and the Newlands cricket oval opened in 1888. In 2003 it hosted the Cricket World Cup opening match. There are a number of fun options here run by Newlands Tours. You can visit the rugby stadium and enter through the players' entrance, see the changing rooms and run through the players' tunnel. At the cricket ground you can walk across the pitch and visit the scorer's and third umpire's booths.

Opposite Newlands and also on Boundary Road, **Josephine Mill** ① *T021-686 4939, www.josephinemill.co.za, Mon-Fri 1000-1600, Sat 1000-1400, R10, milling demonstrations Mon-Fri 1100 and 1500, R20,* the only surviving watermill in Cape Town, has been restored as a working flour mill; note the massive iron waterwheel. The building is in the style of a Cornish red-brick mill, built by a Swede, Jacob Letterstedt in 1840, and named in honour of his Crown Princess, Josephine. The mill is tucked away near the rugby stadium and has a shop selling organic stone-milled flour and bread and a peaceful tea garden and deli.

Kirstenbosch National Botanical Garden

① *Off Rhodes Dr (M3) and clearly signposted, T021-799 8783, www.sanbi.org, Sep-Mar 0800-1900, Apr-Aug 0800-1800, R45, children (6-17) R10, under 6s free. By far the easiest way of getting here is by car. Otherwise there are trains to the nearest station at Mowbray, 10 mins from the city centre. From here there is an erratic bus service or a very long walk. Alternatively, take a Rikki Taxi – they will pick up and drop off at any time other than rush hour. Most of the organized city tours also include the garden on their itinerary and the City Sightseeing bus stops here.*

Kirstenbosch, 13 km south of the city centre is South Africa's oldest, largest and most exquisite botanical garden. The gardens stretch up the eastern slopes of Table Mountain, merging seamlessly with the fynbos of the steep slopes above. Cecil Rhodes bought

Kirstenbosch farm in 1895 and promptly presented the site to the people of South Africa with the intention that it become a botanical garden. It was not until 1913 that it was proclaimed a National Botanical Garden – the Anglo-Boer War had caused the delay. The first director of the gardens was Professor Harold Pearson, who died just three years after the garden's creation. A granite Celtic Cross marks his grave in the Cycad garden. There is a fitting epitaph: "If ye seek his monument, look around you." The real development was under Professor RH Compton, who cared for the gardens for 34 years. The herbarium, named after him, houses over 250,000 specimens, including many rare plants.

A great deal of time and effort has been put into making the gardens accessible to the general public, ensuring they provide pleasure for both serious botanists and families enjoying a day out on the slopes of Table Mountain. In the **Fragrance Garden** herbs and flowers are set out so as to make appreciating their scents effortless. On a warm day, when the volatile oils are released by the plants, there are some rather overpowering aromas. The plaques are also in Braille. The **Dell** follows a beautifully shaded path snaking beneath ferns and along a stream. Indigenous South African herbs can be inspected in the **Medicinal Plants Garden**, each one identified and used by the Khoi and San peoples in the treatment of a variety of ailments. The plants' uses are identified on plaques, and it seems that most ailments are covered – kidney trouble, rheumatics, coughs, cancer, piles and bronchitis. For a sense of the past, it is worth visiting what is known as **Van Riebeeck's Hedge**. Back in 1660 a hedge of wild almond trees (*Brabejum stellatifolium*) was planted by Van Riebeeck as part of a physical boundary to try and prevent cattle rustling. Segments still remain today within the garden. The **Skeleton Path** can be followed all the way to the summit of Table Mountain. It starts off as a stepped path, but becomes fairly steep near the top. It involves a climb up a rocky waterfall; take special care in the wet season.

Perhaps the most enjoyable way of experiencing the gardens is at one of the Sunday sunset concerts held throughout summer (see Music, page 62). Also available for a small fee are eco-adventure tours, and tours by motorized golf cart. Just beyond the entrance is a shop and café on the courtyard terrace. The shop has the usual collection of curios, along with a good choice of books on South Africa and a selection of indigenous plants. With far nicer views is the **Kirstenbosch Tea Room** (see page 60) inside the gardens, which serves good meals (until 1700). And, for a reasonable price, you can have a ready-made picnic with wine and join the Capetonians on the lush lawns.

Cape Town listings

For hotel and restaurant price codes and other relevant information, see pages 10-13.

🏠 Where to stay

Cape Town has an excellent selection of accommodation from large flashy 5-star hotels to good-value small guesthouses and backpacker hostels. Book well ahead for Christmas and the New Year when Cape Town is especially popular with domestic tourists. All accommodation options can organize airport transfers.

Several agencies specialize in **medium- and long-term holiday lets** of private homes or self-catering flats. These are good value for families or groups. Try www.sa-venues.com or www.capeletting.com.

City Bowl *p30, maps p22, p31 and p33*
City centre
$$$$ Taj Cape Town, Wale St, T021-819 2000, www.tajhotels.com. Impressive offering from the Taj luxury hotel group opposite St George's Cathedral; the façades of the old South African Reserve Bank have been kept. 177 palatial rooms. **Bombay Brasserie** is a superb Indian restaurant, there's a champagne and oyster bar, gym and spa.
$$$$ Westin Cape Town, Convention Sq, Lower Long St, T021-412 9999, www.westincapetown.com. This huge grey-glass structure overlooks the convention centre and has 483 rooms, in modern and minimalist style. Facilities include popular rooftop spa, gym and pool, 5 restaurants and bars, and service is impressively swift and efficient.
$$$$-$$$ Hilton Cape Town, 112 Buitengracht St, T021-481 3700, www3.hilton.com. Modern Hilton with top-class facilities and 137 rooms, outdoor heated pool, 3 restaurants: **Signal Hill Terrace**, Arabic food and shisha pipes, **Mezbaan**, Indian food, and **Bistro 126**

for Mediterranean and seafood. Walking distance to museums and Bo-Kaap district.
$$$ Cape Heritage Hotel, Heritage Sq, 90 Bree St, T021-424 4646, www.capeheritage.co.za. Charming hotel set in a rambling renovated town house dating from the late 17th century. The 17 huge rooms are individually styled, with muted coloured walls and contemporary decor, but retain the high teak ceilings and yellowwood floors.
$$$ Grand Daddy, 38 Long St, T021-424 7247, www.granddaddy.co.za. Long St's most eccentric boutique hotel, with 45 rooms and, like its sister hotel, **Daddy Long Legs** (see below), it is decorated throughout by local artists and the design element is simply stunning. Talk of the town are the 7 vintage Airstream trailers (**$$**) on the roof that are again individually decorated; it's a unique way to sleep in Cape Town. **Daddy Cool** is a sexy and stylish cocktail bar and the Showroom Cafe offers good food with an organic and low-calorie slant.
$$$ Urban Chic, corner of Long and Pepper streets, T021-426 6119, www.urbanchic.co.za. Italian-owned hotel with 20 rooms (prices rise the higher you go, as the mountain views improve). Beautiful, airy decor, with pale colours and modern art on the walls, on the 1st floor is the stylish **Blue Horizon Sushi & Grill** with a covered glass-fronted balcony overlooking bustling Long St.
$$$-$$ Cape Town Lodge, 101 Buitengracht St, T021-422 0030, www.capetownlodge.co.za. A striking tower block with 119 rooms with CBD views. Rooftop swimming pool, gym, 2 bars, excellent steak restaurant – **The Famous Butcher's Grill** on the ground floor decorated with photos of District Six.
$$$-$$ Protea Hotel Fire & Ice! corner of New Church and Victoria streets, T021-488 2555, www.proteahotels.co.za. Fashionable place with spacious modern lobby with cocktail bar, restaurant specializing in gourmet burgers, a cheeky smoking room

where seats are fashioned as coffins, and themed elevators (Table Mountain cableway or a shark cage-dive). The 189 rooms are small but neat with all mod cons.

$$ Cape Diamond Boutique Hotel, corner of Longmarket and Parliament streets, T021-461 2519, www.africanskyhotels.com. Round the corner from Government Av and a short walk from Long St and set in a restored Art Deco diamond dealership with 60 small but comfortable and good-value rooms, contemporary decor, bar and restaurant. The rooftop terrace has excellent views of Table Mountain and the City Bowl.

$$ Daddy Long Legs, 134 Long St, T021-422 3074, www.daddylonglegs.co.za. Described as an art hotel, with 13 rooms spread across a town house, offering funky, artistic rooms – each is individually themed and designed by a local artist. Rooms are small, but the stylish, original decor makes up for it. Good value and refreshingly different.

$$ Inn on the Square, 10 Greenmarket Sq, T021-423 2050, www.threecities.co.za. Set in the historical Shell building right on Greenmarket Sq, 165 rooms with pleasant neutral decor. Small pool deck on the 8th floor with view of Table Mountain, restaurant and cigar bar, the **Dish**, on the ground floor with tables overlooking the market.

$ Long St Backpackers, 209 Long St, T021-423 0615, www.longstreetbackpackers.co.za. Sociable hostel with 80 beds in cramped dorms and doubles spread around leafy courtyard, fully equipped kitchen, TV/DVD lounge, pool room, internet, travel centre, balcony overlooking Long St; can be noisy but handy for nightlife.

Gardens and Tamboerskloof

$$$$ Cape Cadogan, 5 Upper Union St, Tamboerskloof, T021-480 8080, www.cape cadogan.com. Ultra-elegant 2-storey 19th-century mansion with 12 spacious rooms, private terraces, 4-poster beds and stone walk-in showers for 2. Shady courtyard with small pool, and a startlingly all-white dining room.

$$$$ Mount Nelson, 76 Orange St, Gardens, T021-483 1000, www.mount nelsonhotel.co.za. Cape Town's famous colonial hotel which opened in 1899 and has always welcomed celebrity guests, with 209 luxurious rooms in 6 wings overlooking Table Mountain, the parkland-type gardens, or 1 of the 2 vast heated swimming pools. Rates vary widely from R3700-13,400 depending on room and season. The celebrated **Planet Restaurant** serves Cape specialities and contemporary fare to live jazz, while the **Oasis Restaurant** is well worth visiting for the daily cream teas on the veranda.

$$$ 15 On Orange, 15 Orange St, Gardens, T021-469 8000, www.africanpridehotels. com. Great location near sights and restaurants, sleek glass-and-steel hotel with 112 large rooms. Vast 7-storey central atrium with white marble floors and retro furnishings, bar, restaurant and luxury spa.

$$$ Cape Milner, 2a Milner Rd, Tamboerskloof, T021-426 1101, www.cape milner.com. Fashionable hotel with 57 rooms with neutral pale grey decor and slick dark-wood furniture. Small infinity pool and cocktail bar. It's a popular local meeting place and has a decent restaurant serving good Capetonian cuisine.

$$$ Kensington Place, 38 Kensington Gardens, Higgovale, T021-424 4744, www.kensingtonplace.co.za. Cape Town's original luxury boutique hotel in a quiet, leafy area with excellent and friendly service and great views over the city. The 8 beautiful and good-sized rooms are individually styled with Afro-chic furnishings. Bar, small pool in tropical gardens, breakfast is served until a decadent 1300.

$$$-$$ Parker Cottage, 3 Carstens St, Tamboerskloof, T021-424 6445, www.parker cottage.co.za. Award-winning B&B set in 2 restored Victorian bungalows, 10 rooms, with claw-foot baths, fireplaces, polished wood floors, lots of antiques and flamboyant colours. Gay-friendly and an easy stroll to restaurants on Kloof St.

$$ Leeuwenvoet House, 93 New Church St, Tamboerskloof, T021-424 1133, www.leeuwenvoet.co.za. Historical guesthouse in cottage built in 1892, with original Oregon pine floors and doors, antique decor, 12 a/c rooms, some with Victorian baths. Heated swimming pool, easy walking distance to shops and restaurants but retains a peaceful atmosphere.

$$-$ Ashanti Lodge, 11 Hof St, Gardens, T021-423 8721, www.ashanti.co.za. One of Cape Town's best-known and most popular hostels, not least for its party atmosphere. Dorms and doubles in huge old house with polished wooden floors and communal balconies. There's a courtyard and small pool and a couple of spaces for camping. Lively bar serving good snacks, with pool table and DSTV, plus good booking centre. Also has a guesthouse (**$$**) nearby with smart en suite double rooms and spotless kitchen, and a 2nd hostel setup at 23 Antrium Rd in Green Point.

$$-$ The Backpack, 74 New Church St, Tamboerskloof, T021-423 4530, www.backpackers.co.za. Cape Town's 1st hostel and today one of the best run in town. Set across several houses with spotless dorms, doubles and singles. Polished wood floors, upmarket decor, tiled courtyard and pool, lovely bar with TV, meals and snacks served throughout the day, one of the best backpacker travel centres around.

$$-$ Zebra Crossing Backpackers, 82 New Church St, T021-422 1265, www.zebra-crossing.co.za. Quiet, friendly backpacker hostel straddling 2 Victorian bungalows, spotless dorms plus small double rooms, Wi-Fi and travel centre, shady courtyard café, bar and good views of Table Mountain.

De Waterkant and Green Point
p41, map p42

$$$$-$$$ Cape Royale, 47 Main Rd, Green Point, T021-430 0500, www.caperoyale.co.za. Impressive new block but with a Victorian façade, 95 1- to 2-bedroom

suites with contemporary furniture and luxurious fabrics, kitchenettes, balconies with V&A Waterfront views. Excellent **1800°**, restaurant, rooftop bar and pool with Table Mountain views, gym and spa.

$$$ Village Lodge, 49 Napier St, De Waterkant, T021-421 1106, www.thevillagelodgesa.com. Spread across 2 converted houses with 15 smallish a/c rooms, decor is trendy greys and white, with shimmery black-stone bathrooms and magnificent Table Mountain views. **Soho** restaurant serves breakfasts and Thai food. Also has a choice of cottages and apartments in the area.

$$$-$$ De Waterkant Village, reception, **The Charles**, 137 Waterkant St, De Waterkant, central reservations, T021-490 2500, www.dewaterkant.com. **Village and Life** manage over 40 historical Bo-Kaap style houses and apartments in trendy De Waterkant, each stylishly and individually decorated in either cutting-edge modern decor or with traditional antiques, sleeping 1-6, many have delightful roof terraces. They also have **De Waterkant House (**$$**)**, www.dewaterkanthouse.com, a guesthouse with 9 chic rooms, a splash pool, beautiful lounge and terrace, and **The Charles (**$$**)**, www.thecharles.co.za, a gay-friendly guesthouse with 9 lovely bright rooms, some with Victorian bath, and good views from the spacious wooden decks, which also serves as the central reception.

$$ Hotel Graeme, 107 Main Rd, Green Point, T021-434 9282, www.hotelgraeme.co.za. Well located on Main Rd, a few mins' walk to the V&A and directly opposite the stadium, with 34 rooms and 4 self-catering apartments sleeping 2-6, all with a/c and DSTV, small pool deck at back, Wi-Fi, breakfast served in a glazed courtyard; also has the popular **Slug & Lettuce** pub facing onto the street.

$$-$ Big Blue Backpackers Lodge, 7 Vesperdene Rd, Green Point, T021-439 0807, www.bigblue.za.net. An airy backpacker hostel set in a gorgeous mansion dating from 1885, with 86 beds in spacious dorms, single or doubles (some en suite). Pleasant breakfast room, bar, small pool, Wi-Fi, travel centre, TV room, kitchen.

$ Sunflower Stop, 179 Main Rd, Green Point, T021-434 6535, www.sunflowerstop. co.za. Dorms with a bit more room than most, smallish doubles, kitchen, garden with swimming pool and outdoor bar with braai, tours and travel advice. Good location close to restaurants and bars on Main Rd.

Sea Point p41

$$$$ Ellerman House, 180 Kloof Rd, T021-430 3200, www.ellerman.co.za. Award-winning luxury boutique hotel with sweeping ocean views, 9 elegant suites with quality furnishings and fabrics, valuable South African art on the walls, balconies. Beautiful well-tended gardens, pool, spa and gym, gourmet dining and wine cellar with a staggering 7500 labels.

$$$$-$$$ The Clarendon, 67 Kloof Rd, T021-434 6854, www.clarendon.co.za. Luxurious guesthouse with 10 grandly furnished rooms, some with views of Lion's Head. Large pool, breakfast and afternoon tea served on terrace, and beautiful lounge. Also has a similar upmarket guesthouse nearby in Bantry Bay at 158 Kloof Rd.

$$$ Winchester Mansions, 221 Beach Rd, T021-434 2351, www.winchester.co.za. A well-run hotel in Cape Dutch style with 76 mountain- or ocean-view rooms, some with 2 bedrooms for families. Pleasant pool deck and **Ginkgo Spa**. Also has **Harvey's** restaurant, offering fusion cuisine and jazz brunches on Sun.

$$$-$$ The Glen, 3 The Glen, T021-439 0086, www.glenhotel.co.za. Gay-friendly boutique hotel in an Italian-style villa with views of Signal Hill, 24 rooms with classy decor. Tropical garden with palm trees and pool, steam room, and can organize temporary gym membership.

$$ The Ritz Hotel, corner Main and Camberwell roads, T021-434 0809, www.cape-town-ritz-hotel.com. A bright silver high-rise and a landmark in Sea Point, this 3-star hotel is popular with tour groups and has a holiday atmosphere, with 222 simple but recently refurbished rooms with amazing ocean views. Facilities include large pool and the rooftop **Top of the Ritz**; the only revolving restaurant in Cape Town (see Restaurants, page 58). Excellent value.

$$-$ Mountview Guesthouse, 208 High Level Rd, T021-434 3335, www.mountviewspa.co.za. Friendly set-up with just 6 rooms and generous healthy breakfasts, the garden has a pool and decor features stylish African touches. An easy walk to shops on Main Rd and the Sea Point promenade.

V&A Waterfront p42, map p44

Generally hotels at the V&A Waterfront are aimed at the high-spending foreign visitor, and all are expensive. For cheaper accommodation with easy access to the V&A, consider Green Point, above.

$$$$ Cape Grace, West Quay Rd, T021-410 7100, www.capegrace.com. One of the most luxurious hotels in Cape Town, and an iconic feature of the V&A. 122 enormous rooms with plush decor, balconies have mountain or harbour views. 2 bars and the celebrated **Signal** restaurant, attractive swimming pool and deck, and there's a lovely rooftop spa.

$$$$ One&Only, Dock Rd, T021-431 5888, www.oneandonlyresorts.com. Sol Kerzner's (of Sun City fame) super-luxury 131-room hotel and as you can imagine it's stunning. Rooms have balconies or terraces overlooking Table Mountain, the ocean, 2 islands in the marina have a clutch of villas – if you are in this league you can park your yacht outside – plus a vast heated swimming pool (the largest in Cape Town) and a tranquil spa. The giant lobby has a cocktail bar, which is also used for high tea, a branch of famed Japanese restaurant **Nobu**, and the gourmet **Reuben's** restaurant, which has a wall of 5000 bottles of wine (also see Restaurants in Franschhoek, page 111).

$$$$ Radisson BLU Hotel Waterfront,
Beach Rd, Granger Bay, T021-441 3000,
www.radissonblu.com/hotel-capetown.
Quality large hotel in an unbeatable location
right on the ocean's edge and a short walk
from the V&A. All 177 rooms are spacious
with sunny decor. Infinity pool, state-of-the-
art spa and **Tobago's** restaurant and bar is
very popular for sundowners.

$$$$ The Table Bay, Quay 6, T021-
780 7878, www.suninternational.co.za.
Enormous luxury offering from the Sun
International Group, with 329 top-notch
rooms; what they lack in character they
make up for in facilities and comfort.
Large pool and sun deck, spa, bar and
good restaurant. Efficient service but feels
ostentatious (note the sculpture by the
main entrance commemorating the stays
of celebrities and politicians).

$$$ Victoria & Alfred, Pierhead, T021-419
6677, www.newmarkhotels.com. Stylishly
converted warehouse (1904) with 96
rooms, spacious with contemporary and
comfortable furnishings, some rooms
have jacuzzis on the balconies. Excellent
restaurant serving seafood and steaks, pool,
gym and spa. Also has a similar properties:
the 35-room **Queen Victoria Hotel ($$$$)**,
and the 34-room **Dock House Boutique
Hotel ($$$)**, in the precinct of heritage
buildings on Portswood Ridge, accessed
from Portswood Rd.

$$ Protea Hotel Breakwater Lodge,
Portswood Rd, T021-406 1911, www.protea
hotels.com. Housed in what was once the
Breakwater Prison (1859), this is the least
expensive option at the V&A. The 191 rooms
are fairly small but comfortable in appealing
muted grey colours, some have 2 bedrooms
for families, 2 restaurants, bar, gym, and
Wi-Fi in the 2 lounges.

Woodstock and Observatory *p47*
$$ DoubleTree by Hilton Cape Town –
Upper Eastside, 31 Brickfield Rd, Woodstock,
T021-404 0570, www.uppereastsidehotel.
co.za. The Hilton brand aimed at business

travellers with 183 small rooms, an impressive
lobby built of steel girders and white pillars,
colourful upholstery and modern pictures,
and excellent value. Bar and restaurant.
Free shuttle to the V&A 4 times a day.

$ Green Elephant Backpackers, 57 Milton
Rd, Observatory, T021-448 6359, www.green
elephant.co.za. Long-established and relaxed
backpacker joint set across 3 old Observatory
houses. Dorms and doubles, kitchen, garden
with pool and jacuzzi, small bar and Wi-Fi.
Short stroll to cafés and bars on Lower Main
Rd in Observatory.

South of Rondesbosch *p49*
$$$$-$$$ Vineyard Hotel & Spa, Colinton
Rd, off Protea Rd, Newlands, T021-657 4500,
www.vineyard.co.za. Set around a country
house originally built for Lady Anne Barnard
in 1799, with 208 a/c rooms set in 2.5 ha
of lovely landscaped parkland full of birds.
Top-class facilities include spa, gym, indoor
and outdoor heated pools, **The Square** and
Myoga restaurants (see page 59).

$$$ Andros Boutique Hotel, corner Phyllis
and Newlands roads, Upper Claremont,
T021-797 9777, www.andros.co.za. Grand
old Cape Dutch house built in 1908 by
Herbert Baker with 8 elegant rooms, white
and cream decor, relaxing terrace, pool,
sauna and spa. The smart restaurant has
candlelit tables and marble floors and a
French-influenced menu.

$$ Harfield Guest Villa , 26 1st Av,
Claremont, T021-683 7376, www.harfield.
co.za. Award-winning, elegant B&B with
9 individually designed rooms, with views
of Table Mountain. Lounge/bar, sun deck
and pool, breakfast room and dinner on
request. Walking distance to Cavendish Sq
shopping mall.

❷ Restaurants

The best source of restaurant listings are
the annual *Eat Out* magazine (www.eatout.
co.za), available at **Exclusive Books** and
other bookshops, and the website **Dining**

Out (www.dining-out.co.za). Hotels often offer an excellent choice for dining.

City Bowl *p30, maps p22 and p31*
City centre

\$\$\$ 95 Keerom, 95 Keroom St, T021-422 0765, www.95keerom.com. Thu-Fri 1200-1430, Mon-Sat 1830-2230. Beautifully presented and expensive Italian Milanese cuisine and favourites include the meat and fish wafer-thin carpaccio, soft polenta with parmesan, and *osso buco* (braised veal shanks). The restored façade is part of the original stables and slave quarters of the Company's Garden that date to 1682.

\$\$\$ Africa Café, Heritage Sq, 108 Shortmarket St, T021-422 0221, www.africacafe.co.za. Open 1800-2300. African-themed restaurant geared at tour groups, offering an excellent introduction to the continent's cuisines. The menu is a set 'feast' and includes 13 dishes from around Africa, such as Egyptian-smoked fish, Kenyan maize patties, Cape Malay mango chicken curry and springbok stew. A great experience, but it's pricey and very touristy.

\$\$\$ Bukhara, 33 Church St, T021-424 0000, www.bukhara.com. Mon-Sat 1200-1500, daily 1830-2300. Cape Town's best Indian, which also has branches at Victoria Wharf in the V&A Waterfront and Grand West Casino. Delicious melt-in-your-mouth aromatic north Indian dishes, plush decor, superb service and award-winning wine list. You can watch the chefs in the open kitchen.

\$\$\$ Savoy Cabbage, Heritage Sq, 101 Hout St, T021-4242626, www.savoycabbage.co.za. Mon-Fri 1200-1430, Mon-Sat 1900-2230. One of the best restaurants in Cape Town, serving beautifully prepared contemporary South African cuisine. The menu changes daily, and includes dishes such as gemsbok carpaccio, free-range duck breast and a gorgeous soft-centred chocolate pudding. Bookings essential.

\$\$ Keenwä, 50 Waterkant St, between Bree & Buitengracht streets, T021-419 2633, www.keenwa.co.za. Mon-Fri 1030-1600, Tue-Sat 1830-2300. Cape Town's only Peruvian restaurant with upstairs bar serving cocktails made from Pisco – a fiery grape brandy. Start with ceviche (fish marinated in lime and chili), followed by hearty traditional meat and poultry dishes cooked with potato, rice and beans.

\$\$ Mama Africa, 178 Long St, T021-424 8634. Tue-Fri 1200-1600, Mon-Sat 1900-late. Popular restaurant and bar serving 'traditional' African dishes with a great atmosphere and often with live music. The food is tasty, despite the notoriously slow service. Centrepiece is a bright green carved mamba-shaped bar.

\$\$ Marco's African Place, 15 Rose St, T021-423 5412, www.marcosafricanplace.co.za. Tue-Sun 1500-late. Good-value 'African' menu covering everything from slow-roasted Karoo lamb to samp and beans, plus popular Pan-African platter with assortment of grilled game. Live music in the evening when a cover charge is added to the bill.

\$\$-\$ Dias Tavern, 15 Caledon St, off Buitenkant St, T021-465 7547, www.diastavern.co.za. Mon-Sat 1130-1500, 1800-2200. Old fashioned pub near the Fugard Theatre so ideal for a quick pre-show meal. Serves authentic Portuguese fare like peri peri chicken, chorizo sausage, sardines, trinchado (beef in red wine) and espetada (a towering steak skewer).

\$ Biesmiellah, 2 Upper Wale St, T021-423 0850, www.biesmiellah.co.za. Open 0930-2300. Lacking in trimmings, but a prime position in colourful Bo-Kaap, this is one of the better-known and well-established Cape Malay restaurants. Try the sweet lamb and chicken curries and sticky malva pudding. No alcohol, but wash a meal down with a *falooda* – milk, rosewater and almonds.

\$ Eastern Food Bazaar, entrances on both Darling and Longmarket streets, T021-461 2458, www.easternfoodbazaar.co.za. Open 1000-2100. On the ground floor of the Wellington Fruit Growers building designed by Herbert Baker's office in 1902,

this food emporium has a long line of self-service counters for delicious and very cheap Indian, Turkish and Cape Malay spicy food. No alcohol and strictly halaal.
$ Royale Eatery, 273 Long St, T021-422 4536, www.royaleeatery.com. Mon-Sat 1200-2300. Ultra-trendy eatery specializing in over 50 gourmet burgers – try the 'Miss Piggy' with bacon and guacamole, served with sweet potato fries. **The Waiting Room**, upstairs, is a popular bar with balcony and great views of Long St.

Cafés
Café Mozart, 37 Church St, T021-424-3774 www.themozart.co.za. Mon-Fri 0700-1600, Sat 0900-1530. With tables spilling out among the stalls of Church St Antiques Market, this 30-year-old café serves excellent breakfasts, filled baguettes and croissants, and mains of seafood and inventive salads.
Mr Pickwicks, 158 Long St, T021-423 3710. Open 0800-0200. Trendy spot, a favourite with pierced and tattooed Long St locals, and sells tickets to Cape Town's major club nights and gigs. Excellent baguettes, toasties, healthy salads, large pasta portions and milkshakes.

Gardens and Tamboerskloof
$$$ Aubergine, 39 Barnet St, Gardens, T021-465 4909, www.aubergine.co.za. Tue-Fri 1200-1400, Mon-Sat 1900-2230. Sophisticated and award-winning menu, with a modern slant on classical European dishes such as foie gras and quail, the 3- to 5- course degustation menu is an elaborate affair when wine is paired to food.
$$$ Miller's Thumb, 10b Kloof Nek Rd, T021-424 3838, www.millersthumb.co.za. Tue-Fri 1230-1430, Mon-Sat 1830-2230. Beloved by locals, bookings essential, this place serves delicious seafood, plus steaks and some veggie choices, lots of spices and a Creole or Mozambique twist on some dishes.
$$ Saigon, corner of Camp and Kloof streets, T021-424 7670. Sun-Fri 1200-1430, daily 1800-2230. Superb Vietnamese and

Japanese cuisine, very popular place set on a corner overlooking busy Kloof St and roof terrace with views of Table Mountain. Good choice for vegetarians and sushi bar.
$$ Societi Bistro, 50 Orange St, Gardens, T021-424 4100, www.societi.co.za. Mon-Sat 1200-2300. A neighbourhood favourite with a bistro-style menu and cosy rooms with bare brick walls and fireplaces, snug bar with leather couches, and garden with tables under palms. On some weekday nights does a meal deal with movie tickets at the nearby Labia Cinema (see page 62).
$$ Yindee's, 22 Camp St, Tamboerskloof, T021-422 1012, www.yindees.com. Mon-Fri 1230-1430, Mon-Sat 1830-2300. An excellent Thai restaurant serving authentic spicy curries, stir-fries, soups and unusual deep-fried coconut ice cream for dessert. Served in a sprawling Victorian house with traditional low tables.
$$-$ Arnold's, 60 Kloof St, Gardens, T021-424 4344, www.arnolds.co.za. Open 0745-2300. Bustling good-value spot on busy Kloof St, good salads, pastas, burgers and more substantial meals like ostrich steak. Fast, friendly service, happy hour 1630-1830, may have to queue for a table at weekends for the legendary cooked breakfasts.
$$-$ Chef Pon's Asian Kitchen, 12 Mill St, Gardens, T021-465 5846, www.chefpons. co.za. Mon-Sat 1800-2230. Long menu of favourite dishes from across Asia, and everything arrives freshly cooked and sizzling hot but it's the Thai food that wins hands down. Decor is simple and dark, but cosy on a winter's night, and lingering after your meal is discouraged if they need the table (which they frequently do).

Cafés
Manna Epicure, 151 Kloof St, Tamboerskloof, T021-426 2413, www.mannaepicure.com. Tue-Sat 0800-1700, Sun 0800-1600. A white and bright café in an old house on trendy Kloof St. Great for elaborate breakfasts, open sandwiches made from the famous Manna's artisanal breads, and gooey cakes and

pastries. Also a takeaway bakery, **Vida e Caffè** www.vidaecaffe.co.za. Mon-Fri 0700-1800, Sat-Sun 0700-1700. The original of what has become South Africa's most successful coffee chain, with its trademark quirky atmosphere, excellent coffees and a choice of muffins and melting hot paninis. The minimalist red and white interior is packed throughout the day.

De Waterkant and Green Point
p41, map p42

$$$ Grand Café & Beach, Granger Bay Rd, Granger Bay, T021-425 0551, www. grandafrica.com. Tue-Sat 1200-late, Sun 1200-1600. Set in a restored warehouse adjacent to the V&A with its own beach created between the rocks of Granger Bay and lovely interior design. Interesting fusion menu but overpriced, better for sundowner cocktails on sofas in the sand.
$$$ Wafu & Wakame, Beach Rd, Mouille Point, T021-433 2377, www.wakame. co.za. Open 1200-1500, 1800-2230. Pair of Asian-inspired restaurants over 3 floors with unbeatable views of Robben Island and open rooftop lounge. **Waku** has a long list of steamed and fried tapas like dim sum, while **Wakamu** has mains like seared tuna or Peking duck.
$$ Mano's, 39 Main Rd, Green Point, T021-434 1090, www.mano.co.za. Mon-Sat 1200-2200. The affable Mano oversees this small Mediterranean restaurant with simple decor and a short but pleasing menu. The steak and pommes frites and lamb cutlets are always popular and there's a good choice of wine.

Cafés
Giovanni's, 103 Main Rd, Green Point, T021-434 6593. Open 0730-0900. Cape Town's best and busiest deli, and a favourite with regulars who come to chat at the coffee bar and buy the imported cheese, cold meats and olives, fresh bread and pastries and hard to come buy groceries from Italy and the UK. The delicious ready meals can be eaten here or taken away.

La Petite Tarte, Shop A11, Cape Quarter, Dixon St, De Waterkant, T021-425 9077. Mon-Fri 0830-1630, Sat 0830-1500. Charming French-style sidewalk café decorated with antique furniture, floral cushions and shelves of dainty china, serves breakfasts, light lunches and cakes, best known for the croque monsieur and chocolate gateau.

Sea Point *p41*
$$$ La Perla, corner Church and Beach roads, T021-434 2471, www.laperla.co.za. Open 0900-2300. Long-term Sea Point favourite opened in 1959, with an extensive and traditional Italian menu with over 200 dishes of seafood, excellent anitpasto, plenty of vegetarian options, and wonderful desserts.
$$$ Top of the Ritz, at the The Ritz Hotel, see Where to stay, page 51, T021-439 6988, www.ritzrestaurants.co.za. Daily 1730-2230, Sun lunch 1200-1530. Iconic revolving restaurant on the 21st floor with gorgeous views of Table Bay, Robben Island, Cape Town Stadium and the Sea Point high-rises; the floor moves a full circle every 75 mins. The menu is a throwback to the 1970s when it opened – prawn cocktail, lobster bisque, chateaubriand and crêpes suzettes. Booking essential.
$$ Posticino, 323 Main Rd, T021-439 4014, www.posticino.co.za. Open 1200-2300. Popular with local residents and always has a buzzy atmosphere, this good-value Italian is well known for its thin-based pizzas and you can make up your own pasta sauce.

V&A Waterfront *p42, map p44*
With over 80 restaurants and cafés, the Waterfront is one of the most popular districts in Cape Town for eating out and gets very busy. There is a wide range of places to eat but they generally charge unashamedly high tourist prices. Nevertheless, to experience superb cuisine and impeccable service with unparalleled harbour and mountain views, a V&A restaurant is usually on most visitors' agendas.

$$$ Baia, Victoria Wharf, T021-421 0935, www.baiarestaurant.co.za. Open 1200-1500, 1900-2300. Fine seafood restaurant spread over 4 terraces with views of Table Mountain. Expensive but delicious seafood dishes follow a Mozambique theme – try the spicy coconut prawns – and some rare wine vintages.

$$$ Balducci's, Victoria Wharf, T021-421 6002, www.balduccis.co.za. Open 0900-2230. Contemporary restaurant with seats overlooking the harbour, good choice of pasta dishes and mains ranging from ostrich steak and luxury lamb burgers, to confit de canard and blackened kingklip.

$$$ Belthazar, Victoria Wharf, T021-421 3753, www.belthazar.co.za. Open 1200-2300. Top-of-the-range steakhouse with tables overlooking the harbour. Excellent Karan dry- and wet-cured steaks, plus range of seafood and a staggering 600 South African wines.

$$$ Cape Town Fish Market, Victoria Wharf, T021-413 5977, www.ctfmco.za. Open 1100-2300. Now a quality chain found in the other main cities and there's a branch in London; this is the original. Seafood restaurant with a fisherman's theme, but the best reason to come here is to watch the Japanese chefs at the revolving sushi bar and teppanyaki table.

$$$ Den Anker, Pierhead, T021-419 0249 www.denanker.co.za. Open 0900-2300. Popular Belgian restaurant with a bar with Belgian beer on tap, views across Alfred Basin. Best known for tin pots of mussels with crispy bread and steak tartare with pommes frites.

$$$ Emily's, Clock Tower Centre, T021-421 1133, www.emily-s.com. Mon-Sat 1200-2200. Restaurant attached to a catering school serving excellent French-style cuisine with a daily changing menu, superb wine list, great views from balcony overlooking the Waterfront.

$$ Quay Four, Quay 4, T021-419 2008, www.quay4.co.za. Open 1100-2400. Hugely popular tavern and bistro with great views over the water from the broad wooden deck. Seafood

is the focus and the calamari and fish and chips served in giant frying pans are excellent value. There's often live music in the evening.

$$ Wang Thai, Victoria Wharf, T021-421 8702, www.wangthai.co.za. Open 1130-2300. Great Thai restaurant serving mouth-watering stir-fries, well known for its spicy curries with coconut milk and lemon grass. Decor is all things Buddha inspired.

Cafés

San Marco, Victoria Wharf, T021-418 5434, www.eatalian.co.za. Open 0830-2300. Alfresco tables with views of the mountain and the V&A's street performers serving a full menu of coffees and alcoholic drinks, enormous salads, stuffed paninis and gelato ice cream.

Woodstock and Observatory *p47*

$ Pancho's, 127 Lower Main Rd, Observatory, T021-447 4854, www.panchos.co.za. Mon-Sat 1730-late. Mexican dishes in a lively atmosphere, all the usual tacos and fajitas. Tasty cocktails – try the strawberry margarita.

Cafés

Obz Café, 115 Lower Main Rd, Observatory, T021-448 5555, www.obzcafe.co.za. Kitchen 0900-2230, bar until 0200. Popular student haunt open all day for light meals, coffee or cocktails, great salads and sandwiches, also has main meals in the evenings and occasional live music and stand-up comedy.

South of Rondesbosch *p49*

$$$ Myoga, Vineyard Hotel, see Where to stay, page 51, T021-657 4545, www.vineyard.co.za. Tue-Sat 1130-1500, 1830-2230. A very smart award-winning hotel restaurant with a great global fusion menu. Lunch is buffet style with a weigh-by-plate charging system and dinner is à la carte. The desserts are very creative – think violet ice cream with dissolving candy floss.

$$ Barristers Grill, corner of Kildare and Main streets, Newlands, T021-671 7907, www.barristersgrill.co.za. Mon-Fri 1100-late, Sat 0900-late, Sun 1100-2200. A popular mock-Tudor steakhouse that has expanded into a bistro/café during the day with plenty of alfresco tables. Given that it's in Newlands, it's a popular spot on a Sat afternoon to watch rugby on the giant TVs.

Cafés

The Kirstenbosch Tea Room, Kirstenbosch National Botanical Garden, T021-797 4883, www.ktr.co.za. Open 0830-1700. Lovely terrace with views of the gardens and mountain looming behind. Offers breakfasts, sandwiches and salads and lunchtime mains like sweet and spicy bobotie and ostrich burgers. The cakes, scones and artisan breads are baked on the premises. Also offers a picnic hamper service.

♦ Bars and clubs

City Bowl *p30, maps p22 and p31*
There's plenty of edgy youthful nightlife around Long St and this is the place to come for local live music and the latest dance sounds. The best source of advice on gigs and club nights is in the cafés on Long St where you can pick up fliers. The more sophisticated bars and clubs are in Green Point, the V&A Waterfront and Camps Bay. Nightclubs charge an entry fee and bars a cover charge for live music.
Assembly, 61 Harrington St, T021-465 7286, www.theassembly.co.za. Wed, Fri-Sat 2100-0400. Cavernous place in a converted loft with a very long bar, a mixed bag of music from DJs and live bands.
The Bang Bang Club, 70 Loop St, T021-426 2011, www.thebangbangclub.co.za. Wed-Sat 2100-0400. Upmarket spot with leather couches and banquettes, upstairs VIP seating and downstairs dance floors, 3 bars, house and lounge music, gets packed at weekends.
Chrome, 6 Pepper St, between Long and Loop streets, T021-422 3368, www.chromect.com. Wed-Sun, 2200-0500. Aimed firmly at the serious dance crowd, mostly hip hop and R&B, large dance floor, sophisticated lighting and sound system.

Jo'burg, 218 Long St, T021-422 0142. Open 1700-0330. Trendy neon-lit bar with industrial decor serving pints and cocktails to a mixed crowd, gay friendly, relaxed during the week but gets very busy at weekends when DJs play hip hop and commercial house.
Mercury Live & Lounge, 43 de Villiers St, T021-465 2106. Mon, Wed-Sat 2100-0200. With a stage and a bar in a darkened room, this is Cape Town's leading live indie music venue for rock, punk and hip hop acts, with a lively, young crowd.
Zula, 196 Long St, T021-424 2242, www.zulabar.co.za. Tue-Sat 1200-late. Fashionable bar and cocktail lounge with several small rooms, great balcony overlooking Long St, and occasional live music. Sells snacks like pizzas, burgers and nachos and non-alcoholic smoothies.

Gardens and Tamboerskloof

Rafiki's, 13 Kloof Nek Rd, Tamboerskloof, T021-426 4731, www.rafikis.co.za. Open 1200-0200. Popular bar overlooking Kloof Nek with a huge wrap-around balcony perfect for a sundowner. DJs and occasional live music in the evenings, simple food like pizzas and burgers.
Rick's Café Américain, 2 Park St, Gardens, T021-424 1100, www.rickscafe.co.za. Mon-Sat 1100-0200. Just off fashionable Kloof St, in a rambling old Victorian house decorated with cushion-laden couches, mirrors and elaborate candlesticks. Cocktails, beer on tap, and good inexpensive food including tapas.

De Waterkant and Green Point
p41, map p42
Buena Vista Social Café, 14 Alfred House, Portswood Rd, Green Point, T021-421 0348, www.buenavista.co.za. Open 1200-1200. Cuban-themed bar and restaurant where a fashionable crowd tuck into a mix of tapas and Tex-Mex-style dishes washed down with mojitos. Splashes of vibrant colour and fireplaces create a warm atmosphere.

Café Manhattan, 74 Waterkant St, De Waterkant, T021-421 6666, www.manhattan.co.za. Open 1000-late. Cape Town's most established gay venue in a bright yellow building with a wrap-around balcony and long bar, good varied food, especially the burgers.

Crew Bar, 30 Napier St, De Waterkant, T021-418 0118. Mon-Sun 1900-0400. Popular gay club in a historic De Waterkant house with 2 dance floors, balconies with Table Mountain views. Mostly men but women are welcome and may also appreciate the bare-chested gogo-dancers.

Fireman's Arms, corner Buitengracht Mechau Sts, T021-419 0207, www.firemansarms.co.za. Mon-Sat 1200-2300. Historic pub set in what was Cape Town's first fire station built in 1864, still complete with fire pole and fireman's hats. Best known as a place to watch sports and its get packed out on rugby match days. Good homely menu of pub grub such as liver and onions or bangers and mash.

V&A Waterfront *p42, map p44*
Ferryman's Tavern, East Pier Rd, T021-419 7748, www.ferrymans.co.za. Open 1100-2300. A popular haunt with restaurant upstairs, huge outside seating area, TV continually showing sports action, a lively mixed crowd.

Bascule Whiskey, Wine & Cocktail Bar, Cape Grace (see Where to stay, page 54), www.capegrace.com. Open 1000-2400. Overlooking the gleaming yachts in the V&A Waterfront's marina, social butterflies meet for sundowners at this glamorous bar. Has over 400 whiskies, numerous Cape wines, and the light menu features savoury and sweet tapas.

Mitchell's Scottish Ale House, East Pier Rd, T021-419 5074, www.mitchells-ale-house.com. Open 1100-2300. Next door to **Ferryman's** this is an English-style wood-panelled pub and it brews its own beer including bitter and stout, which are not common in South Africa. Sports are shown on TV and there's simple pub fare.

Tobago's, Radisson BLU Hotel Waterfront, (see Where to stay, page 55), T021-441 3000, www.radissonblu.com. Open 0900-2300. Super-stylish hotel bar set around an infinity pool, with great ocean views, a long list of cocktails. A perfect spot for sundowners and attracts a mixed crowd of tourists and after-work drinkers.

South of Rondesbosch *p49*
Forester's Arms, 57 Newlands Av, T021-689 5949, www.forries.co.za. Open 1100-late. Old-fashioned English-style pub, popular with sports fans who come to watch important matches. A fun-loving, boozy scene with a leafy beer garden and fire inside in winter.

Tiger Tiger, 103 Main Rd, Claremont, T021-683 2220, www.tigertiger.co.za. Tue, Thu-Sat 2030-late. This is the Southern Suburbs' most commercial and modern nightclub with several bars, plenty of seating areas, a large sunken dance floor and mainstream pop music. Attracts the odd local rugby or cricket star given its proximity to Newlands.

⚫ Entertainment

Casino
GrandWest Casino & Entertainment World, 1 Vanguard Dr, Goodwood, T021-505 7777, www.suninternational.com. Most facilities 1000-2400, casino 24-hr. Around 12 km to the east of the city centre in Goodwood, this multifaceted Vegas-style entertainment complex has a casino, a 6-screen Nu Metro cinema, ice-rink, 10-pin bowling alley, several restaurants and bars, and the 5000-seat Grand Arena that regularly hosts pop and rock concerts and comedy from international artists.

Cinema
The 2 major cinema groups are **Nu Metro**, www.numetro.co.za, and **Ster-Kinekor**, www.sterkinekor.com. There are multi-screen cinemas in all the large shopping malls including Canal Walk, the V&A Waterfront

and Cavendish Sq. The latter 2 also have a separate **Cinema Nouveau**, which screens international and art-house films (information and bookings also at Ster-Kinekor). For film festivals, see Festivals, below.

Labia Cinema, 68 Orange St, Gardens, T021-424 5927, www.labia.co.za. Cape Town's most enjoyable cinema, showing independent international films in a historic building that used to be the Italian Embassy's ballroom and was named after an Italian princess. It has a café serving good pre-movie snacks that is licensed, so you can take your glass of wine into the movie.

Music

All tickets for live performances can be purchased online from **Computicket**, T011-340 8000, www.computicket.com, or there are kiosks at the V&A Waterfront and Cavendish Sq and the other larger malls, as well as in Checkers and Shoprite supermarkets.

See also Bars and clubs, page 60, for live music venues.

Cape Town Opera, see Artscape (below), T021-410 9807, www.capetownopera.co.za. The acclaimed Cape Town Opera's season is usually from May-Nov, and includes at least one well known crowd pleaser, such as *Madame Butterfly*.

Cape Town Philharmonic Orchestra, T021-410 9809, www.cpo.org.za. Based at Artscape (see below) where they accompany the Cape Town Opera and Cape Town City Ballet; the orchestra also plays symphonies in the City Hall.

Kirstenbosch Summer Concerts, at Kirstenbosch National Botanical Garden (see page 49), T021-799 8782, www.sanbi.org. Nov-Mar every Sun at 1700. Summer concerts from folk and jazz to classical and opera, and the occasional international pop star, in an idyllic setting where you can picnic on the lawns. The programme is published at the beginning of Oct and ticket prices vary but include garden entry.

Theatre

Tickets from **Computicket**, see above.
Artscape, DF Malan St, Foreshore, T021-410 9800, www.artscape.co.za. Cape Town's major complex offering opera, ballet, theatre and music, with several stages and a main theatre seating 1500.
Baxter Theatre, Main Rd, Rondebosch, T021-685 7880, www.baxter.co.za. Hosts community theatre and children's performances, as well as international productions and musicals.
Fugard Theatre, Caledon St, off Buitenkant St, City Centre, T021-461 4554, www.thefugard.com. Cape Town's newest theatre named after renowned South African playwright Athol Fugard is located in the restored historical Sacks Futeran Building, which used to house tailors and seamstresses in the District Six days. Shows musicals, plays and comedy.
Theatre on the Bay, Link St, Camp's Bay, T021-483 3301, www.theatreonthebay.co.za. Interesting mix of plays, comedy and musicals. The restaurant here is good and there's the option of a pre-show dinner and then dessert in the interval.

⊙ Festivals

There are a number of events throughout the year; many of which fall over public holiday weekends. See www.capetown.travel for full listings. Islamic holidays are celebrated across Cape Town as the majority of Cape Coloureds are Muslim, while the Christian holidays are celebrated by other communities.
2 Jan Karnaval (also known as **Kaapse Klopse**). This carnival, staged by the Cape Coloured community, begins in Bo-Kaap, ends up near the Green Point Stadium, and includes a procession of competing minstrel bands, with painted faces, straw boaters and bright satin suits.
Jan J&B Metropolitan Handicap, last Sat in Jan, www.jbmet.co.za. South Africa's major horse racing meet at Kenilworth Race Course, where everyone is expected to dress

up and there's plenty of TV coverage for the fashion and social events.

Feb/Mar Cape Town Pride, www.cape townpride.org. The biggest gay event in town, with floats and a parade around Green Point culminating in a street party in De Waterkant.

Mar Cape Town Carnival, www.capetown carnival.com. A fabulous and extravagant 1-km procession of floats, dancers and musicians along Somerset Rd in Green Point between De Waterkant and the Cape Town Stadium followed by a street party with local DJs. Cafés and street vendors serve snacks and beverages along the route. In just a few years since its conception, this has become one of Cape Town's most popular annual events.

Mar Cape Town Festival, www.capetown festival.co.za. Music festival held over the weekend of the Human Rights' Day public holiday on 21 Mar at various venues, with a main stage in Company's Garden. It features many of Cape Town's home-grown musicians.

Mar Cape Argus Pick 'n' Pay Cycle Tour, www.cycletour.co.za. The world's largest timed cycling event taking an impressive 109-km route around Table Mountain and along the shores of the peninsula. It's open to international cyclists and attracts some 40,000 participants each year.

Apr Two Oceans Marathon, www.two oceansmarathon.org.za. Dubbed as one of the most beautiful marathons in the world, it runs on a 56-km route around the Cape Peninsula, and attracts over 26,000 runners; there's also a half marathon and a number of fun runs, and again they are open to international competitors.

Apr Cape Town International Jazz Festival, www.capetownjazzfest.com. Held at the Cape Town International Convention Centre (CTICC), where 5 stages host a huge array of local and international jazz artists and on 1 night there's a free concert in Greenmarket Sq. This celebrated event now attracts in excess of 30,000 people.

May Taste of Cape Town, www.tasteof capetown.com. Held at the Cape Town Cricket Club in Green Point next to the Cape Town Stadium with stalls and marquees, some of the city's top gourmet restaurants showcase their food; buy a book of coupons and a wine glass for tastings.

May Cape Times V&A Waterfront Wine Affair, www.waterfront.co.za. You can taste over 350 wines from 95 estates, and food is from participating V&A Waterfront restaurants.

May Good Food & Wine Show (2nd weekend). At the Cape Town International Convention Centre (CTICC), this celebrates gourmet food and good wine, with tastings and Cape Town's best restaurants serving up tempting mini-plates, plus hands-on cooking experiences and demonstrations from celebrity BBC chefs from the UK (gourmetsa.co.za).

May Sexpo (2nd weekend). The world's largest health, sexuality and lifestyle show at the Cape Town International Convention Centre (CTICC) attracts a staggering 35,000 each year for shopping, shows, food and wine, even pole-dancing lessons (sexpo.co.za).

Jun Cape Town Book Fair, www.capetown bookfair.com. The Cape Town International Convention Centre (CTICC) is filled with hundreds of thousands of books from South African and international publishers. Events include author talks and children's readings.

Jul Encounters Documentary Film Festival, www.encounters.co.za. Films screened at Nu Metro at the V&A Waterfront.

Aug Arise Cape Town Fashion Week. Runway shows at the Cape Town International Convention Centre (CTICC) showcase young and established designers from across Africa, which conclude with a dazzling display of evening wear. The sponsor, Arise, is a stylish magazine on African fashion (africanfashionint.com).

Sep Chelsea Festival at Kirstenbosch, www.sanbi.org. The best time to see the flowers in full bloom, special events include gardening talks, flower arranging contests and fine art exhibitions, but the real reason to come is to see Kirstenbosch's entry to the Chelsea Flower Show in London, for which they have won countless gold medals.

Sep Out in Africa Festival, www.oia.co.za. Gay and lesbian film festival, with screenings at Nu Metro at the V&A Waterfront.

Sep Hermanus Whale Festival, www. whalefestival.co.za. Marks beginning of calving season of southern right whales, when there is excellent land-based whale watching over Walker Bay from the cliff-tops in Hermanus. This is an easy day trip from Cape Town and features live music, a craft market, and a marquee displaying exhibits on whales. A whale-crier blows his horn when a whale is spotted.

Sep Cape Town Comedy Festival, Baxter Theatre, www.comedyfestival.co.za. A week-long festival with local and international talent.

Oct Cape Town International Kite Festival Africa's biggest celebration of kite-flying on Muizenburg Beach with acrobatic kite displays, giant inflatables, craft market, kiddie's rides, kite-making workshop and food stalls. An excellent family day out (capementalhealth.co.za/kite).

Dec Obz Festival (1st weekend). A huge street party in Observatory with stalls, live music, DJs and all-night parties. It showcases South African alternative music and is popular with students from the University of Cape Town (UCT) (www.obzfestival.com).

Dec Mother City Queer Project, www. mcqp.co.za. The city's biggest annual gay-themed party and a colourful and fun event which attracts thousands. Different venue and different dress-up code each year; there's a no costume, no entry policy.

Dec Kirstenbosch Summer Concerts (every Sun until Mar). This is a perfect way to enjoy the gardens with a picnic on the lawns; the concerts vary from rock, folk and jazz to classical and opera. A popular venue for international stars (www.sanbi.org).

O Shopping

Arts, crafts and curios

African Image, 52 Burg St, T021-423 8385, www.african-image.co.za. Mon-Sat 0900-1700. Excellent alternative to the tired souvenir shops, this sells contemporary African art, such as bags made from traditional weavings and beautiful baskets, plus quirky souvenirs like coke-bottle-top bags and old township signs.

Church St Antiques Market, on Church St, between Long and Burg streets. Mon-Sat 0900-1400. Offbeat antiques, nautical equipment, crockery and jewellery.

Greenmarket Square. Mon-Sat 0900-1600. A lively arts and crafts market selling goods from across Africa on the picturesque square flanked by several terrace cafés.

Green Point Market, on Helen Suzman Blvd. Sun 0800-1700. A good mixture of curios, especially wooden carvings. Be prepared to take part in some cheerful haggling.

Monkeybiz, 43 Rose St, Bo-Kaap, T021-426 0636, www.monkeybiz.co.za. Mon-Fri 0900-1700, Sat 0900-1300. Something of a local sensation, **Monkeybiz** creates employment for women (many of them HIV positive) in the townships of Mandela Park and Khayelitsha. The women create beautiful and quirky one-off bead works, including figures, animals and accessories.

Out of This World, Victoria Wharf, V&A Waterfront, T021-419 3246. Open 0900-2100. One of the more tasteful selections of the many African arts and crafts shops at the V&A, and there's also carefully chosen ethnic interior decor items collected from around the world.

The Pan African Market, 76 Long St, T021-426 4478, www.thepanafricanmarket. com. Mon-Fri 0900-1700, Sat 0900-1500. 2-storey centre set in a converted Victorian house, selling crafts from across the continent, good local crafts made from recycled material, beadwork, ceramics. Café specializing in African food, plus a book shop and holistic healing area.

Red Shed Craft Workshop, Victoria Wharf, V&A Waterfront. Open 0900-2100. Handful of local craftspeople, goods are of suspect taste, kitsch embroidery and satin cushions.
Streetwires, 77 Shortmarket St, T021-426 2475, www.streetwires.co.za. Mon-Fri 0900-1700, Sat 0900-1300. Another wire-sculpture cooperative supporting local communities, useful place to browse these interesting South African crafts without feeling under pressure from the usual street vendors. You can also meet the artists.

Books and maps
Clarke's Bookshop, 211 Long St, T021-423 5739, www.clarkesbooks.co.za. Mon-Fri 0900-1700, Sat 0900-1300. A mass of antiquarian, second-hand and new books in a muddled old shop, a must for any book lover, and also specializes in books on Southern Africa art.
Exclusive Books, www.exclusivebooks. co.za. National bookshop chain, the best branches are at Victoria Wharf at the V&A Waterfront and Cavendish Sq Mall, which also have cafés. Particularly good for maps, guidebooks and coffee-table books on Cape Town and Africa and carry a full range of international magazines and newspapers.
Select Books, 232 Long St, T021-424 6955. www.selectbooks.co.za. Mon-Fri 0900-1700, Sat 0900-1300. This small friendly bookshop specializes in classics, antiquarian and Africana books, with a strong emphasis on Cape Town's and South African history, plus sports like cricket and rugby.

Music
The African Music Store, 134 Long St, T021-426 0857, www.africanmusicstore. co.za. Mon-Fri 0900-1800, Sat 0900-1400. Stocks an excellent choice of music by major African artists as well as compilations and reggae. The staff are incredibly helpful and are happy to let you listen to any number of CDs before purchasing. Can ship worldwide.
Mabu Vinyl, 2 Rheede St, Gardens, T021-423 7635, www.mabuvinyl.co.za.

Mon-Sat 0900-1800, Sun 1100-1500. A relative Aladdin's Cave of vinyl LPs and 12"s, cassettes, turntables, comics and new CDs of independent South African artists. Can ship worldwide.
Musica, Victoria Wharf, V&A Waterfront, T021-418 4722, www.musica.co.za. Open 0900-2100. The national music and movie store with branches in the larger shopping malls, selling CDs and DVDs. Has an extensive range of South African contemporary and African traditional music.

Shopping malls
Canal Walk, Century Blvd, Century City, Milnerton, T021-555 4444, www.canalwalk. co.za. Open 0900-2100. On the N1 about 10 km north of the city, this is one of South Africa's largest malls with over 400 retail outlets, local chain stores as well as international brands, cinema, entertainment atrium, food court and restaurant piazza.
Cavendish Square, Dreyer St, Claremont, T021-657 5600, www.cavendish.co.za. Mon-Sat 0900-1900, Sun 1000-1700. A stylish mall with 230 stores, 20 restaurants, cinema, food court, the Cavendish Connect section features individual boutiques.
Gardens Centre, Mill St, Gardens, T021-465 1842, www.gardensshoppingcentre.co.za, Mon-Fri 0900-1900, Sat 0900-1700, Sun 0900-1400. Large branches of supermarkets, plus 85 specialist shops for homeware, fashion, decor and gifts.
Victoria Wharf, V&A Waterfront, T021-408 7600, www.waterfront.co.za. Open 0900-2100. With over 400 upmarket shops, this is Cape Town's premier shopping mall with many specialist shops for curios, jewellery and international brand designer fashion, plus over 80 restaurants and 2 cinemas.

⏱ What to do

Abseiling and kloofing
Abseil Africa, T021-424 4760, www. abseilafrica.co.za. Operates one of the world's highest and longest commercial

abseils – 112 m down Table Mountain – R640 excluding cableway fee. Also runs day trips to other abseil points around the Cape and kloofing (canyoning) trips, which involve hiking, boulder-hopping and swimming along mountain rivers.

Cricket

Sahara Park Test Ground, 161 Camp Ground Rd, Newlands, for fixtures and tickets Computicket, T011-340 8000, www.computicket.com. A beautiful cricket oval where a few of the famous old oak trees remain and it is still possible to watch a game from a grassy bank with Table Mountain as a backdrop. You can take a tour of Newlands, see page 49.

Boat tours

See also page 46 for Robben Island Tours and page 89 for boat trips from the Peninsula.

There are more than 20 boats of varying types and sizes operating from Quay 5, the Pierhead or the Clock Tower at the V&A Waterfront. Just take a stroll around and the touts at the various kiosks will tell you what's on offer and when the next departure is. You can choose from a sail on a schooner to Camps Bay, a quick ferry trip across one of the docks, a guided tour of the working harbour, a sunset cruise with champagne, or a fast inflatable jet boat ride. All companies are listed at www.waterfront.co.za.

Tigresse, Quay 5, T021-421 0909, www.tigresse.co.za. Daily departures on luxury catamarans for a 1½-hr sail out to Table Bay; R140, R220 with champagne, discounts for children (4-12).

Waterfront Boat Company, Quay 5, T021-418 5806, www.waterfrontboats.co.za. 86 boats to choose from including a large catamaran and stylish schooner called the *Spirit of Victoria*, and a range of boat tours including around (not to) Robben Island, whale watching, sunset and dinner cruises. Example prices – ½-hr seal cruise, R60; 1½-hr sunset cruise, R250; 1-hr jet boat, R575.

Golf

For further details visit the website of the **Western Province Golf Union**, www.wpgu.co.za. Expect to pay green fees of around R300-550 for 18 holes and clubs, carts and caddies can be hired:

Metropolitan Golf Club, Fritz Sonnenberg Rd, Green Point, T021-430 6011, www.metropolitangolfclub.co.za. The 1st golf club was founded here in 1885, and after the land was turned into a military camp by the British during the Anglo-Boer War, reopened again as the Metropolitan Golf Club in 1902. In 2010, the course layout was changed to accommodate the new Cape Town Stadium, and now the 18-hole course has a magnificent location immediately beneath the outer rim of the impressive stadium as well as sweeping ocean views.

Rondebosch Golf Club, Klipfontein, Rondebosch, T021-689 4177, www.rondeboschgolfclub.com. A tidy course with the Black River flowing through it and good views of Table Mountain.

Royal Cape Golf Club, 174 Ottery Rd, Wynberg, T021-761 6551, www.royalcapegolf.co.za. An old club with a history dating back to 1885, which has been the venue for major professional tournaments.

Helicopter flights

Without doubt, seeing Cape Town from a low-flying helicopter is an incredible experience. You can pre-book, or if it's a clear wind-free day, just turn up at Quay 5 at the V&A Waterfront where there are several offices. Passengers are transferred from there by golf cart to the helipad beyond the Table Bay Hotel. Flights start from R700 per person for 15-20 mins.

The Hopper, Quay 5, V&A Waterfront, T079-513 2254, www.thehopper.co.za. The 15-min flight goes along the coast to Camps Bay, then turns back through Kloof Nek to see the top of Table Mountain and the City Bowl. Longer 20-, 30- and 60-min flights take in other parts of the peninsula.

The Huey Helicopter Co, Quay 5, V&A Waterfront, T021-419 5907, www.thehuey helicopterco.com. The 30-min loop goes down as far as Noordhoek and across to False Bay and back over Constantia in an ex-US Army Huey that served during the Vietnam War.

Hiking

Downhill Adventures, Shop 10 Overbeek Building, corner Kloof, Long and Orange streets, Gardens, T021-422 0388, www. downhilladventures.com. Guided half-day hikes on Table Mountain for R595. Also organizes a number of other adventure activities; see listings, below.

Kiteboarding

Cabrinha, Eden On The Bay Shopping Centre, corner of Sir Baird & Otto Du Plessis drives, Bloubergstrand, T021-554 1729, www.cabrinha.co.za. Rents out equipment to experienced kiteboarders and offers 2-hr lessons for R495 and a full-day course for R1485 on Langebaan Lagoon, a 1-hr drive north of Cape Town.
Downhill Adventures, www.downhill adventures.com, see above. Beginners' tuition at Dolphin Beach at Table View, north of the city centre from R750 per 2-hr lesson and recommends 3 sessions before going alone.

Mountain biking

Downhill Adventures, www.downhill adventures.com, see above. Organizes the popular Table Mountain double descent, which is a 90% downhill trail around Devil's Peak for R595, as well as rides around Cape Point and the Winelands Meander. Also offers bike and helmet rentals for R160 per day.
Homeland, 305 Long St, T021-689 5431, www.homeland.co.za. Mountain-bike rentals cost R140 for 24 hrs; cheaper rates the longer you hire. Also rents out surf boards, paddle skis, wet suits and camping equipment.

Paragliding

Para-Pax, T082-881 4724, www.parapax.com. Tandem paragliding from Lion's Head is very popular, with gliders landing on Sea Point Promenade. Flights cost R950 and for R200 you get photos and DVD.

Rugby

The rugby season is from mid-May to mid-Jul. International games are played at the **Western Province Rugby Union** ground, Boundary Rd, Newlands, T021-659 4600, www.wprugby.co.za. Tickets through **Computicket**, T011-340 8000, www.computicket.com. You can take a tour of Newlands, see page 49.

Sandboarding

Downhill Adventures, www.downhill adventures.com, see above. Not as fast as snowboarding, but can be a fun day out. Half-day trips to dunes about 1 hr north of Cape Town cost R595.

Scuba-diving

The Cape waters are cold but good for wreck and kelp diving. The best season for diving is during the winter months when the weather ensures the sea is flat as the prevailing winds blow offshore. Water temperatures are 12-18°C; visibility is usually 5-10 m.

For dive operators on the Cape Peninsula, see page 89. A number of dive companies also specialize in great white shark cage-diving offshore from Gansbaai, 165 km southeast of Cape Town. Full-day excursions are available from Cape Town, see page 68. Experienced divers can also dive with sharks in the predator tank in the Two Oceans Aquarium, see page 46.
Table Bay Diving, Quay 5, V&A Waterfront, T021-419 8822, www.tablebaydiving.com. Dive charters and full range of PADI courses.

Skydiving

Skydive Cape Town, T082-800 6290, www.skydivecapetown.za.net. Offers tandem jumps on the West Coast for

R1750; extra R600 for DVD and photos. There are fantastic views back across to Cape Town and Robben Island.

Surfing

Surfing is a serious business in Cape Town, and there are excellent breaks catering for learners right through to experienced surf rats. Some of the best breaks are on **Long Beach**, Kommetjie, **Noordhoek**, Llandudno, Kalk Bay, Muizenberg and Bloubergstrand. To check out the local scene visit www.wavescape.co.za.
Downhill Adventures, www.downhill adventures.com, see above. Organizes day and multi-day courses from R750 per day including equipment and also rents out surfboards, R250 per day, and wet suits (essential), R160 per day, to experienced surfers. As does **Homeland**, see Mountain biking, above.

Swimming

The beaches on the Atlantic Seaboard are almost always too cold to swim in – even during the hottest months, the water temperatures rarely creep above 16°C. Camps Bay has a tidal pool and shady, grassy areas, see page 72. Noordhoek is too rough for swimming, but is a great place for kite-flying or a horse ride, see page 74. False Bay is always a good 5°C warmer, and the main swimming spot is Seaforth Beach, see page 81. Fish Hoek has a pleasant beach with small waves and a playground, see page 80.
Sea Point Swimming Pool, Beach Rd, Sea Point, T021-434 3341. Oct-Apr 0700-1900, May-Sep 0830-1700, R20, children (under 16) R10. Some (probably Cape Town people) regard this as being the most stunning location for a public swimming pool in the world. Indeed, it is a sparkling bright blue outdoor Olympic-sized pool built right on the rocks next to the ocean with superb mountain and sea views. It has 2 splash pools for kids, a springboard diving pool, and terraces for sunbathing.

Tour operators

For information about a city tour in an open-top bus with **Sightseeing Cape Town**, visit www.citysightseeing.co.za, or see Getting around, page 23. There are a diverse range of day tours in and around Cape Town available through the operators below. Expect to pay in the region of R400 for a ½-day tour and R650 for a full day. The 3 most popular are tours of the Cape Peninsula, the Winelands and the townships. Peninsula tours generally go down the west side to Hout Bay and offer an optional boat trip to see the seals on Duiker Island, then go over Chapman's Peak Drive (if its open) and into the Table Mountain National Park to Cape Point. They return to the city on the eastern side with a stop to see the penguins at Boulders Beach. Winelands tours take in about half a dozen vineyards in the Stellenbosch and Paarl regions. Township tours usually begin at the District Six Museum and continue to Langa and Khayelitsha, and companies work with the communities they visit, putting back some of the proceeds. If you want to combine a ½-day township tour with the excursion to Robben Island, all operators will drop off at the ferry. Below is a small selection of the numerous tour operators offering day tours. Any hotel can make recommendations and for a full list of tour operators, visit www.capetown.travel.

Day tours

African Eagle, T021-464 4266, www.day tours.co.za. Offers a full choice of local tours to the Peninsula, townships, Winelands, Whale Coast and 4-day, 3-night tours of the Garden Route. Has regular scheduled departures that single travellers can join.
Andulela Experience, T021-790 2590, www.andulela.com. Very different township tours that focus on music and poetry, jazz and soccer and a day trip in Bo-Kaap that includes a walking tour, Cape Malay cookery lessons and meals.
Cape Capers, T021-448 3117, www.tour capers.co.za. Range of trips, including

½-day tours looking at Cape Town's slave history, District Six and Bo-Kaap tours and the Cape Care Route that goes to social and environmental projects on the Cape Flats.

Cape Discovery Tours, T021-461 9652, www.discoverytours.co.za. Can organize private tailor-made tours for 2-5 people for day trips around Cape Town, plus the West Coast, Garden Route and as far as the private game reserves and Addo Elephant National Park in the Eastern Cape.

Cape Rainbow Tours, T021-551 5465, www.caperainbow.com. Tours in many European languages to the townships, Winelands, Peninsula and, in season, to the West Coast to see the flowers and Hermanus for whales.

Day Trippers, T021-511 4766, www.daytrippers.co.za. Peninsula tours which include 1 or 2 hrs of cycling at Cape Point, Winelands, township, Table Mountain hike and the Whale Coast. Good value and fun, popular with backpackers.

Flamingo Tours, T021-557 4496, www.flamingotours.co.za. Tour operator specializing in disabled travel, tailor-made tours are led by a registered guide and nurse (if necessary) and can organize day tours of Cape Town with sign language.

Footsteps to Freedom, T083-452 1112, www.footstepstofreedom.co.za. From R220 per person depending on group size. A historical 3-hr walking tour of central Cape Town which goes to the Castle, District Six Museum and Company's Garden and can be combined with a township minibus tour later in the afternoon. A good way to learn about the city centre's historical past.

Friends of Dorothy, T021-465 1871, www.friendsofdorothytours.co.za. Gay-friendly tours, including a Four Passes tour, Peninsula, Winelands and whale-watching trips. Gay drivers and guides, max 7.

Hylton Ross, T021-511 1784, www.hyltonross.com. Full range of day tours, Cape Point with optional boat ride to see the seals from Hout Bay, Winelands, township, and longer trips to the Garden Route.

Transport

For details of all Cape Town's public transport – bus, metrorail and minibus taxis – see box, page 22.

Air

See also Arriving in Cape Town, page 21, for details of getting to/from the airport. For details of the international airlines serving Cape Town, see page 6. There are frequent connections throughout the day from Cape Town to all the other South African cities with the domestic airlines. You can either book directly, or through **Computicket**, T011-915 8000, www.computicket.com.

Airlines

British Airways/Comair, www.britishairways.com. **Kulula**, www.kulula.com. **Mango**, www.flymango.com. **South African Airways (SAA)**, www.flysaa.com.

Bus

Intercape, Greyhound and Translux long-distance buses all depart from/arrive at Cape Town railway station on Adderley St. Booking offices are here or book through **Computicket**, T011-915 8000, www.computicket.com.

Budget buses

The Baz Bus has a daily service from Cape Town to **Port Elizabeth**. The service continues from Port Elizabeth to **Durban**, the following day, and then the day after continues to **Johannesburg** and **Tshwane** (**Pretoria**). See page 8 for details.

Bus companies

Baz Bus, www.bazbus.com. Greyhound, www.greyhound.co.za. Intercape, www.intercape.co.za. Translux, www.translux.co.za.

Car hire

It's always a good idea to shop around for rates and pre-book a car in peak seasons.

See page 9 for further advice on car hire and driving.
Around About Cars, T021-422 4022, www.aroundaboutcars.com.
Atlantic Car Hire, T021-385 0178, www.atlanticcarhire.co.za.
Avis, T021-934 0330, www.avis.co.za.
Budget, T021-380 3180, www.budget.co.za.
Britz Africa, T021-385 0403, www.britz. co.za. Contact for camper vans and motorhomes for travel in and beyond South Africa. Good all-inclusive deals.
Cape Car Hire, T021-914 0723, www.capecarhire.co.za.
Europcar, T021-412 9053, www.europcar.co.za.
First Car Rental, T021-934 7499, www.firstcarrental.co.za.
Hertz, T021-935 4800, www.hertz.co.za.
Tempest, T021-481 9860, www.tempestcarhire.co.za.

Motorbike hire
There are a number of places to hire bikes around the city and they are a great way to get around in summer but remember you'll need a licence. A 150cc scooter can cost as little as R190 a day.
Cape Bike Rentals, 189 Buitenkant St, Gardens, T021-465 6883, www.capebike rentals.com. Rents scooters and 650-1200 cc motorbikes from their shop opposite the Gardens Centre shopping mall.
Cape Town Scooter, T082-572 3709, www.capetownscooter.co.za.
Rents scooters and delivers and picks up at hotels or private addresses.
Cape Sidecar Adventures, 2 Glengariff Rd, Sea Point, T021-434 9855, www.sidecars. co.za. Rents vintage ex-Chinese Red Army motorbikes with sidecars
Harley Davidson Cape Town, 9 Somerset Rd, Green Point, T021-401 4260, www.harley-davidson-capetown.com, rents out Harleys and provides route maps for day tours.

Taxi
There are several ranks dotted around town – the most useful ones are outside the railway station on Adderley St, in Greenmarket Sq and on Long St. If you are outside the city centre, you will have to call one in advance or ask your hotel or restaurant to call one for you.
Rikki Taxis, T0861-745 547/021-447 3559 (from an international phone), www.rikkis. co.za. The fleet of London black cabs can be seen buzzing around all over Cape Town, and are a cheaper alternative to regular taxis for getting around the city. You need to call one, but they pick up several people along the route, which brings down costs. They operate 24 hrs, and costs vary from R15-35 depending on the distance. They only operate in the City Bowl and Atlantic Seaboard as far as Camps Bay, but a few people can charter one to get to somewhere like Kirstenbosch, for example. If you see one in the street, you can flag it down.

Train
Cape Town railway station is is on Adderley St in the city centre. For details of Metrorail suburban services, see box, page 23.
For details of train travel, including luxury services between Cape Town and Tshwane (Pretoria), see page 8.

⦿ Directory

Medical services
The most central private hospitals are **Christiaan Barnard Memorial Hospital**, 181 Longmarket St, T021-480 6111, www. netcare.co.za; and **Cape Town Medi-Clinic**, 21 Hof St, Gardens, T021-464 5500, www. mediclinic.co.za. **Netcare Travel Clinic**, 11th floor, Picbel Parkade, Strand St, T021-419 3172, www.travelclinic.co.za, for vaccinations and anti-malaria medication.

Cape Peninsula

The most popular day trip from central Cape Town is a leisurely loop around the Cape Peninsula. The stunning coast road winds its way through the city's swanky suburbs on the Atlantic Seaboard on the western side, down to Cape Point and the Cape of Good Hope at the southern tip of the peninsula, and then up again through the quaint fishing settlements on the False Bay coast on the eastern side. This can be done under your own steam and a day's hire car is an ideal way to explore at your own pace; alternatively, all the tour operators offer the excursion – some take mountain bikes too, for a spot of cycling in the Table Mountain National Park. As well as fine ocean and mountain views, there are a number of attractions to stop for including the boat trip from Hout Bay to see the seals on Duiker Island, the spectacularly scenic Chapman's Peak Drive, climbing to the lighthouse at Cape Point, and the penguins at Boulders Beach. There are also ample places to stop for lunch, be it simple fish and chips or a gourmet meal, and there are many tourist shops, art galleries and roadside stalls to grab your attention along the way.

Atlantic Seaboard → *For listings, see pages 83-90.*

The Atlantic Seaboard refers to Cape Town's wealthy suburbs on the west side of the peninsula. Exclusive Clifton, Camps Bay and Llandudno have some of Cape Town's most sought-after properties and whitewashed modern mansions and luxury apartments with their brilliantly blue swimming pools climb up the hillsides, while the pristine beaches are popular with the beautiful people. Further south the road winds its way above the rocky shoreline and below the magnificent Twelve Apostles, the spine of mountains from the back of Table Mountain. It then drops into Hout Bay and the back end of the Constantia Valley, before continuing south towards Cape Point.

Arriving in the Atlantic Seaboard

The tour operators take the Atlantic Seaboard route on Cape Peninsula day tours, but a car is a logical option if you want to stop and explore the less visited attractions and the beaches. Some minibus taxis from central Cape Town go beyond Green Point and Sea Point as far as the police station on the main seaside strip of Camps Bay. MyCiTi and Golden Arrow buses also ply this route and some continue on to Hout Bay. The **Sightseeing Cape Town** bus (see page 23) goes as far as Hout Bay on its Blue Route. On the False Bay side, there are a few Golden Arrow buses from the Strand Street bus station in the city centre to Simon's Town via Muizenberg and Fish Hoek, or there is also the option of taking a leisurely day trip on the train from the railway station in central Cape Town, also as far as Simon's Town. It goes along a spectacularly scenic route, which in parts couldn't be closer to the sea, and there is a tourism initiative known as the **Southern Line** – a hop-on hop-off ticket designed for tourists visiting the False Bay villages and sights.

Clifton Beach

Cape Town's best-known beaches stretch along Clifton, and are renowned as the playground of the young and wealthy – this is the place to see and be seen. Other than being hotpots of high society, Clifton's four sheltered beaches are stunning, perfect arches of powder-soft white sand sloping gently into turquoise water. The beaches, reached be a series of winding footpaths, are divided by rocky outcrops and are unimaginatively named First, Second, Third and Fourth. Each has a distinct character – if you're bronzed and beautiful, head to First beach. More demure visitors may feel more comfortable on Fourth, which is popular with families and has been an award-winning Blue Flag beach for many years now. The sunbathing and swimming are good on all the beaches and lifeguards are on duty, but note that the water is very cold – usually around 12°C. Most of the relatively small-scale, high-luxury development has been behind the beaches (some impressive houses can be glimpsed from the winding steps leading down). Be warned that there is limited parking in high season, so get here early.

Camps Bay

Following the coast south, you soon skirt around a hill and come out over Camps Bay, a long arch of sand backed by the Twelve Apostles. This is one of the most beautiful (and most photographed) beaches in the world and it also has Blue Flag status, but the calm cobalt water belies its chilliness. The sand is also less sheltered than at Clifton, and sunbathing here on a windy day can be painful. But there are other distractions; the beachfront is lined with excellent seafood restaurants, and a sundowner followed by a superb meal is quite the perfect ending to a day in Cape Town.

The drive between Camps Bay and Hout Bay runs along the slopes of the Twelve Apostles and is beautiful. Apart from the turning to Llandudno, there is no easy access to the coast until you reach Hout Bay. **Llandudno** itself is a small, exclusive settlement with only one road in and out and no shops, and a fine beach and excellent surf but again parking can be difficult on a sunny day.

Hout Bay

Hout Bay, a historical fishing harbour with an attractive beach, attracts swarms of South African families during peak season. Most come for the seafood restaurants and boat trips, but the best reason for heading here is for spectacular Chapman's Peak Drive (see below), which begins just outside town. As the sun sets in the summer months every lay-by along the road is filled with spectators, drink in hand.

Hout Bay itself is fairly attractive, with a busy fishing harbour at the western end of the bay; at the other end is a collection of shops and popular restaurants. By the harbour is a commercial complex known as **Mariners Wharf**, a popular attraction, although looking a little wind-worn these days. It is based upon Fisherman's Wharf in San Francisco, with a whole string of fish and chips restaurants, souvenir shops, boats for hire and **Snoekies Fresh Fish Market**, close to the harbour gates. Even if you're not intending to buy anything it is worth a quick look to see the huge variety of fish that are caught off this coast. Boats also run from here to see the seals on **Duiker Island** (see Boat tours, page 89).

About 600 m to the east of Snoekies at the very end of Harbour Road, and located in a former fish factory, is the **Bay Harbour Market** ① *T082-570 5997, www.bayharbour.co.za, Fri 1700-2100, Sat-Sun 0930-1600*. A fairly new set up that draws a big crowd at weekends for the craft, fashion and decor stalls, but mainly for the fantastic food offered by local producers, organic farmers and artisans. There are more than 100 choices from designer cupcakes or oysters and a glass of fizz, to spit roast Karoo lamb or sushi and paella made from Hout Bay seafood. Drinks include several local ales on tap, organic wine and fruit juice, and cocktails and mocktails. Seating is at communal benches set around roaring fireplaces and a market requirement is that stallholders use biodegradable compostable cutlery and containers, and all market waste is recycled. On Friday evenings there is often live music or comedy on the small stage, and the market is so popular that successful South African bands sometimes play here 'unplugged' (when there's a cover charge).

Back in the town, next to the **tourist office** ① *T021-791 8380, www.capetown.travel, Mon-Fri 0830-1730, Sat-Sun 0900-1300*, is the **Hout Bay Museum** ① *4 Andrews Rd, T021-790 3474, Tue-Sat 1000-1230, 1400-1630, R5*, with displays on the history of the area, aimed at visiting school groups. More popular with families is **The World of Birds** ① *Valley Rd, T021-790 2730, www.worldofbirds.org.za, daily 0900-1700, R75, children (3-16) R40, under 3s free*, with over 400 species of bird housed in impressive walk-through aviaries. There's also the **Monkey Jungle**, populated with squirrel monkeys.

Chapman's Peak Drive

① *T021-791 8220, www.chapmanspeakdrive.co.za, R33 per car, though from the Hout Bay side you can get a day pass for free and drive the 1st 3 km to stop at the viewpoints, but you must go back the same way.*

Chapman's Peak Drive is a breathtaking 9-km route with 114 curves, carved into the cliffs 600 m above the sea. Not surprisingly, it's a favourite spot for filming car commercials. It was the brainchild of Sir Francis de Waal, a former administrator of the Cape Province (De Waal Drive in central Cape Town is named after him), and work began in 1915 and it was opened in 1922. Unfortunately, rock fall caused it to close in 2000, but, following extensive engineering works including the rigging of giant nets to catch falling rocks and an impressive cutaway section of the road right into the mountainside, it was reopened in 2003, and is now a toll road. The best time to drive along here is close to sunset in the summer, but the views of the craggy coastline and thrashing ocean, and the crescent of white sand at Hout Bay on one side, and the vast stretch of Noordhoek Beach on the other, are recommended at any time. The Drive sometimes closes in bad weather; check its up-to-the-minute status on the website.

Noordhoek

The greatest attraction here is the 8-km-long deserted beach, backed by a couple of tidal lagoons which offer excellent birdwatching. There's very little to the village itself, but the **Noordhoek Farm Village** ① *Village Lane, at the bottom end of Chapman's Peak's Drive, T021-789 2812, www.noordhoekvillage.co.za, 0900-1700,* is a collection of replica Cape Dutch whitewashed buildings around a little green and a pleasant spot for a coffee or light lunch, with four family restaurants and a deli to pick up picnic items, the **De Noordhoek Lifestyle Hotel** (see page 83), and a number of shops selling arts and crafts. The beach also offers the Cape's finest setting for horse riding along the shore (see What to do, page 89).

Kommetjie

The small settlement of Kommetjie means 'little basin', a reference to the natural inlet in the rocks which has been developed into a tidal pool. Long Beach is a major surfing spot and always busy with surfers, even in winter. There is an interesting walk (although go in a group as it's quite isolated) along Long Beach to the wreck of the *Kakapo*, offering a rare opportunity to examine a wreck at close quarters without having to don full scuba equipment. The *Kakapo* is a steamship which was beached here in May 1900 on her maiden voyage when the captain apparently mistook Chapman's Peak for Cape Point during a storm. The boiler and shell are still intact about 100 m above the high tide mark. Birdwatchers may be lucky to see oystercatchers roosting on the wreck. The **Slangkoppunt Lighthouse** ① *Mon-Fri 1000-1500, R16, children (under 12) R8,* lies at the southern end of Long Beach and the name, also spelt Slangkop, means 'snake head'. Slender and startlingly white, it was built in 1919 and, at 41 m, is the tallest cast-iron structure in South Africa. You can climb the steep internal staircase for the views from the tiny balcony.

Off the road into the village, **Imhoff Farm** ① *T021-783 4545, www.imhofffarm.co.za. 0900-1700,* is a worthy stop for families. Here are a number of attractions including a small snake and reptile park, the **Higgeldy Piggedly Farmyard** ① *Tue-Sun 1200-1600,* with petting animals, and there are a couple of camels to ride. The farm was built in 1743 by Cape commissioner, Baron Gustav Wilhelm van Imhoff, as a refreshment station for passing ships. The stables, silo, smithy, slave quarters and milking sheds are now occupied by local artists selling crafts and furniture, an excellent farm shop selling organic and free-range produce, and the **Blue Water Café**. The **Imhoff Equestrian Centre** is also here (see page 90).

Scarborough

Scarborough consists of a scattering of weekend and holiday homes on the hillside overlooking the Atlantic. The beach is broad and long but swimming is not a good idea as the water is cold and there are strong currents. Just outside Scarborough, close to the entrance to the Table Mountain National Park, is the **Cape Point Ostrich Farm** ① *T021-*

780 9294, www.capepointostrichfarm.com, 0930-1730, R40, children (6-16) R20, under 5s free, which is worth visiting for its in-depth tours, describing the lifecycle of the ostrich; during breeding season you can watch eggs hatching. There's a pleasant tea garden on site.

Table Mountain National Park → *For listings, see pages 83-90.*

ⓘ *T021-701 8692, www.sanparks.org, www.capepoint.co.za, Oct-Mar 0600-1800, Apr-Sep 0700-1700, R90, children (2-11) R40.*
Formerly the Cape of Good Hope Nature Reserve, this is now part of Table Mountain National Park, and was established to protect the unique flora and fauna of this stretch of coast. In 1928 the area came under threat from developers who were looking to build seaside resorts. Those in favour of a reserve persuaded local families to sell their land, and in 1939 the reserve came into existence. Some game animals were introduced and the land has since been left to its own devices. Today, it is a dramatically wild area of towering cliffs, stupendous ocean views, some excellent hiking and, to top it all off, beautiful, deserted beaches.

Arriving in Table Mountain National Park
Getting there Given its location at the southern tip of the peninsula, you can approach the reserve from two directions: along the False Bay shoreline via Muizenberg and Simon's Town; or by the quieter M65 via Kommetjie and Scarborough. It is about 70 km from Cape Town centre to the reserve gates. There is no public transport to the reserve.

Getting around The reserve is visited as part of day trips from the city or you can self drive. A **funicular railway** ⓘ *0900-1700, R49 return, R39 single, R21/16 children (6-16), under 6s free,* takes visitors up from the main car park to the original lighthouse. The walk is about 500 m, is fairly steep and takes about 20 minutes. Next to the car park is the **Two Oceans Restaurant** ⓘ *T021-780 9200, www.two-oceans.co.za, 0900-1700,* specializing in seafood and there is also a takeaway cafeteria.

Around the reserve
The Cape of Good Hope is an integral part of the Cape Floristic Kingdom, the smallest but richest of the world's six floral kingdoms. A frequently quoted statistic is that within the 7750 ha of the reserve there are as many different plant species as there are in the whole of the British Isles. In addition to all this there are several different species of antelope: eland, bontebok, springbok, cape grysbok, red hartebeest and grey rhebok, as well as the elusive cape mountain zebra, snakes, tortoises and pesky baboons.

Although the strong winds and the low-lying vegetation are not ideal for birds, over 250 species have been recorded here. There are plenty of vantage points where you can watch seabirds such as the Cape gannet, shy albatross, Sabine's gull and Cory's shearwater.

Cape Point → *For listings, see pages 83-90.*

Cape Point Lighthouse is nothing special in itself, but the climb is well worth it for spectacular views of the peninsula. On a clear day the ocean views stretching all around are incredible – as is the wind, so be sure to hold on to hats and sunglasses. You can take the funicular to the top, but the 20-minute walk allows better views of the coast. There are plenty of viewpoints, linked by a jumble of footpaths.

The first lighthouse came into service in May 1860, but it quickly became apparent that the most prominent point on a clear day was far from ideal in poor weather. It was quite often shrouded in cloud while at sea level all was clear. In 1872 the Lighthouse Commission decided on a lower site, but it was only after the Portuguese ship, the *Lusitania*, struck Bellows Rock in April 1911, that work started on a new lighthouse. This was built just 87 m above sea level, close to Diaz Rock and remains the Cape's most important lighthouse today. The current beam can be seen up to 63 km out to sea, and 18 km out there is a red lamp that warns ships that they are in the danger zone.

From the top point of the railway there are still approximately 120 steps to the old lighthouse where you get some of the finest views. If you are reasonably fit and have a good head for heights, there is a spectacular walk to the modern lighthouse at Diaz Point. From the renovated old lighthouse you can see the path running along the left side of the narrow cliff that makes up the point. The round trip takes about 30 minutes, but do not attempt it if it is windy – the winds around the Cape can reach up to 55 knots.

Diaz Beach
Apart from visiting Cape Point and the Cape of Good Hope there are a few minor attractions dotted about the reserve as well as three excellent walks, probably the best way of appreciating the splendour of the coastline. You can drive down to the Cape of Good Hope and then walk to beautiful **Diaz Beach** via Maclear's Peak, a very steep walk in parts. You can also approach Diaz Beach via a 253-step staircase. **Diaz Cross**, further inland, is a memorial to the explorer Bartholomew Diaz. Note how it is painted black on one side so that sailors can see it against the horizon.

Hiking around the Cape of Good Hope
Hiking is encouraged within the reserve. There are several marked paths and maps are available from the information centre. One of the most spectacular routes is along the coast from Rooikrans towards Buffels Bay. Look out for the wreck of *Tania* (1972). On the west side close to Olifants Bay there are a couple of walks; one to the inland lake, Sirkels Vlei, the other along the coast where you can see the wrecks of the *Thomas Tucker* (1942) and *Nolloth* (1964). You can light a braai at one of the designated areas at Buffels Bay and Bordjiesrif, but again watch out for the baboons.

False Bay → *For listings, see pages 83-90.*

On the eastern side of the peninsula lies False Bay, a popular stretch of coast thanks to the warmer waters – temperatures can be as much as 8°C higher. The area is also more sheltered and well developed for tourism, although some of the landscape seems almost dull after the Atlantic seaboard. Nevertheless, the area has some excellent beaches and gets busy with domestic tourists in summer. In spring, False Bay is the favoured haunt of calving whales, offering excellent opportunities to see southern right, humpback and Bryde whales. There are also some interesting fishing villages. False Bay is also known for its population of white sharks. A shark watch service operates from Muizenberg, signalling alerts when sharks come in proximity of bathers and surfers.

Arriving in False Bay
False Bay is easily accessed from the city centre by the M3, which runs around the mountain and along the coast. There are also two routes across the mountainous spine linking the

roads that hug the coast around the peninsula: you can cross from Noordhoek to Fish Hoek via the M65 and Sun Valley or, further south, take the Red Hill road from Scarborough to Simon's Town. Each route is convenient if your time is short, but the most scenic route is to follow the M65 along the coast from the Atlantic seaboard to False Bay. It is impossible to get lost as there is only one road along the shoreline.

Alternatively, **Metrorail** ① *T0800-656463, www.capemetrorail.co.za, for up-to-date times; see also box on page 22*, has a line running from central Cape Town through the southern suburbs to Simon's Town – the stretch following False Bay is spectacular and this may be the only place in the world where you can spot whales from a train carriage window. Trains go as far as Simon's Town and leave every 30 minutes, and take one hour and 15 minutes without stops, with the last trains leaving Simon's Town at around 1930. The **Southern Line** initiative is a hop-on hop-off rail ticket designed for tourists. Tickets, R30 for a one-day pass and R50 for a two-day pass, allow unlimited travel on the line and can be purchased from any of the stations and are valid 0830-1600 (outside of commuter hours). Many of the attractions for tourists in Observatory, Newlands, Muizenberg, Kalk Bay, Fish Hoek and Simon's Town, are within walking distance (or no more than a short taxi ride) from each of the stations. Brochures can be downloaded from the Metrorail website.

Constantia
South of Kirstenbosch National Botanical Garden and the city's southern suburbs, lies the verdant area of Constantia and its winelands. This historical district was the first site of winemaking in South Africa and today it is an attractive introduction to the country's wines, as well as offering some fine examples of Cape Dutch architecture. There are five estates here, of which Groot Constantia (see below) is the best known and definitely worth a visit. **Buitenverwachting** ① *T021-794 5190, www.buitenverwachting.co.za*, is a working estate with an excellent restaurant that also offers picnic baskets during the summer (November-April) from 1200-1600. **Klein Constantia** ① *T021-794 5188, www.kleinconstantia.com*, is a beautiful hilly estate with a great tasting centre, and is famed for its dessert wine, Vin de Constance, allegedly Napoleon's favourite wine. **Constantia Uitsig** ① *T021-794 1810, www.constantia-uitsig.com*, has excellent wines, luxury accommodation and two restaurants (see pages 84 and 87). **Steenberg** ① *T021-713 2222, www.steenberghotel.com*, also offers superb wines as well as having luxurious lodgings, a good restaurant and a golf course (see pages 84, 87 and 89).

Groot Constantia
① *T021-795 5140, www.grootconstantia.co.za, www.iziko.org.za, Mon-Fri 0900-1800, Sat-Sun 1000-1800, free entrance to the main estate and orientation centre, museum 1000-1700, R30, children (6-18) R15, under 5s free, 2 restaurants: Jonkershuis has traditional Cape food; Simon's serves burgers, salads and seafood. Wine tastings at the sales centre, R30 for 5 wines; cheese platters available. Cellar tours every hour on the hour.*
This old wine estate has some of the finest Cape Dutch architecture in South Africa, and with its rolling, vineyard setting and wine-tasting centre is a delightful place to spend an hour or two – although it does get swamped with tour buses in high season.

The main Manor House was originally home to Cape Governor Simon van der Stel between 1699 and 1712. He named the estate after Constantia, the daughter of the company official who had granted the land to him. Before his death, van der Stel planted most of the vines, but it was not until 1778 that the estate became famous for its wines. During this period the estate was unable to meet the demand from Europe, especially

France. The house is now a museum full of period furniture and a booklet is available giving a brief description of the objects on show. The magnificent wine cellar behind the main house was designed by the renowned French architect, Louis Thibault, and today has displays on brandy and winemaking. There are two impressive giant oak vats each with a capacity of over 4000 litres. The **Orientation Centre** near the car park has some interesting storyboards on the history of the estate.

Tokai Forest

ⓘ *Take the M3 out of town towards the southern suburbs. Just before Muizenberg, turn right into Tokai Rd and follow signs, T021-712 7471, Apr-Sep 0800-1700, Oct-Mar 0700-1800, R10, children (under 16) R5, R10 car.*

Tokai was set up as a forest nursery in 1883 to start a programme of reforestation. Due to this, large parts of the Constantiaberg Mountains are covered in pine trees and as they are non-indigenous there is some debate as to whether they should remain. Today, the forest is part of Table Mountain National Park. The arboretum contains 40 tree species – there are two walking trails, and horse riding and mountain biking are possible in the low-lying section (permits from the main gate).

Muizenberg

Travelling out from the city centre on the M3, Muizenberg is the first settlement you reach on False Bay and as such has long been a popular local bathing spot. The Battle of Muizenberg was a small but significant military affair that began in June 1795 and ended three months later with the (first) British occupation of the Cape. Cecil Rhodes bought a holiday cottage here in 1899 and many other wealthy people followed, building some fine Victorian and Edwardian cottages along the back streets and attracting the likes of Agatha Christie and Rudyard Kipling to its shores. Although the resort had decayed significantly over the last decade, various recent regeneration projects have meant that the area is starting to look like its old cheerful self again. The beach certainly remains beautiful: a vast stretch of powdery white sand sloping gently to the water. It is safe for swimming as there is no backwash, and it is very popular with surfers who head out to the bigger breakers. At low tide you can walk into the shallow sea for more than 300 m without having to swim.

The walk along Main Street towards St James is known locally as the **Historic Mile** and will take you past a number of interesting old buildings. Some of these are national monuments, but most are closed to the public. The first of note is the **Station building**, a fine example of art-deco architecture built in 1912. Further along on the right is the thatched and stone squat **Het Post Huijs (The Post House)**, thought to be the oldest building in False Bay, dating back to 1742 and built by the Dutch East India Company as a toll-house to levy taxes on farmers passing by to sell their produce to ships moored in Simon's Bay. One of the early post holders was Sergeant Muys, from whom Muizenberg is thought to have got its name.

The next building of note is **Rhodes Cottage** ⓘ *246 Main St, T021-788 9140, 1000-1600, entry by donation*, which is surprisingly small and austere for someone as wealthy as Cecil Rhodes. It has been restored and now contains many of his personal items, including his diamond-weighing scale and the chest in which he carried his personal belongings, and there are displays on his life and achievements. It's a pleasant place to wander around, with a lovely garden around the side. This is where he died on 26 March 1902, and his body was transported by train with great ceremony to the Matobo Hills outside Bulawayo in Zimbabwe, where he was buried in a giant rock outcrop. The volunteers that keep the place open make charismatic and enthusiastic guides.

St James

Just beyond Muizenberg lies the more upmarket resort of St James, an appealing village with characteristic brightly coloured bathing huts lining the tidal pool. The village is named after a Roman Catholic church which was built here in 1854 to save Catholics having to travel as far as Simon's Town to attend services – interestingly, some of the early settlers were Catholic Filipino fishermen. There is a small sheltered beach and reasonable surf off **Danger Beach** and the tidal pool is a safe place for a swim.

Kalk Bay

Kalk Bay is one of the most attractive settlements on False Bay, with a bustling fishing harbour and a bohemian vibe. The town is named after the lime kilns that produced kalk from shells in the 17th century (the name Kalk is derived from the Dutch for lime). Until the arrival of the railway in 1883, the local fishermen hunted whales, seals and small fish. Today it remains a fishing harbour, worked mainly by a coloured community which somehow escaped the Group Areas Act under Apartheid. Between June and July the harbour is busy with the snoek season – look out for returning deep-sea fishing boats around the middle of the day. In the harbour itself you can see seals, who cheekily hop up to try and get to the fish at the counters. Also at the harbour, **Kalky's** (see Cafés, page 87), in a colourful wooden shed, serves up great fish and chips. **Main Road** is an appealing spot, lined with bric-a-brac and antiques shops and a handful of arty cafés. On the other side of the road is Kalk Bay's most popular attraction, the **Brass Bell**, a pub wedged between the railway tracks and the water (see Restaurants, page 87).

High up behind the town is **Boyes Drive**, an alternative route connecting Kalk Bay with Muizenburg, offering sweeping views of False Bay and it takes just 10 minutes to complete – look out for the signs from Main Road as you head out of Kalk Bay towards Simon's Town.

Silvermine Nature Reserve

ⓘ *At the top of Ou Kaapseweg Rd (M64) between Westlake (at the end of the M3 from Cape Town) and Noordhoek, T021-780 9002, www.sanparks.org, 0700-1900, R30, children (under 11) R15.*

This is a popular local reserve split into two sections by the Ou Kaapseweg Road as it crosses the Kalk Bay Mountains. By car you can approach either from the Cape Town side or from Noordhoek and Fish Hoek. Note that this road is windy and has one of Cape Town's highest accident rates, so take care when driving. Silvermine is now part of the Table Mountain National Park, but not often visited by overseas visitors. Table Mountain and Cape Point tend to dominate the open-air attractions, and rightly so, but this reserve is well worth a visit if you enjoy hiking, plus there are great views across False Bay and the Atlantic Ocean.

Like much of the Cape, the reserve encompasses one of the oldest floral kingdoms in the world. Over 900 rare and endangered species have been recorded in the mountains, including many types of proteas, ericas and reeds. In addition to the plants there are a couple of patches of indigenous forest in the Spes Bona and Echo valleys. Ornithologists should look out for black eagles, ground woodpeckers, orange-breasted sunbirds and rock kestrels. If you're extremely lucky, you may also come across small shy mammals such as lynx, porcupine and various species of mongoose.

A tarred road leads from the western sector gates to the Silvermine Reservoir built in 1898 to supply Kalk Bay and Muizenberg with water until 1912. There is a boardwalk at the edge of the dam suitable for wheelchairs and prams and a shady picnic site under some pine trees. One of the more popular walks from here is to **Noordhoek Peak** (754 m), a circuit of about 7 km from the dam. The path is marked by stone cairns. At the summit there are spectacular views of the Sentinel and Hout Bay. Another interesting walk is from the car park to **Elephant's Eye Cave** covered with ferns and hanging plants. En route you pass the **Prinz Kasteel waterfall**. Allow about three hours for the round trip.

Fish Hoek

The centre of Fish Hoek with its cheap shops and fish and chip takeaways is fairly unremarkable, but the village is best known for its fine beach – perhaps the best for swimming after Muizenberg – which stretches almost 2 km across the Fish Hoek valley. Swimming is safe at the southern end of the bay, and boogie-boarding and kayaking are also popular. From mid-August to October, there is a good chance of catching a glimpse of whales from here. The valley which stretches behind the town joins with Noordhoek beach on the Atlantic coast. In recent geological times this was flooded and all the lands towards Cape Point were in fact an island.

Glencairn

It is easy to drive through this coastal resort without realizing you've actually been here, although it does have a small family beach with a tidal pool by the railway station. At low tide you can occasionally see the remains of a steamship, the *Clan Stuart*. She was blown aground on 20 November 1914 while the crew drank in the local hotel, which today is still a popular pub **The Glen**.

Glencairn, Simon's Town & Boulders Beach

Where to stay

Boulders Beach Lodge
& Restaurant **3**
Central Hotel Guesthouse **4**
The Glen **5**
Moonglow Guesthouse **7**
Quayside **12**
Simon's Town Backpackers **1**
Whale View Manor
Guesthouse **6**

Restaurants

Bertha's **1**
Black Marlin **5**
Salty Sea Dog **3**
The Sweetest Thing **4**

Bars & clubs

Two & Sixpence Tavern **2**

Just Nuisance

An enormous great dane and adored by Simon's Town sailors, Just Nuisance was officially registered as personnel aboard *HMS Afriander* in 1939. His favourite spot was to lie on the deck at the top of the gangplank. No one could easily get past him and he was loathed to move, hence the name. Although he never went to sea, like all new sailors, he underwent a medical examination, which he duly passed, and was declared fit for active duty. He signed his enlistment papers with a paw print. All able seamen were entitled to free travel on the train and Just Nuisance liked nothing better than to make the journey from Simon's Town to Cape Town and he carried his rail pass in his collar. Sometimes, if he found a drunken sailor on the train, he would escort the man back to his bunk in the naval quarters in Simon's Town. However, he was also guilty of several misdeeds. His conduct sheet (on display in Simon's Town Museum along with his collar and official papers), records that he travelled on the train without his pass, went AWOL, lost his collar, resisted eviction from pubs at closing time, and slept on a Petty Officer's bed – for the latter he was deprived of bones for seven days. He died in 1944, and he is the only dog in history to have been given a full military burial and a solemn ceremony included a firing party of Royal Marines and a lone bugler. A simple granite headstone marks his grave on the mountainside above Simon's Town. There's a bronze statue of him on Jubilee Square.

Simon's Town

This is the most popular town on False Bay, with a pleasant atmosphere and numerous Victorian buildings lining Main Street. If you want a break from Cape Town, this makes for a good alternative base from which to explore the southern peninsula. It's also a good place to spot whales in False Bay and notice the statue of a real-size southern right whale on the quayside of the waterfront. For information, there's a **tourist office** ① *Simon's Town Museum (below), T021-786 3046, www.simonstown.com, Mon-Fri 1000-1600, Sat 1000-1300.*

Take some time to wander up the hill away from the main road – the quiet, bougainvillea-bedecked houses and cobbled streets with their sea views are a lovely retreat from the bustling beaches. The main swimming spot is **Seaforth Beach**, not far from Boulders. To get there, turn off St George's Street into Seaforth Road after passing the navy block to the left. The swimming is safe, as there is no surf due to offshore rocks which protect the beach. For children there is a water slide and a wooden raft in the water. Look out for some giant pots, a legacy from whaling days, when they were used for melting whale blubber.

Simon's Town is named after Simon van der Stel, who decided that an alternative bay was needed for securing ships in the winter months as Table Bay suffered from the prevailing northwesterly. However, because of the difficult overland access, the bay was little used in the early years. It was not until 1743 that the Dutch East India Company finally built a wooden pier and some barracks here. In 1768 the town transferred into British hands, and following the end of the Napoleonic Wars in Europe, the British decided to turn Simon's Town into a naval base. It remained as such until 1957 and is now a base for the South African Navy. The two-day **Naval Festival** is held in April each year, when some of the ships are opened to the public.

Just before you hit the town centre, the **Simon's Town Museum** ① *Old Residency, Court Rd, T021-786 3046, Mon-Fri 1000-1600, Sat 1000-1300, entry by donation*, has displays related to the town's history as a naval base for the British and South African navies. Several displays are dedicated to Just Nuisance, a great dane who became something of a local hero in the 1930s (see box, page 81), who is now Simon's Town unofficial mascot. Also of interest is the **Peoples of Simon's Town Exhibit**, a collection referring to the forcible removal of coloured families from the area in the 1960s and 1970s, photographs, family trees and household goods. The building itself was built in 1777 as the winter residence of the Governor of the Cape.

Nearby, the **South African Naval Museum** ① *Naval Dockyard, St George's St, T021-787 4686, 1000-1600, entry by donation*, includes a collection of model ships, gunnery displays, information on mine-sweeping, a modern submarine control room plus relics from the Martello Tower.

In the centre of town, the **Quayside Centre** is a smart development on St George's Street, next to Jubilee Square in the centre of town, which has greatly enhanced the seafront. Above the shops and restaurants is the comfortable **Quayside Hotel** (see Where to stay, page 85). Cruises in the harbour can be booked here (see page 89).

Just round the corner from Jubilee Square, and worth a quick peek, is the **Warrior Toy Museum** ① *St George's St, T021-786 1395, daily 1000-1600, entry by donation*, a tiny museum with an impressive collection of model cars, trains, dolls and toy soldiers. This is a great little place and definitely worth a stop – nostalgic for adults and fun for kids. New and old model cars are also for sale.

The nearby **Heritage Museum** ① *Amlay House, St George's St, T021-786 2302, Tue-Fri 1100-1600, Sat 1100-1300, entry by donation*, faithfully charts the history of the Muslim community in Simon's Town. The town was designated a 'white' area during the Group Area Act and over 7000 people classified as coloured were relocated. The Amlay family were the last to be forcibly removed from Simon's Town in 1975 and were the first to return in 1995. The exhibition consists mainly of pictures and artefacts dating back to the turn of the 20th century.

Boulders Beach

About 2 km south of Simon's Town is a lovely series of little sandy coves surrounded by huge boulders (hence the name).

The attraction here is the colony of African penguins that live and nest between the boulders. **Boulders Visitor Centre** ① *T021-786 2329, www.sanparks.org, Apr-Sep 0800-1700, Oct-Nov and Feb-Mar 0800-18300, Dec-Jan 0700-1930, R45, children (2-11) R20*, has been created to protect the little creatures, and their numbers have flourished. One of the highlights of a visit to Cape Town is watching them happily go about their business of swimming, waddling and braying (their characteristic braying was the reason they were, until recently, known as jackass penguins). This is one of two colonies on mainland Africa, the other being in Betty's Bay (see page 120), and is now a protected area as part of Table Mountain National Park. From the visitor centre a (wheelchair accessible) boardwalk leads you down to viewpoints over the beach. Look out for the little concrete half moon huts that have been installed for the penguins to nest in and look up from the beach where you're likely to see a single penguin contemplating life from the top of a boulder. Every visitor gets a leaflet telling the story of the colony – it started from just two breeding pairs in 1985 and now numbers some 3000 penguins – and the shop sells all things 'penguiney'. If you want to swim, go to the adjoining Seaforth Beach, which is a lovely sandy cove with a picnic lawn and you may bump into a stray penguin in the water.

Miller's Point

This is the last easy access to the sea on this side of the peninsula. Miller's Point has two sandy coves and a tidal pool. There is a good restaurant, the **Black Marlin** (see Restaurants, page 88), which is a popular lunch stop for coach tours of the Cape Peninsula. The road then climbs above the sea before rounding the mountains by **Smitswinkel Bay**. On a clear day you can look back to a perfect view of the cliffs plunging into the sea. A short distance from the shore is the Table Mountain National Park entrance to Cape Point.

Beyond Miller's Point be on the lookout for baboons. They are not shy and will approach cars. Wind windows up and remember they can be vicious.

A number of **boat trips** to the Cape of Good Hope originate from Simon's Town harbour. Taking a trip from here allows views of the spectacular coastline and its hinterland from a different angle.

Cape Peninsula listings

For hotel and restaurant price codes and other relevant information, see pages 10-13.

● Where to stay

Camps Bay *p72*

$$$$ The Bay, 69 Victoria Rd, T021-438, www.thebay.co.za. Set just across the road from the beach, with 78 modern deluxe a/c rooms all with views across the bay, pleasant contemporary feel, large pool with deck and cocktail bar, spa and beach-facing restaurant.

$$$$ Twelve Apostles, Victoria Rd, T021-437 9000, www.12apostleshotel. com. In a gloriously scenic spot just to the south of Camps Bay beneath the **Twelve Apostles**, this 70-room 5-star hotel, has a commanding position overlooking the ocean and features an award-winning spa, pool, excellent restaurant, bar that also offers afternoon tea, and a small cinema.

$$$-$$ Camps Bay Resort, 32 Camps Bay Drive, T021-437 9708, www.campsbayresort. com. One of the most affordable options in Camps Bay, the resort manages 48 units spread around the blocks behind Victoria Road, no more than 150 m from the beach, from simple budget rooms and sea-facing doubles, to self-catering studios and apartments sleeping up to 6. There's access to 2 swimming pools. Breakfast vouchers are arranged at one of the restaurants.

Hout Bay *p73*

$$$$ Hout Bay Manor, Baviaanskloof, off Main Rd, T021-790 0116, www.houtbay manor.com. A beautifully restored manor house built in 1871, with 20 luxury a/c rooms. The decor throughout is stunning and best described as Afro-chic with bright splashes of colour. There's a pool, spa, gorgeous bar and lounge and celebrated **Pure**, restaurant (see Restaurants, page 85).

$$$$ Tintswalo Atlantic, 2 km south of Hout Bay, reservations T011-300 8888, www.tintswalo.com. Luxury option right by the waves beneath Chapman's Peak Drive, with 10 suites. Long wooden deck with pool, jacuzzi and jaw-dropping views, and there's a restaurant and bar with open kitchen where guests can interact with the chefs.

$$$-$$ Chapman's Peak Beach Hotel, Chapman's Peak Drive, T021-790 1036, www.chapmanspeakhotel.co.za. This has 10 double rooms in the original historical building and 21 stylish more expensive rooms in a new block, with sea views. Excellent restaurant (see Restaurants, page 85), and great location just across from the beach and at the start of Chapman's Peak Drive.

$$ Cube Guest House, 20 Luisa Way, T071-441 8161, www.cube-guesthouse. com. Set high up in the valley above Hout Bay with sweeping views of the mountains and named after its modern gleaming white block architecture, 6 comfortable rooms, designer decor, pool in tropical gardens, gourmet breakfasts.

Noordhoek *p74*
$$$-$$ Monkey Valley Resort,
Mountain Rd, T021-789 1391, www.monkey valleyresort.com. Family resort set in woodland overlooking Noordhoek Beach, with attractive self-catering thatched log cottages sleeping 2-8 with superb views. The restaurant specializes in pizzas and seafood and serves breakfast all day.

$$ De Noordhoek Lifestyle Hotel, at the Noordhoek Farm Village (page 74), Village Lane, T021-789 2760, www.denoordhoek. co.za. Newly built but in traditional Cape Dutch style, this has 20 sleekly modern a/c rooms, a comfortable lounge with bar and fireplace. Restaurants are in the farm village. Strong on environmental policies – water is heated by solar energy, everything is recycled, the gardens have been designed in a water-wise way.

Kommetjie *p74*
$$$$ The Last Word Long Beach,
1 Kirsten Av, T021-799 6561, www.thelong beach.com. 6 modern luxury suites with views over Long Beach, spacious airy decor in pale blues and pinks, stunning swimming pool right on the sand dunes, bar, rates include all drinks, lunch and dinner on request or a chauffeur service is available to take guests to restaurants on the peninsula.

Constantia *p77*
The original Cape Dutch homestead and vineyard that gave the area its name is today surrounded by one of Cape Town's most exclusive suburbs, dotted with luxury hotels. All are superb, in lovely settings and with impeccable service, but are firmly in the upper price category.
$$$$ Cellars-Hohenort Hotel,
93 Brommersulei Rd, T021-794 2137, www.collectionmcgrath.com. One of the most luxurious hotels in Cape Town, set in 2 converted manor houses in 9.5 ha of beautiful gardens on a wine estate with views of False Bay. 49 individually decorated spacious suites, 3 excellent restaurants (see Restaurants, page 87), 3 heated swimming pools, tennis courts, 9-hole golf course and spa.

$$$$ Constantia Uitsig, Spaanschemat River Rd, T021-794 6500, www.constantia-uitsig.com. On the well-known wine estate, with 16 luxurious cottages with views across vineyards to the mountain. Activities include horse riding and vineyard walks, there's a stunning spa, and 2 excellent restaurants of which La Colombe (see Restaurants, page 87) is considered one of the best in South Africa.

$$$$ Steenberg Hotel, Tokai Rd, T021-713 2222, www.steenberghotel.com. Country hotel with 24 elegant rooms in converted farm buildings overlooking manicured gardens and working vineyards. Swimming pool, gym, spa, and the beautiful 18-hole golf course has sweeping views of False Bay. The award-winning Catharina's Restaurant (see Restaurants, page 87) has an excellent reputation.

$$$ Alphen Boutique Hotel, Alphen Drive, T021-795 6300, www.alphen.co.za. Set on an elegant 18th-century Cape Dutch estate, the 19 rooms are decorated with fine antiques and have polished floors and log fires. Gourmet meals in the formal 5 Rooms Restaurant in the manor house and there's also a bistro, garden bar and swimming pool.

Muizenburg *p78*
$$-$ Bluebottle Guest House, 18 Mount Rd, T021-788 6100, www.blue-bottle.co.za. 6 neat B&B rooms with floor-to-ceiling glass windows, modern decor with bright colours, self-catering kitchen, bar, gardens planted with indigenous plants. You need to be fit, as there are 131 steps to climb but the sweeping views over False Bay make it worthwhile.

Kalk Bay p79
$$ Chartfield Guesthouse, 30 Gatesville Rd, T021-788 3793, www.chartfield.co.za. A turn-of-the-20th-century house with verandas, 13 rooms, DSTV, uncluttered decor of original wooden floors and fireplaces and retro furniture, good harbour views, pool, walking distance to restaurants.

Fish Hoek p80
$$ Tranquillity Guesthouse, 25 Peak Rd, T021-782 2060, www.tranquil.co.za. A peaceful option, 600 m above the town, with jaw-dropping views, 4 stylish rooms with huge showers, balconies, nice touches include fruit platters and fresh roses. Watching the sunrise over the mountains on the other side of False Bay is quite special.

Glencairn p80, map p80
$$ Moonglow Guesthouse, 7 Bennett Close, T021-786 5902, www.moonglow.co.za. 6 individually decorated rooms with hand-embroidered percale linen and TV, balconies with fabulous views over Glencairn Beach and False Bay, cosy lounge and bar with library, breakfast room.
$$-$ The Glen, 12-14 Glen Rd, T021-782 0315, www.theglenlodgeandpub.co.za. Delightful historical hotel in turn-of-the-20th-century building set a short walk from the sea, with 8 good-value rooms with high ceilings, dark polished wood floors, one is a budget room with 4 bunks. Bar and restaurant serving pub meals, seafood and grills.

Simon's Town p81, map p80
$$$-$$ Quayside Hotel, Jubilee Sq, St George's St, T021-786 3838, www.quayside.ahagroup.co.za. In a great central location overlooking the harbour, with 26 spacious rooms, bright and sunny marine blue and white decor, good views of False Bay. Buffet breakfasts and within walking distance of restaurants in Jubilee Sq for other meals.
$$ Central Hotel Guesthouse, 96 St George's St, T021-786 3775, www.central hotelguesthouse.com. The **Central** first opened in 1828, now restored with an authentic historical feel, 11 rooms with Victorian antiques, characterful old-fashioned dining room with elaborate sideboards and paintings, generous breakfasts that can be taken on the lovely balcony.
$ Simon's Town Backpackers, 66 St George's St, T021-786 1964, www.capepax.co.za. An easy walk from the train station, a 38-bed backpacker joint with small dorms and fairly pleasant doubles, small kitchen, bar, braai on balcony overlooking the main street and harbour, bikes for hire and can organize sea kayaking.

Boulders Beach p82, map p80
$$$ Whale View Manor Guesthouse, 402 Main Rd, Murdoch Valley, T021-786 3291, www.whaleviewmanor.co.za. 1 km south of Boulders and across the road from the lovely Fisherman's Beach. 10 stylish rooms with either ocean or mountain views, some with balconies, excellent meals and decadent high tea is served in the garden. There's also a day spa open to non-guests.
$$$-$$ Boulders Beach Lodge, 4 Boulders Pl, T021-786 1758, www.bouldersbeachlodge.com. This friendly, well-run guesthouse is a firm favourite, with 10 double rooms and 2 family rooms, the upstairs rooms have sea views. At night you're likely to see penguins exploring the grounds after everyone has gone home. Good restaurant and the **Curious Penguin** souvenir shop.

❶ Restaurants

Clifton Beach p72
$$$ Koi, 34 Victoria Rd, Bantry Bay, T021-439 7258, www.koirest.co.za. Open 1200-2230. Sophisticated restaurant with magnificent ocean views, especially at sunset. Offers Japanese and Chinese favourites with a Western twist like butternut and spinach dim sum or

Norwegian salmon with wasabi puree. Free valet parking.

Camps Bay *p72*

$$$ Blues, Victoria Rd, T021-438 2040, www.blues.co.za. Open 1200-2300. Popular restaurant and lounge/bar with superb views and a super luxurious all-white interior. Californian-style seafood menu served to a beautiful crowd, and the long cocktail menu features the signature Blues Bellini.

$$$ The Codfather, 37 The Drive, T021-438 0782, www.codfather.co.za. Open 1200-2300. Stylish laid-back place offering a range of superbly fresh seafood. No menu – the waiter takes you to a counter and you pick and choose whatever you like the look of. Also has an excellent sushi bar.

$$$ The Roundhouse, Kloof Rd, T021-438 4347, www.theroundhouserestaurant.com. Tue-Sat 1200-1600, 1830-2300. High above Camps Bay and also accessed from the city from Kloof Nek Rd, this building has its origins as a guard house built in 1786 and was later a hunting lodge for Lord Charles Somerset. Now well known for its modern French cuisine on the curved balcony with sweeping ocean views.

$$ Tuscany Beach, 41 Victoria Rd, T021-438 1213, www.tuscanybeachrestaurant.com. 0700-2300. Overlooking the beach, open all day from breakfast. Delicious seafood specials – don't miss the kingklip espetadas or the paella. Also serves wood-fired pizzas, salads, burgers and steaks. Trendy place, gets very busy for sundowners.

Hout Bay *p73*

$$$ Pure, Hout Bay Manor (see Where to stay, page 83). Tue-Sat 1900-2130, Sun 1200-1500. A beautifully decorated restaurant almost entirely in sliver with glittering chandeliers, with 3-, 5- and 7-course tasting menus, each paired with wine, or an à la carte menu of gourmet dishes including veal, scallops, lobster, tuna and game meat.

$$ Chapman's Restaurant, Chapman's Peak Beach Hotel, see Where to stay, page 83, T021-790 1036. Open 1100-2200. A lively restaurant and bar with wood-panelled interior, serving good seafood dishes in frying pans, also grills and pub fare. The outside terrace gets packed in summer.

$$ Dunes, Hout Bay Beach, T021-790 1876, www.dunesrestaurant.co.za. Mon-Fri 1200-2300, Sat 0900-2300, Sun 0900-1800. Sprawling restaurant overlooking the dunes with breezy outdoor tables in the sand. Excellent seafood including Namibian oysters and West Coast mussels and popular breakfast venue at the weekend.

Cafés

Fish on the Rocks, 1 Harbour Rd (about 600 m beyond Snoekies Market), T021-790 1153, www.fishontherocks.co.za. Open 1000-1900. Delicious fresh fish and chips, deep-fried calamari and prawns, eaten from cardboard boxes at wooden tables overlooking the fishing boats in the harbour.

Noordhoek *p74*

$$$-$$ The Foodbarn, Noordhoek Farm Village (page 74), Village Lane, T021-789 1390, www.thefoodbarn.co.za. Open 1200-1430, Wed-Sat 1900-2130. A French restaurant with lovely white linen-clad tables in an old barn and outside on the farm stoep. The short menu features well-thought-out dishes such as bouillabaisse or crusted rack of lamb in truffle jus. There's also a deli (**$**, open 0800-1700) on the other side of the village green.

$ Red Herring, Beach Rd, signposted off Chapman's Peak Drive, T021-789 1783, www.theredherring.co.za. Mon 1600-2200, Tue-Sun 1200-2200. Cosy country-style restaurant in an old farmstead with adjoining craft shops, the outdoor deck is ideal for sundowners overlooking Noordhoek Beach. Good wood-fired pizzas and fish and chips, and daily specials on the chalk-board.

Kommetjie p74

$$-$ Fisherman's, corner Main Rd and Somerset Way, T021-783 1496, www.fishermans-restaurant.co.za. Mon-Fri 1100-2400, Sat-Sun 1000-2400. Restaurant and pub with wooden bench tables under milkwood trees where a live band plays on Sun afternoon. As the name suggests, a good choice of seafood including combos and platters, plus beers on tap.

Constantia p77

$$$ Catharina's, Steenberg Hotel, see Where to stay, page 84. Open 1200-1500, 1900-2130. One of the finest restaurants in the area, where meals are served outside under the oaks or in the contemporarily decorated dining room. The menu features gourmet South African fare such as West Coast mussels, Knynsa oysters and springbok loin, and there's a fine wine list.

$$$ The Greenhouse, The Cellars-Hohenort Hotel, see Where to stay, page 84. Open 0730-2200. 1 of 2 highly rated restaurants at this 5-star hotel, set in a pretty conservatory with white wicker furniture. The Michelin-trained chef produces top-quality fare – mostly modern South African, so expect fish and game. Excellent wine to match.

$$$ La Colombe, Constantia Uitsig, see Where to stay, page 84. Mon-Sat 1230-1430, 1930-2130. French menu with strong Provençal flavours and some Asian influences, and expect the likes of rabbit, duck, fish and game dishes, with emphasis on rich sauces, jus and foams. Also here is the **Constantia Uitsig Restaurant** and the **River Café**.

Muizenburg p78
Cafés

Empire Café, 11 York Rd, T021-788 1250, www.empirecafe.co.za. Mon-Sat 0700-1600, Sun 0800-1600. A little tatty but popular with local surfers, this serves eclectic breakfasts including omelettes (try the famous bacon, banana and honey) and

specials like line-caught fish or saucy pastas for lunch.

Kalk Bay p79

$$$ Harbour House, Kalk Bay Harbour, T021-788 4133, www.harbourhouse.co.za. Open 1200-1600, 1800-2200. Perched right on the rocks overlooking the ocean with great views of the jaunty fishing boats, with bright white decor and wooden decks, this is well known for its seafood including grilled crayfish. There's another branch at Quay 4 at the V&A Waterfront.

$$ Cape to Cuba, Main Rd, T021-788 1566, www.capetocuba.com. Open 1100-2300. Atmospheric Cuban restaurant serving good-value seafood with Caribbean flavours. Great setting on water's edge with tables overlooking the harbour. Bar open till 0200 if there is the demand and cocktails include mojitos and daiquiris.

$$-$ Brass Bell, by the railway station, T021-788 5455, www.brassbell.co.za. Open 1000-2300. A very popular pub and restaurant in a great location. Downstairs gets packed around sunset, great for a cool beer outside close to the waves, serves pub meals and good pizzas and fish and chips, more expensive restaurant upstairs serves fresh fish and steak.

Cafés

Kalky's, Kalk Bay Harbour, T021-788 1726. Open 0800-2100. Simple seafood and chips at plastic tables, freshly cooked, counter service and then listen for your number to be called out. You'll rub shoulders with Kalk Bay's characterful fishermen here, and look for seals in the harbour.

Olympia Café & Deli, 134 Main Rd, T021-788 6396. Open 0700-2100. A Kalk Bay institution, this laid-back café serves some of the freshest bread on the peninsula, plus light lunches, fabulous cakes and daily specials. Expect to chalk your name on the blackboard and queue for a table at weekends.

Simon's Town *p81, map p80*
$$$ Black Marlin, Miller's Point, 2 km from Simon's Town, T021-786 1621, www.blackmarlin.co.za. Open 1200-1600, 1800-2100. Set in an old whaling station, this place is a good lunch stop on the way to or from Cape Point. Fabulous sea views and wide range of fresh seafood – try the delicious crayfish and oysters or the signature kingklip skewers. It can get busy with tour buses in summer so reservations are essential.
$$ Bertha's, Jubilee Sq, T021-786 2138, www.berthas.co.za. Open 0700-2200. Tables at the water's edge are perfect to enjoy fresh seafood and watch the yachts and naval ships in the harbour. There's also a long menu of breakfasts such as French toast with syrup or eggs Benedict.

Cafés
Salty Sea Dog, next to Quayside Centre, T021-786 1918. Mon-Sat 1000-2100, Sun 1000-1630. Cheap and cheerful place serving fresh grilled or battered fish and calamari and chips on trestle tables in the little shack or on outside tables overlooking the harbour. Friendly and swift service and sells wine. Popular with tour groups.
The Sweetest Thing, 82 St George's St, T021-786 4200, www.thesweetestthing.co.za. Mon-Fri 0800-1700, Sat 0900-1700, Sun 0900-1600. An elegant patisserie and café offering sweet and savoury tarts, muffins and pastries, plus gooey éclairs, brownies and meringues. The aromas from the bakery at the back are wonderful. Decor is bright red with Tibetan prayer flags on the walls.

Boulders Beach *p82, map p80*
$$ Boulders Beach Restaurant, Boulders Beach Lodge, see Where to stay, page 85. Open 0800-1115, 1200-1500, 1800-2130. Homely place with wooden floors and broad outside deck, serving good English breakfasts, cocktails (including 'Pickled Penguins'), delicious seafood platters or gourmet salads for a light meal.

Bars and clubs

Camps Bay *p72*
Easily the hottest place to be seen in Cape Town, Victoria Rd in Camps Bay is one long line of neon-lit restaurants and bars and the city's favourite place to watch the sun sink over the Atlantic.
Grand Café, 35 Victoria Rd, T021-438 4253, www.grandafrica.com. Open 0900-late. Sister venue to the **Grand Café & Beach** in Granger Bay (page 58), with sophisticated soft pink decor, silver candlesticks, ornate fireplaces, and balconies on 2 floors to watch the sunset. Creative cocktails and champagnes include Dom Pérignon and Cristal.
Café Caprice, Victoria Rd, T021-438 8315, www.cafecaprice.co.za. Open 0900-late. Popular café and bar with outdoor seats, great fresh fruit cocktails. Gets packed and very noisy around sunset, loud house music played until late by a DJ every night in season and at the weekends in winter.
Dizzy Jazz Café, 41 The Drive, T021-438 2686, www.dizzys.co.za. Open 1200-late. Busy bar and music venue, popular at the weekend, mostly jazz but has everything from funk to rock and is a platform for local bands, comfortable couches, low tables, food includes sushi and pizza.

Hout Bay *p73*
Pakalolo, 10 Main Rd, T021-790 0700, www.pakalolo.co.za. Open 0900-late. An always vibey bar/restaurant with outside terraces, chill-out lounge, bar with TV for sports, regular live music and comedy. Food includes Mexican specialities like fjitas and chilli con carne, plus burgers, BBQ ribs and surf 'n turf.

Noordhoek *p74*
The Toad in the Village, Noordhoek Farm Village (page 74), Village Lane, T021-789 2973, www.thetoad.co.za. Open 1100-2400. Cosy pub and sports bar, gets busy and excitable at the weekend when there's an important match on, pub grub

like steaks, spare ribs and *eisbein*, plus wood-fired pizzas. One of the owners is former Springbok rugby player Bobby Skinstad.

Simon's Town *p81, map p80*
Two and Sixpence Tavern, 88 St George's St, T021-786 5735, www.twoandsixpencetavern.co.za. Open 1000-2400. British-style pub serving standard bar food such as burgers, bangers and mash, ploughman's, Sun roasts and curry nights. Has pool tables, occasional live music and 1960-70s sing-alongs on Sun night.

What to do

For tour operators running day tours around the Cape Peninsula, see Cape Town, page 68.

Boat tours
Pleasure cruises depart from Hout Bay Harbour, and the most popular on a day trip around the peninsula is to see the Cape fur seal colony on Duiker Island just offshore. Some boats have underwater cameras or glass bottoms. Boats generally depart 0830-1100 (there are additional later departures in summer), which means that this determines in which direction you go around the peninsula if you want to include a morning seal excursion. The trip takes 30-40 mins and costs around R70, children (under 12) R35; no need to book just turn up at the harbour.
Drumbeat Charters, Hout Bay Harbour, T021-791 4441, www.drumbeatcharters.co.za.
Nauticat, Hout Bay Harbour, T021-790 7278, www.nauticatcharters.co.za.
Simon's Town Boat Company, Simon's Town Harbour, T082-257 7760, www.boat company.co.za. In whale-watching season, trips go out daily at 1030 and 1400, R850, children (under 12), R500, booking essential. Weather permitting, they also offer fast speed boat rides to Cape Point for R450, children (under 12) R250, and the round 2½-hr trip includes a stop on the seaward side of Boulders Beach (page 82) to watch

the penguins in the water. There are also short boars tours around the harbour area for R50, children (under 12) R20, on the *Spirit of Just Nuisance*, which include entertaining stories about the famous dog (see box, page 81) and the history of Simon's Town, and a visit to the naval dockyard.

Diving
Pisces Divers, Good's Shed, Simon's Town railway station, Main Rd, Simon's Town, T021-786 3799, www.piscesdivers.co.za. A PADI dive centre offering shore, reef and kelp forest dives in False Bay and further afield including to several wrecks off Cape Point.
Scuba Shack, T072-603 8630, www.scubashack.co.za. Full range of PADI-instruction and equipment hire and arranges shore dives from various points in Simon's Town and boat dives in False Bay with launches from Miller's Point.

Golf
Simon's Town Country Club, St George's St, Simon's Town, T021-786 1233, www.simonstowncountryclub.com. A 9-hole, 18-tee links course on the seafront, just by the turning for Boulders Beach. This is a narrow course and is a real test for anyone not used to playing in very windy conditions.
Steenberg Hotel, Tokai Rd, Constantia, T021-713 2222, www.steenberghotel.com. Beautiful 18-hole course with views of False Bay and the Constantia vineyards, known for its challenging 14th hole, which, at 76 m long, has the largest green in Africa.

Fishing
Hooked on Africa, T021-790 5332, www.hookedonafrica.co.za. Charter deep-sea fishing trips from Hout Bay Harbour, all gear is supplied. The most common catches are mako shark, long-fin tuna and yellowtail.
Nauticat Charters, T021-790 7278, www.nauticatcharters.co.za. Game fishing and boat charters, also operates from Hout Bay Harbour.

Horse riding

Trotting through the surf on the 8-km beach at Noordhoek is very popular and there are great views looking up to Chapman's Peak. Both these charge around R450 for a 2-hr ride and have horses suitable for novice riders. Departure times depend on season.

Imhoff Equestrian Centre, Imhoff Farm, Kommetjie, T082-774 1191, www.horseriding.co.za.
Sleepy Hollow Horse Riding, Sleepy Hollow Lane, Noordhoek, T021-789 2341, www.sleepyhollowhorseriding.co.za.

Winelands

The Winelands is South Africa's oldest and most beautiful wine-producing area, a fertile series of valleys quite unlike the rest of the Western Cape. It is the Cape's biggest attraction after Cape Town, and its appeal is simple: it offers the chance to sample several hundred different wines in a historical and wonderfully scenic setting.

This was the first region after Cape Town to be settled, and the towns of Stellenbosch, Paarl and Franschhoek are some of the oldest in South Africa. Today, their streets are lined with beautiful Cape Dutch and Georgian houses, although the real architectural gems are the manor houses on the wine estates. While the wine industry flourished during the 18th and 19th centuries, the farmers built grand homesteads with cool wine cellars next to their vines. Most of these have been lovingly restored and today can be visited as part of a Winelands tour – many have even been converted into gourmet restaurants or luxury hotels.

Winelands

To Ceres via
Bain's Kloof
Pass

To Rawsonville, Worcester & Great Karoo

ape Chamonix
Franschhoek
Pass

ubertsgat
Bridge

To Villiersdorp

Theewaterskloof
Dam

To Villiersdorp

To Caledon & Swellendam

N

5 km
5 miles

Where to stay 🛏
Bellevue Manor **1**
Berg River Resort **2**
Country Guest House **7**
Diemersfontein Wine &
   Country Estate **9**
Eben-Haëzer Country
   Manor **10**
Franschhoek Country
   House **11**
Lanzerac Manor **4**
L'Avenir Country Lodge **3**
Lekkerwijn **13**
Lord Charles **14**
Palmiet Valley Estate **15**
Spier **6**
Wedgeview Country
   House & Spa **5**

Restaurants 🍴
96 Winery Road **1**
Goatshed **2**
Harvest at Laborie **5**
La Petite Ferme **3**
La Vigna **4**
Monneaux **7**
Moyo **6**
Oude Wellington **12**
Seasons **10**
Wilderer's **11**

Arriving in the Winelands

Getting there

The N2 highway goes past Cape Town International airport, 22 km east of the city, and then continues along the northern fringes of the Cape Flats, home to the sprawling townships of Mitchells Plain, Nyanga and Khayelitsha. Beyond these the R310 left turning is the quickest route to Stellenbosch, the heart of the Winelands, 16 km from the N2. The N2 continues east splitting the towns of Strand and Somerset West before climbing over the Hottentots Holland Mountains into the Overberg via Sir Lowry's Pass (see page 102). The R44 is an alternative route from Strand to Stellenbosch. Paarl and Wellington are best accessed by the N1 from Cape Town, and Franschhoek by either route. The wine estates in the region are far too numerous to list in full, but on an organized tour (see pages 68 and 115) or a self-drive trip (with a designated driver), there is ample opportunity to visit several estates in one day.

Tourist information

Cape Town Tourism ⓘ *www.capetown. travel (see page 21)*, can provide brochures and maps, and the website is a good source of information for the Winelands. There are also tourist offices in the regional towns. For a list of tour operators offering day tours to the Winelands from Cape Town, see page 68. Wine estates charge a small tasting fee of about R10-30, which often includes a free wine glass.

Strand and Somerset West

→ *For listings, see pages 107-116.*

Although principally an industrial area, Strand is a popular seaside resort and commuter town with an excellent 5-km white-sand beach. It mainly caters for domestic tourists and, despite its proximity to Cape Town, the Winelands and the Whale Coast, it holds little appeal. Further inland,

Somerset West is a prosperous town and again a major commuter centre. It has a beautiful location on the slopes of the Helderberg Mountains, with unimpeded views of False Bay and, occasionally, Cape Point, but again there's little interest for visitors. However the unmissable giant 200-shop **Somerset Mall** ① *T021-852 7114, www.somersetmall.co.za, Mon-Sat 0900-1800, Sun 0900-1600*, at the intersection of the N2 and R44, is a useful stop on the way to somewhere else.

Cheetah Outreach

① *Paardevlei, De Beers Ave, T021-851 6850, www.cheetah.co.za, 0900-1700, Mon-Fri R10, Sat-Sun R5 per person, adult cheetah encounters R120, children (under 14) R70, cheetah cub encounters R220 per person, bat-eared fox encounters R50, children (under 14) R35. To get here from the N2, turn off on to the R44 and head south past Somerset Mall for about 1.5 km; De Beers Ave is the second turning on the right from the N2.*

Most of South Africa's remaining wild cheetahs live in unprotected areas of remote farmland in South Africa's northern provinces. They rarely prey on livestock, but when rural farmers lose their animals to other predators they often blame and kill cheetahs. Cheetah Outreach is home to several adult cheetahs, and seasonally cubs, that act as 'ambassadors' for South Africa's free-roaming cheetah to inform the public about the problems they face, and to raise funds for conservation initiatives. These include a breeding and placement programme for Turkish Anatolian Shepherd dogs that are given to farmers to look after their herds, ensuring that predators find other sources of food and farmers can retain their livelihood. The centre is also home to many smaller predators, like meerkats, caracal, serval, bat-eared fox and black-backed jackal – typical animals that share the same habitat as cheetah. Visitors can stroll between the enclosures and walkways, stroke an adult cheetah, and a cute cub (when available), or visit the bat-eared foxes and go on a guided tour with one of the project's many enthusiastic volunteers. There is a café and souvenir shop.

Vergelegen Estate

① *T021-847 1334, www.vergelegen.co.za, 0930-1600, R10, children (under 16) R5, wine tasting R30, cellar tours R20. From Somerset West take the R44, turn right at the traffic lights and after 1 km turn left into Lourensford Rd; the estate is 4 km on the right. There is a shop, displays on the history of the estate, a smart wine-tasting room and 2 restaurants: Camphors at Vergelegen is the formal à la carte restaurant, lunch Mon-Sun 1200-1500, dinner Fri-Sat 1830-2100, booking essential, T021-847 1346; Stables at Vergelegen is a café/bistro open for breakfast, lunch and teas 0930-1600. There is also a picnic hamper service.*

This is one of the Cape's finest estates and the highlight is a visit to the magnificent manor house filled with beautiful period furniture and historical paintings, similar to the collection at Groot Constantia. At the front of the house are five **Chinese camphor trees** that were planted by Willem van der Stel between 1700 and 1706. They are the oldest living documented trees in South Africa and are now a national monument. Behind the house is a walled octagonal garden – many of the plants were planted here by Lady Phillips (wife of Sir Lionel Phillips, owner for 25 years from 1917), who wished to recreate a typical English garden, complete with herbaceous border. Look out for the collection of roses next to the main house. The surrounding parkland, much of it similar to an English country estate, is also open for exploration.

Stellenbosch → *For listings, see pages 107-116.*

Stellenbosch, the centre of the Winelands, is the oldest and most attractive town in the region, with a large university giving it a liveliness which is lacking in other nearby towns. The centre has a pleasing mix of architectural styles: Cape Dutch, Georgian, Regency and Victorian houses line broad streets, dappled with shade from centuries-old oak trees, and furrowed with water ditches which still carry water to the gardens. It's a fairly large place but, with its handful of good museums and fun nightlife, is a perfect base for visiting the wine estates.

Arriving in Stellenbosch

The town is served by the suburban Metro railway from Cape Town, but for safety reasons, this is best avoided. Hiring a car is the best way of getting here as you then have the freedom to explore the surrounding wine estates. The trip from Cape Town takes about an hour, either along the N1 or the N2. Stellenbosch itself is perfect for exploring on foot as many of the interesting sights are concentrated in a small area along Church, Dorp and Drostdy streets. **Stellenbosch Tourist Office** ① *36 Market St, T021-887 9150, www. stellenbosch.travel, Mon-Fri 0800-1800, Sat 0900-1700, Sun 1000-1600 (in Jun and Aug the office opens 1 hr later and closes 1 hr earlier)*, is a professional and helpful office, which provides maps and can help with accommodation bookings, tour information and wine routes. **Stellenbosch On Foot** ① *T021-887 9150, or book at the tourist office, R100 per person (minimum 3 people)*, offers 90-minute guided walks that leave from the tourist office every day at 1100 and 1500.

Background

In November 1679, Governor of the Cape Simon van der Stel left Cape Town with a party of soldiers in order to explore the hinterland. There was already a great need for additional land to be brought under cultivation to supply both Cape Town and passing ships calling for fresh supplies. On the first night the group camped beside a stream they named the Kuilsrivier. The stream turned out to be a tributary of a much larger river, the Eersterivier. As they followed the Eersterivier towards the mountains they found themselves in a fertile alluvial valley. There was no sign of human habitation, the waters were cool and clean and everything seemed to grow in abundance – exactly the type of land Van der Stel had been sent to discover. Several days after entering the valley the group camped under a large tree on an island formed by two branches of the Eersterivier. The camp was named Van der Stel se Bosch (Van der Stel's Wood).

Six months later, in May 1680, eight families from Cape Town moved into the area, tempted by the offer of as much free land as they could cultivate, and by the summer of 1681 Stellenbosch was a thriving agricultural community. This became the first European settlement in the interior of southern Africa. By the end of 1683 more than 30 families had settled in the valley, a school had been built and a *landdrost* (magistrate) had been appointed. Throughout his life, Simon van der Stel maintained a close interest in the development of the town. One of his greatest legacies was to order the planting of oak trees along the sides of every street. Canals were also built to bring water to the town gardens. Today, a number of the original oaks are still standing and some have been proclaimed national monuments.

It is difficult to picture it today, but at the end of the 17th century this new settlement was a frontier town. For the next 100 years the magistracy had dealings with the explorers, hunters, adventurers and nomadic peoples who lived beyond the Cape, and the authority extended over 250,000 sq km. In the meantime, the town prospered as an agricultural centre and also emerged as a place of learning. In 1859 the Dutch Reformed Church started a Seminary which in 1866 became the Stellenbosch Gymnasium, renamed Victoria College in 1887. After the creation of the Union of South Africa in 1910, there was pressure on the new government to establish a single national university. By this stage Victoria College had emerged as a respected Afrikaner school, and Stellenbosch itself was regarded as an important centre of Afrikaner culture. In 1915 a local farmer, Johannes Marais died and left £100,000 towards higher education in Stellenbosch. This bequest finally persuaded the government to yield to public pressure and in April 1918 the Victoria College became the University of Stellenbosch.

Places in Stellenbosch

Stellenbosch offers two approaches to sightseeing: walking around the town centre viewing public buildings, oak-lined streets and stately homes; or going on a wine tour, visiting any number of the roughly 130 wineries and private cellars. Spend a couple of days in Stellenbosch and you'll get to do both. No other town in South Africa has such an impressive concentration of early Cape architecture. However many of the earliest buildings were lost to fires in the 18th and 19th centuries; what you see today is a collection of perfectly restored buildings. Following each fire, the destroyed buildings were recreated

Stellenbosch

Where to stay 🛏
Dorpshuis
 & Spa **5**
D'Ouwe Werf **7**
Eendracht **4**

Labri Manor **2**
Ryneveld Country
 Lodge **10**
Stellenbosch **11**

Restaurants 🍴
Big Easy **1**
Dorp Street Deli **4**
Jan Cats **3**
Volkskombuis **5**

with the help of photographs, original plans and sketches, although the technology and materials of the day were used. This is perhaps why they appear to have survived in such good condition. This restoration process is not unusual: the town of Tulbagh in the Breede River Valley was completely destroyed by an earthquake in 1969, but today it has the look and feel of an unspoilt quaint Victorian village.

Dorp Street, which runs east–west in the southern part of town, has all the classic features – an avenue of oak trees, running water in open furrows and carefully restored white-walled buildings. A walk from the **Libertas Parva** building to the Theological College takes you through the oldest parts of town and past some of the best-preserved old buildings. Libertas Parva (No 31), is a beautifully restored classic H-shaped manor house built in 1783, though the present front gable and twin front doors date from the late Georgian period. Continue east along Dorp Street, where you'll pass the famous **Oom Samie se Winkel (Uncle Samie's Store)** ① *No 84, T021-887 0797, 0830-1700*, a Victorian-style general store that is still functioning as a shop today. It became most famous between 1904 and 1944 when the store was owned and run by Samuel Johannes Volsteedt, when he stocked virtually anything and everything the townspeople could possibly need. The shop still sells a wide range of goods and retains it character with items hanging from all corners, and old cabinets full of bits and pieces. Also of particular note on Dorp Street are the town houses just past the junction with Helderberg Street. **Hauptfleisch House** (No 153), **Bakker House** (No 155), **Loubser House** (No 157), and **Saxenhof** (No 159), are regarded as the best-preserved street façades in old Stellenbosch.

Branching off from Dorp Street is Drostdy Street, dominated by a building with a tall tower. Also in this street is the town church, the **Moederkerk**; its current steeple church was designed by Carl Otto Hagen and built in 1862. Inside, it is worth admiring the pulpit and the unusually thick stained-glass windows.

Turn right at the top of Drostdy Street into Van Riebeeck Street, then left into Neethling Street to reach the **Botanical Gardens** ① *0800-1700, free, tea room and bookshop 1000-1700*. These were established in the 1920s and are part of the University of Stellenbosch, with a fine collection of ferns, orchids and bonsai trees. One of the more unusual plants to look out for is the *Welwitschis* from the Namib Desert.

Heading west back along Van Riebeeck Street brings you to Ryneveld Street, where you'll find the entrance to the engaging **Village Museum** ① *T021-887 2948, www. stelmus.co.za, Mon-Sat 0900-1700, Sun 1000-1600, R30, children (under 16) R5*. The complex currently spreads over two blocks in the oldest part of town. If you

Wijnhuis **13**

Fandango **7**
Osetra Tapas &
Champagne Lounge **8**

Bars & clubs ①
Brazen Head **9**
Dros **6**

follow the guide numbers you will be taken through four houses, each representing a different period of the town's history. The oldest of these is **Schreuderhuis** (1709), one of the earliest houses to be built in Stellenbosch. The simple furniture and collection of household objects are all of the same period. The house was built by Sebastian Schreuder, a German. **Blettermanhuis** (1789) is a perfect example of what has come to be regarded as a typical H-shaped Cape Dutch home. The furnishings are those of a wealthy household between 1750 and 1780. The house was built by Hendrik Lodewyk Bletterman, the last *landdrost* to be appointed by the Dutch East India Company. Notice the contrast in furnishings between Schreuder the messenger and Bletterman the magistrate. The third building in the museum to have been restored is **Grosvenor House** (1803), in Drostdy Street. This is an excellent example of the two-storeyed town houses that once dominated the streets of Cape Town. The home was built by Christian Ludolph Neethling, a successful farmer, in 1782. The fourth and final house is the fussy **OM Bergh House** (1870), which once had a thatched roof. All four houses are set in neat kitchen gardens which have been recreated to reflect the popular plants of each period. Guides dressed in period clothes are at hand answer any questions and point out interesting details.

Much of the town's activity today takes place around the **Braak**, at the western end of Church Street. This is the original village green, and one-time military parade ground. On the western edge by Market Street is the **VOC (Vereenigde Oost-Indiesche Compagnie) Kruithuis** ① *T021-887 2948, www.stelmus.co.za, Sep-May, Mon-Fri 0930-1300, R5, children (under 16) R2*, or Powder House, built in 1777 as a weapons store. Today it is a military museum. A short distance north, on the corner of Alexander Street, is the **Burgerhuis** ① *T021-887 0339, Mon-Fri 0800-1630, Sat 1000-1300, 1400-1600, free*, a classic H-shaped Cape Dutch homestead built by Antonie Fick in 1797, that is now decorated to represent the house of a well-to-do Stellenboscher in the Victorian era.

Two churches overlook the Braak, **Rhenish Church**, built in 1832 as a training school for coloured people and slaves, which has a very fine pulpit, and **St Mary's-on-the-Braak**, an Anglican church completed in 1852. A little to the west, on Market Street just behind the tourist office, is the **Toy and Miniature Museum** ① *T021-887 2948, www.stelmus.co.za, Mon-Sat 0930-1700, Sun 1400-1700, R5, children (under 16) R2*, a small but fairly diverting collection of antique toys including a working model of the Blue Train, and a set of rooms devoted to miniatures. Most interesting are the tiny replicas of furniture, clothes and household items for dolls' houses that you can buy in the shop.

Stellenbosch wine route

① *Maps and brochures on the wine route can be picked up at the tourist offices in Stellenbosch and Cape Town or visit www.wineroute.co.za. Remember the drink-drive laws in South Africa; when wine tasting, you may be offered up to 15 different wines to sample at each estate, so make sure one of you stays sober.*

This was the first wine route to open in South Africa, in April 1971. It was the idea of three local farmers: Neil Joubert, Frans Malan and Spatz Sperling. It has been hugely successful, attracting tens of thousands of visitors every year, and today the membership comprises more than 200 private cellars. It's possible to taste and buy wines at all of them, and the cellars can arrange for wine to be delivered internationally. Most of the estates have excellent restaurants as well as providing very popular picnic lunches with wine – at weekends it is advisable to book in advance – and many also have guest accommodation.

Delaire Graff ① *R310, T021-885 8160, www.delairewinery.co.za, sales and tastings: Mon-Sat 1000-1700, Sun 0930-1600; restaurant: daily 1200-1430, Wed-Sat 1830-2100.* This small estate on the crest of the Helshoogte Pass has some of the best views in the valley, and on a clear day visitors are rewarded with views of the Simonsberg Mountains. Their flagship Merlot is very popular, while the Chardonnay remains a favourite export label. The estate provides accommodation in 10 private luxury houses (**$$$$**).

Delheim ① *Knorhoek Rd, off the R44, T021-888 4600, www.delheim.com, sales and tastings: 0900-1700, cellar tours: 1030 and 1430, restaurant: 0930-1630.* The restaurant has a beautiful setting with views towards Cape Town and Table Mountain, and serves breakfasts, lunches and teas, and offers picnic baskets to eat at benches next to the river. Tastings are conducted in a cool downstairs cellar. There are six farm-style B&B rooms for accommodation on the property (**$$**).

Eikendal ① *R44, T021-855 1422, www.eikendal.com, sales and tastings: 1000-1600; cellar tours: Mon-Fri, 1000 and 1430; restaurant: Tue-Sun 1200-1530.* The microclimate on the western slopes of the mountain is ideal for viticulture, and there is a wide selection of both whites and reds. Lunch is served in the wine-tasting room or the gardens; Swiss-owned so expect unusual European dishes on the menu. There are nine comfortable suites for accommodation (**$$$-$$**).

Hartenberg ① *Botterlary Rd, T021-865 2541, www.hartenbergestate.com, sales and tastings: Mon-Fri 0900-1715, Sat 0900-1500; cellar tours: by appointment; lunches: 1200-1400.* The first vines on this estate were planted in 1692, and today is best known for its Gravel Hill Shiraz. During the summer, lunches are served in the shade and peace of the gardens; come winter the tasting room doubles up as a restaurant with warming log fires. Picnic baskets are available to enjoy on the lawns, or picnic backpacks can be taken on a short walking trail through a wetland area on the estate.

Neethlingshof ① *R310, T021-883 8988, www.neethlingshof.co.za, sales and tastings: Mon-Fri 0900-1700, Sat-Sun 1000-1600; cellar and vineyard tours: by appointment; lunches: Tue-Sun 1000-1530.* With its fine Cape Dutch buildings and grand pine avenue (which features on the labels of the wines), this estate is a very pleasant one to visit. The first vines were planted here in 1692 and the manor house was built in 1814 in traditional Cape Dutch H-style. Today this has been converted into the **Lord Neethling** restaurant renowned for its venison and veal. The **The Palm Terrace** has outside tables with beautiful views of the gardens.

Saxenburg ① *Polkadraai Rd, T021-903 6113, www.saxenburg.co.za, sales and tastings: Mon-Fri 0900-1700, Sat 1000-1630, Sun 1000-1600; restaurant: Wed-Sun 0900-1600.* Saxenberg has a long history, starting in 1693 when Simon van der Stel granted land to a freeburgher, Jochem Sax. Sax planted the first vines and built the manor house in 1701, and the estate has been producing ever since. It produces a small number of cases each year; its Private Collection of red wines is very good. The **Guinea Fowl** restaurant is in part of the original wine cellar and accommodation is in three self-catering apartments on the estate (**$$**).

Spier ① *R310, T021-809 1100, www.spier.co.za, sales and tastings: 1000-1630; meals are available throughout the day and evening at 2 restaurants; picnics and a deli are also available.*

This is the Winelands' most commercial wine estate, offering an array of activities as well as wine tastings. Their Private Collection Chenin Blanc and Chardonnay are especially good and frequently win awards. There is and a birds of prey area, craft market, children's play areas and beautiful grounds dotted with lakes and streams. **Moyo**, is one of the best restaurants in the Winelands, see Restaurants, page 111, and accommodation is at the **Spier Hotel**, see Where to stay, page 108.

Simonsig ① *Kromme Rhee Rd, M23, T021-888 4900, www.simonsig.co.za, sales and tastings: Mon-Fri 0830-1700, Sat 0830-1600, Sun 1100-1500; cellar tours: Mon-Fri 1000 and 1500, Sat 1000; restaurant: Tue-Sat 1200-1500, Sun 1200-1400.* This large estate has been in the Malan family for 10 generations, and in recent years has produced some exceptionally fine wines. There is an attractive outdoor tasting area with beautiful views out over the mountains. One wine worth looking out for is the Kaapse Vonkel, a sparkling white considered the best of its kind in South Africa. The **Cuvée**, restaurant has a more modern menu than most and a terrace under oak trees.

Franschhoek Valley → *For listings, see pages 107-116.*

Franschhoek

This is the most pleasant of the Wineland's villages, with a compact centre of Victorian whitewashed houses backed by rolling vineyards and the soaring slopes of the Franschhoek Mountains. It does, however, have an artificial feel to it as most of the attractions here have been created to serve the tourist industry. The outlying wine estates all have their individual appeal, but the village itself is made up of restaurants and touristy craft shops. Nevertheless, Franschhoek is famed for its cuisine and dubs itself the 'gourmet

Franschhoek

Where to stay	La Fontaine 9	Restaurants
Auberge Bligny 1	Le Quartier Français 4	Café de Arts 1
Auberge La Dauphine 3	Lekkerwijn 10	French Connection Bistro 2
Franschhoek Country	Mont Rochelle 12	Mange Tout 4
House 5	Otter's Bend 6	Reuben's 6
Klein Oliphants Hoek 14	Protea Franschhoek 7	Tasting Room and
La Cabrière Country		Common Room 7
House 8		

capital of South Africa', so a visit here should guarantee an excellent meal accompanied by a fine glass of wine.

Arriving in Franschhoek Franschhoek is 71 km from Cape Town (via the N1), 26 km from Paarl and 31 km from Stellenbosch. There is no regular public transport so you will need a car. Most of the tour operators offering Winelands tours don't usually include Franschhoek. The **tourist office** ① *62 Huguenot Rd, T021-876 3603, www.franschhoek.org.za, Mon-Fri 0800-1700, Sat 0900-1700, Sun 0900-1600,* has helpful staff with a good knowledge of accommodation and restaurants. The office also has the Franschhoek wine route desk (see below).

Background Although the first Huguenots arrived at the Cape in 1688, the village of Franschhoek only took shape in 1837 after the church and the manse had been built. The first immigrants settled on farms granted to them by Simon van der Stel along the Drakenstein Valley at Oliphantshoek in 1694. Franschhoek is built on parts of **La Motte** and **Cabrière** farms. The village became the focal point of the valley but the oldest and most interesting buildings are to be found on the original Huguenot farms and estates.

Places in Franschhoek The **Huguenot Memorial Museum** ① *T021-876 2532, www. museum.co.za, Mon-Sat 0900-1700, Sun 1400-1700, R10, children (under 16) R5,* is housed in two buildings either side of Lambrecht Street. The main building, to the left of the Huguenot Monument, is modelled on a house designed by the French architect, Louis Michel Thibault, built in 1791 at Kloof Street, Cape Town. The displays inside trace the history of the Huguenots in South Africa. There are some fine collections of furniture, silverware and family bibles, but the most interesting displays are the family trees providing a record of families over the past 250 years. One of the roles of the museum today is to maintain an up-to-date register of families, so that future generations will be able to trace their ancestors.

Next door to the museum is the rather stark and unattractive **Huguenot Monument**, a highly symbolic memorial built to mark 250 years since the first Huguenots settled in the Cape. It is set in a peaceful rose garden with the rugged Franschhoek Mountains providing a contrasting background. The three arches represent the Trinity, and the golden sun and cross on top are the Sun of Righteousness and the Cross of Christian Faith. In front of the arches, a statue of a woman with a bible in her right hand and a broken chain in her left symbolizes freedom from religious oppression. If you look closely at the globe you can see objects carved into the southern tip of Africa: a bible, harp, spinning wheel, sheaf of corn and a vine. These represent different aspects of the Huguenots' life, respectively their faith, their art and culture, their industry and their agriculture. The final piece of the memorial, the curved colonnade, represents tranquillity and spiritual peace after the problems they had faced in France.

Franschhoek wine route

All the vineyards lie along the Franschhoek Valley, making it one of the most compact wine routes in the region. There are now 42 wine estates on the route, and again many estates have opened their own excellent restaurants and several also offer luxury accommodation. Maps and information on all the estates are available at the tourist office.

Allée Bleue ① *R45, T021-874 1021, www.alleebleue.com, sales and tastings and restaurant: Mon-Fri 0900-1700, Sat 1000-1700, Sun 1000-1600.* This estate is a good place to drop in for

Four Passes

One of the popular recommended day drives from Cape Town is known as the Four Passes route. This takes you through the heart of the Winelands, and, as the name suggests, over four mountain passes. It is a wonderful day out from Cape Town, especially if combined with fine wine and gourmet food in Franschhoek. The first stop on the drive is Stellenbosch. From here you take the R310 towards Franschhoek. Driving up out of Stellenbosch you cross the first pass – **Helshoogte Pass**. After 17 km you reach a T-junction with the R45: a left turn would take you to Paarl, 12 km, but the route continues to the right. This is a pleasant drive up into the Franschhoek Valley. The road follows a railway line and part of the Berg River. After passing through Franschhoek, take a left in front of the Huguenot Monument and climb out of the valley via the **Franschhoek Pass**. This pass was built along the tracks formed by migrating herds of game centuries earlier, and was originally known as the Olifantspad (elephant's path). One of the more surprising aspects of this drive is the change in vegetation once you cross the lip of the pass, 520 m above the level of Franschhoek. As the road winds down towards Theewaterskloof Dam, you pass through a dry valley full of scrub vegetation and fynbos – gone are the fertile fruit farms and vineyards.

Take a right across the dam on the R321 towards Grabouw and Elgin. An alternative but much longer route back to Cape Town is to take a left here, onto the R43. This is the road to Worcester, 50 km, the principal town in the Breede River Valley. From Worcester follow the N1 back to Cape Town.

The Four Passes Route continues across the Theewaterskloof Dam and then climbs **Viljoens Pass**, the third of four. To the right lies the Hottentots Holland Nature Reserve, a popular hiking region. The country around here is an important apple-growing region. At the N2 highway turn right and follow the road back into Cape Town. The fourth and most spectacular pass is **Sir Lowry's Pass**, which crosses the Hottentots Holland Mountains. From the viewpoint at the top you will be rewarded with a fine view of the Cape Flats with the brooding Cape Peninsula behind.

some quick wine tasting if you haven't the time to see a whole vineyard. Tastings include four wines and the estate also produces olives and olive oil which are available to taste. There is a small fashionable bistro and picnic baskets are available.

Anthonij Rupert Wines (formerly L'Ormarins) ① *R45, T021-874 9000, www.rupertwines. com, sales and tastings: Mon-Sat 1000-1630.* The original land was granted to the Huguenot, Jean Roi, in 1694, who named the farm after his village in the South of France. The present homestead was built in 1811 – from its grand marble halls and staircases you look out across an ornamental pond and neat gardens. Cheese platters and high teas are served on the veranda. Among the classic range of wines, is the Italian varietal range, Terra del Capo. Also here is the **Franschhoek Motor Museum** ① *Mon-Fri 1000-1600, Sat-Sun 1000-1500, T021-874 9000, www.fmm.co.za, R60 per person*, which has over 80 vintage and classic cars on display plus other vehicles such as an 1898 tricycle. Any car enthusiast will enjoy a visit here and the valuable cars are displayed in chronological order from pre-1900 models up to a 2003 Ferrari.

Boschendal ① *R310, T021-870 4272, www.boschendal.com, sales and tastings: 0830-1630; vineyard and cellar tours: 1030, 1130 and 1500 by appointment.* Boschendal has been producing wine since 1687 and is today one of the most popular and beautiful estates in the region, not least for its excellent food and pleasant wine-tasting area underneath a giant oak. The restored H-shaped manor house (1812) is one of the finest in South Africa, and is open as a museum to the public. The restaurant serves an excellent buffet lunch (1200-1500), **Le Pique Nique** (1215-1330) offers picnic hampers in the gardens between November and April, and **Le Café** (1000-1700) has light meals and afternoon teas.

Cape Chamonix ① *Uitkyk St, T021-876 2494, www.chamonix.co.za, sales and tastings: 0930-1700; cellar tours: by appointment; restaurant: 1200-1430.* This is one of the largest farms in the valley, with an underground cellar providing pleasantly cool tours at the height of summer. Wine tastings are held in the Blacksmith's Cottage; you can also try their fruit schnapps or the Chamonix mineral water. The restaurant is highly rated and has a warming fire inside in winter. Food is prepared on a stove built in Paris in 1908. Accommodation is in 13 comfortable whitewashed self-catering cottages (**$$**).

Mont Rochelle ① *Dassenberg Rd, T021-876 2770, www.montrochelle.co.za, sales and tastings: 1000-1900; cellar tours: Mon-Fri 1100, 1230 and 1500; restaurant 1200-1800.* This estate has one of the most attractive settings in the region with beautiful views of the valley and it produces some good full bodied red wines and a couple of whites. Tastings are informal and friendly and can be combined with wine-pairing lunches at the Country Kitchen restaurant in the wine-tasting centre and picnic baskets are available. The estate is also home to a hotel with the **Mange Tout** restaurant (see Where to stay, page 109, and Restaurants, page 112).

La Motte ① *R45, T021-876 3119, www.la-motte.co.za, sales and tastings: Mon-Sat 0900-1700, restaurant Tue-Sun 1100-1700, Thu-Sat 1830-2230.* The original manor house was built in 1752 and the grand old cellars can be viewed through glass walls from the tasting room. The museum and gallery has interesting exhibits on Cape Dutch architecture and some valuable local art. The restaurant with its pleasant conservatory has a good choice of traditional South African dishes. There's a 5-km circular hiking trail on the estate which takes about two hours to complete.

Paarl Winelands → *For listings, see pages 107-116.*

Paarl

While Paarl is home to two of South Africa's better-known wine estates, KWV and Nederburg (see page 106), the town itself is fairly staid and is not as interesting as Stellenbosch or as fashionable as Franschhoek. All of the attractions and restaurants are strung out along Main Street at the base of Paarl Mountain. When the first European arrival, Abraham Gabbema, saw this mountain in October 1657 it had just rained; the granite domes sparkled in the sunlight and he named the mountains *paarl* (pearl) and *diamandt* (diamond). The first settlers arrived in 'Paarlvallei' in 1687 and, shortly afterwards, the French Huguenots settled on four farms, **Laborie**, **Goede Hoop**, **La Concorde** and **Picardie**. The town grew in a random fashion along an important wagon route to Cape Town. Several old buildings survive, but they are spread out rather than concentrated in a few blocks as in Stellenbosch. There is a helpful **tourist office** ① *216 Main St, T021-872 4842, www.paarlonline.com, Mon-Fri 0800-1700, Sat-Sun 1000-1300.*

Places in Paarl The 1-km walk along Main Street will take you past some of the finest architecture in Paarl. Here you'll find one of the oldest buildings, the **Paarl Museum** ① *303 Main St, T021-876 2651, Mon-Fri 0900-1600, Sat 0900-1300, R5, children (under 16) free.* This 18th-century U-shaped Cape Dutch former parsonage houses a reasonably diverting

Paarl

Where to stay 🛏
Eben-Haëzer
  Country Manor **1**
Grande Roche **2**
Lemoenkloof Guest
  House **3**
Pontac Manor **4**
Zomerlust Guest
  House **13**

Restaurants 🍴
Bosman's **5**
Café du Pontac **6**
Harvest at Laborie **3**
Noop **7**
Proviant Kaapse Tafel
  en Spens **4**

collection of Cape Dutch furniture and kitchen copperware plus some more delicate silver. There is also a small section outlining Paarl during Apartheid, although the fact that Nelson Mandela spent his final years in prison near Paarl is barely mentioned. Only a few hundred metres away, in Gideon Malherbe House, the **Afrikaans Language Museum** ① 11 *Pastorie St, T021-872 3441, www.taalmuseum.co.za, Mon-Fri 0900-1600, Sat 0900-1300, R15, children (under 16) R10*, gives a detailed chronicle of the development of the Afrikaans language and the people involved. The house itself was built in 1860 by a wealthy wine farmer of the same name and the downstairs rooms have been decorated with period furniture donated by his descendents.

Paarl Mountain Nature Reserve

① *Jan Philips Mountain Drive, T021-872 3658, Nov-May 0700-1900, Apr-Oct 0700-1800, free.* Paarl runs along the eastern base of Paarl Mountain, a giant granite massif, which in 1970 was declared the Paarl Mountain Nature Reserve. Within the 1900-ha reserve is a network of footpaths, a circular drive and a couple of dams. The vegetation differs from the surrounding countryside because of the bedrock – the granite mass is not as susceptible to veld fires and many of the fynbos species grow exceptionally tall. The domed summit is easy to climb, and near the top is an old cannon dating from the early days of the Cape Colony. Just below the summit a mountain stream flows through the **Meulwater Wild Flower Reserve**. This garden was created in 1931, and contains specimens of the majority of flowers found around Paarl Mountain including 15 species of protea.

Set high on the slopes of Paarl Mountain amongst granite boulders and indigenous trees stands the controversial **Afrikaanse Taalmonument** ① *Gabbema Doordrift St, follow signs off Main St just after the R45 enters the south of town from the N1, T021-863 0543, www.taalmuseum.co.za, 0800-1700, Oct-Mar 0800-2000, R15, children (under 16) R10, coffee shop 0800-1700*, three concrete columns linked by a low curved wall. This is the Afrikaans Language Monument, inaugurated in October 1975 and designed by Jan van Wijk. Built to celebrate 100 years of Afrikaans being declared as a different language from Dutch, it is thought to be on the only monument in the world dedicated to a language. Each column represents different influences in the language. The phrase *Dit is ons erns*, roughly meaning 'this is our earnestness' is inscribed on the pathway leading up to the monument. There are excellent views across the Berg River Valley from here, and on a clear day you can see False Bay, Table Mountain and all the vineyards. As well as light meals, the coffee shop organizes cheese platters and picnic baskets to take on walks; phone ahead, T021-863 2800.

Those with little children in tow may wish to visit **Butterfly World** ① *on the R44 at junction 47 of the N1, T021-875 5628, www.butterflyworld.co.za, 0900-1700, R53, children (3-16) R31, under 3s free, family of 4 ticket R137*, the largest such park in South Africa, with butterflies flying freely in colourful landscaped gardens. They are at their most active on sunny days. There are also spiders, scorpions, chameleons, tortoises and meerkats to see and you can buy packets of seeds for children to feed the goats, ducks and chickens in the garden. There is a craft shop and the **Jungle Leaf Café** on site.

Paarl wine route

① *Maps and information can be picked up at the tourist office or visit www.paarlwine.co.za.* The route was set up in 1984 by local producers to help promote their wines and attract tourists into the area. The programme has been a great success and some of the estates have opened their own restaurants. Today there are 30 members; below is a short selection.

Backsberg ① *R45, T021-875 5141, www.backsberg.co.za, sales and tastings: Mon-Fri 0800-1700, Sat 0930-1630, Sun 1030-1630; cellar tours by appointment; restaurant: 0930-1530.* This is a very pleasant estate located along the lower slopes of the Simonsberg Mountains midway between Paarl and Franschhoek, where the Back family has been producing wine since the 1920s. Lunches are served under the oaks and at weekends there is a traditional lamb on the spit accompanied by a guitarist. Picnic platters are available. Also offers vineyard tours by tractor and a mountain-bike challenge is held on the estate in September.

Fairview ① *Suid-Agter-Paarl Rd, off the R101, T021-863 2450, www.fairview.co.za, wine and cheese sales and tastings and restaurant: 0900-1700.* This popular estate has a rather unusual attraction in the form of a goat tower, a spiral structure which is home to two pairs of goats. In addition to a variety of good wines (look out for the popular Goats do Roam label – a humorous dig at French wines) visitors can taste delicious goat cheeses, which are now produced from a herd of over 700 goats and sold in South African supermarkets. Their Camembert consistently wins awards as the best in the world at the annual World Cheese Awards. Meals are served in **The Goatshed** restaurant (see Restaurants, page 113).

The Laborie ① *Taillefer St, T021-807 3390, www.laboriewines.co.za, sales and tastings: 0900-1700, Sun 1100-1500; restaurant: 1200-1500, Wed-Sat 1830-2130.* Part of KWV (see below), this is a beautifully restored original Cape Dutch homestead – in many ways the archetypal wine estate, and developed with tourism firmly in mind. It's an attractive spot, with a tasting area overlooking rolling lawns and vineyards, and a highly rated restaurant (see Restaurants, page 112). As well as a good range of wines they produce an award-winning brandy. Accommodation is in seven B&B rooms in restored farm buildings (**$$**) and one deluxe room in the manor house (**$$$**).

KWV Wine Emporium ① *Kohler St, T021-807 3007, www.kwvwineemporium.co.za, sales and tastings: Mon-Sat 0900-1630, Sun 1100-1600; cellar tours: Mon-Sat 1000, 1015 (in German), 1030, 1415, Sun 1100; café: Mon-Sat 0930-1600.* A short distance from the Laborie estate is the famous **KWV Cellar Complex** which contains the five largest vats in the world. The **Ko-operative Wijnbouwers Vereniging van Zuid-Afrika** (Cooperative Wine Growers' Association) was established in Paarl in 1918 and is responsible for exporting many of South Africa's best-known wines. They are also well known for their brandy and tastings are served with Belgian chocolates.

Nederburg ① *Sonstraal Rd, T021-862 3104, www.nederburg.com, sales and tastings: Mon-Fri 0900-1700, Sat 1000-1600, Nov-Mar Sun 1000-1400; cellar tours Mon-Fri 1030 and 1500, Sat-Sun 1100; restaurant: Mon-Sat (and Sun Oct-Apr) 1100-1600* This is one of the largest and best-known estates in South Africa. Their annual production is in excess of 650,000 cases and their wines win countless annual awards. As such a large concern they are involved in much of the research in South Africa to improve the quality of the grape and vine. Every April the annual Nederburg Auction attracts buyers from all over the world and is considered one of the top five wine auctions in the world. The estate's 1000 sq m auction hall also doubles up as the kitchen and studio for the popular TV show MasterChef South Africa™. The homestead was built in 1800, and today is a National Monument and home to the bistro-style restaurant which has a terrace with fine views of the Drakenstein Mountains. Picnic baskets are available to enjoy on the lawns.

Rhebokskloof ① *Northern Agter-Paarl Rd, T021-869 8386, www.rhebokskloof.co.za, sales and tastings and restaurant: Mon-Fri 0900-1700, Sat-Sun 1000-1500.* This old estate is now a thoroughly modern outfit. Informal tastings are accompanied by cheese and biscuits and the terrace café is popular with tour groups and on Sundays they offer a family buffet lunch. There are occasional music concerts on summer weekends (check the website for the programme) and the stage is set up on the lawns next to the estate's dam; picnic baskets are available. The estate is also home to Wine Valley Horse Trails (see page 115).

Wellington district → *For listings, see pages 107-116.*

Wellington

Wellington, 11 km north of Paarl on the R301, like the other Winelands towns, is surrounded by beautiful countryside and has a number of fine historic buildings, with the added bonus of far fewer tourists thronging the streets. Nevertheless, there is little in the town to keep visitors for long – there are a few wine estates in the surrounding area, but the town is best known for its dried fruit. (The other important fruit centres, Ceres and Tulbagh, are on the eastern side of the Limietberg. They can be visited via the magnificent Bain's Kloof Pass, see box, page 102.) To the north, the countryside opens up into the rolling Swartland, an important wheat region. The **Wellington Tourism Bureau** ① *104 Main St, T021-873 4604, www.wellington.co.za, Mon-Fri 0800-1700, Sat-Sun 1000-1300,* is housed in the Old Market Building next to the Dutch Reformed Church.

The shady **Victoria Park** in Church Street is notable for its roses. Look out for the archway which was built to commemorate the coronation of King Edward VII in 1902. The fountain in **Joubert Square** was unveiled in 1939 as a memorial to the Huguenot settlers in the valley. The **Wellington Museum** ① *Church St, T021-873 4710, Mon-Fri 0900-1700, Oct-Feb, Sun 0900-1300, R5, children (under 16) free,* has a small collection on the history of the town and the Huguenot farms in the district. The archives of the Huguenot Seminary are kept here. Oddly, there are a few ancient Egyptian relics on display.

Winelands listings

For hotel and restaurant price codes and other relevant information, see pages 10-13.

◐ Where to stay

Most hotels in the Winelands can organize airport transfers.

Strand and Somerset West
p93, map p92
$$$ Lord Charles Hotel, corner Main Rd and R44, Somerset West, T021-855 1040, www.nh-hotels.co.za. Pleasant 4-star traditional hotel in expansive beautifully kept grounds with dam and gazebos. 198 smart a/c rooms with good mountain views, full range of facilities including 2 pools, beauty salon, gym, pub and La Vigna restaurant (see Restaurants, page 111).

$$$-$$ The Country Guesthouse, 96 Winery Rd, 7 km north of Somerset West off the R44 towards Stellenbosch, T021-842 2945, www.thecountryguesthouse.co.za. On a working wine estate, with 12 cottages set in immaculate gardens, some have fireplaces, all have private terraces and contemporary décor. Swimming pool, beauty treatments and fine restaurant (see Restaurants, page 111).

Stellenbosch and around
p95, maps p92 and p96
In town
$$$ Dorpshuis & Spa, 22 Dorp St, T021-883 9881, www.proteahotels.com.

A smart Victorian townhouse with 27 individually decorated a/c rooms with antiques, marble-clad bathrooms and private patios, heated swimming pool and the **Oak Leaf** à la carte restaurant.

$$$-$$ D'Ouwe Werf Hotel, 30 Church St, T021-887 4608, www.ouwewerf.com. Converted Georgian house with 44 a/c rooms an 5 apartments with kitchenettes, all individually decorated with Cape-style furniture and DSTV. Good-sized pool and vine-shaded terrace where breakfast and lunch are served. The **1802** restaurant has a good reputation.

$$$-$$ Labri Manor, 71 Victoria St, T021-886 5652, www.labrimanor.co.za. A fine Victorian house with 10 luxury rooms with DSTV, polished wooden floors, huge 4-poster beds, subtle yellow walls and dark wood antiques. Spa room, cobbled courtyard, dinner and picnic baskets on request.

$$ Eendracht, 161 Dorp St, T021-883 8843, www.eendracht-hotel.com. Housed in a reconstruction of what was one of Stelllenbosch's oldest houses, this boutique hotel has 12 rooms with modern understated decor and luxuries like silk-filled duvets, pool, bar and the small restaurant serves traditional South African dishes such as *water-blommetjiebredie*.

$$ Ryneveld Country Lodge, 67 Ryneveld St, T021-887 4469, www.ryneveldlodge.co.za. Friendly B&B in a beautiful late 19th-century house full of antiques with breakfast room, shady terrace and small pool, 10 a/c rooms, some in more expensive cottages have additional kitchenettes and are suitable for families.

$$ Stellenbosch Hotel, 162 Dorp St, T021-887 3644, www.stellenboschhotel.co.za. Central hotel with 32 a/c rooms and 6 self-catering apartments in buildings with restored façades dating to 1815. Although small with plain decor, good value and centrally located. Friendly bar popular with locals, bright dining room with tables on terrace overlooking the street (see Restaurants, page 111).

Out of town

$$$$ Lanzerac Manor, Jonkershoek Rd, 2 km from town centre T021-887 1132, www.lanzerac.co.za. Very expensive but fittingly luxurious hotel set around an 18th-century Cape Dutch manor house on a wine estate, tastings and cellar tours on offer. 48 spacious and plush suites with private patios and all mod cons, 2 restaurants: the formal **Governor's Hall**, and the more relaxed **Lanzerac Terrace** for alfresco dining during summer. There's an extensive spa with a separate pool overlooking the vines which is also popular with non-guests for a day of pampering.

$$$ Spier Hotel, Spier Wine Estate (see page 99), T021-809 1100, www.spier.co.za. Condo-style buildings set around courtyards with private pools for each section, 155 large rooms with stylish decor in strong colours and polished concrete floors, beautiful bathrooms stocked with aromatherapy products, restaurant, wine bar and spa.

$$$ Wedgeview Country House & Spa, The Bonniemile, 5 km south of town, T021-881 3525, www.wedgeview.co.za. Set in 1.5 ha of attractive grounds surrounded by vineyards with 13 garden thatched suites, main house has snooker room, bar, lounge and breakfast room, 2 swimming pools and beauty spa. Rates are for B&B, restaurant for light lunches and snacks and 3-course dinners on request.

$$$-$$ L'Avenir Country Lodge, 5 km north of Stellenbosch off the R44 towards the N1 and Paarl, T021-889 5001, www.lavenir-lodge.com. A peaceful setting on a smart wine farm with 11 a/c rooms with contemporary African decor, good views of the farm dam, pool. Price includes breakfast and wine tasting, meals arranged on request.

$$ Bellevue Manor, 5 km south of Stellenbosch on the R44, T021-880 1086, www.bellevuestellenbosch.co.za. Peaceful farm with 8 purpose-built a/c thatched B&B cottages in Cape Dutch style with pleasant country-style furnishings, TV, fireplace, private terrace, good-sized pool with braai area.

Franschhoek Valley
p100, maps p92 and p100
In town
$$$$ Le Quartier Français, 16 Huguenot Rd, T021-876 2151, www.lqf.co.za.
A superb hotel and impeccable service with 17 enormous luxury rooms with fireplaces, plush furnishings and views over the pool and peaceful, shady courtyard, some have private splash pools and lofts for children. The Screening oom, is a private cinema, and The Treatment Room, an intimate spa. The restauants, **The Tasting Rooom** (see Restaurants, page 111) is considered one of Franschhoek's best.

$$$$ Mont Rochelle, Dassenberg Rd, T021-876 2770, www.montrochelle.co.za.
24 luxury suites and rooms set in the main manor house or in garden units, elegantly decorated with enormous bathrooms, superb award-winning restaurant (see Restaurants, page 112), cigar bar, swimming pool, gym and sauna, attentive service, good mountain views and pleasant rolling gardens.

$$$ La Cabrière Country House, Park Lane, off Middagkrans Rd, T021-876 4780, www.lacabriere.co.za. Small luxurious and stylish guesthouse set just outside town in formal lavender and herb gardens, 6 a/c rooms with Provençal decor, limed-wood furniture, views of vineyards and mountains, swimming pool.

$$$-$$ Klein Oliphants Hoek, 14 Akademie St, T021-876 2566, www.kleinoliphantshoek.co.za. A fine guesthouse close to the centre of Franschhoek which was originally a missionary hall built in 1888, with 8 small but comfortable a/c rooms. The vast, high-ceilinged lounge, once the original meeting hall, has a fireplace and is filled with antiques, and there's a veranda for afternoon tea overlooking pretty gardens.

$$$-$$ La Fontaine, 21 Dirkie Uys St, T021-876 2112, www.lafontainefranschhoek.co.za. One of the finest guesthouses in Franschhoek with 14 rooms set in a Victorian house near the village centre, elegant decor with antiques, polished wooden floors and Persian rugs, some rooms are set in the garden around the pool and the stables have been converted into a family unit.

$$$-$$ Auberge Bligny, 28 Van Wijk St, T021-876 3767, www.bligny.co.za.
A beautifully restored house dating from 1861, 9 rooms, and apart from the TVs, with furniture specifically from the period with brass beds, patchwork quilts, and Victorian claw-foot baths. Lounge with open fire in winter, neat gardens with pool.

$$ Auberge La Dauphine, at La Dauphine Wine Estate off Excelsior Rd, T021-876 2606, www.ladauphine.co.za. One of the most peaceful locations in the valley, wih 5 luxury a/c B&B rooms each with a spacious lounge and patio in a carefully restored wine store, plus 3 self-catering farm cottages sleeping 4, surrounded by beautiful gardens and vineyards. Large swimming pool and fishing in the farm dam can be arranged.

$$ Protea Hotel Franschhoek, 34 Huguenot Rd, T021-876 3012, www.proteahotels.co.za. A quality offering from Protea and in an excellent location right in the village centre, though there are more atmospheric places to stay. The 30 individually decorated rooms are arranged around the swimming pool, and there's a decent restaurant and bar.

$ Otter's Bend, Dassenberg Rd, T021-876 3200, www.ottersbendlodge.co.za. Budget accommodation in 5 small en suite log cabins, and a self-catering flat sleeping 4 in a lovely wooded spot around a swimming pool. Communal fully equipped kitchen with fireplace and braai. Breakfast extra.

Out of town
$$$$-$$$ Franschhoek Country House, Huguenot Rd, 1 km east of town, T021-876 3386, www.fch.co.za. Very elegant boutique hotel with 14 rooms and 12 suites, some with fireplace, private verandas, the newer suites are 100 sq m and very luxurious with

French-style furniture, dramatic drapes and candelabras, 2 swimming pools, spa, lovely fountains in the grounds, excellent restaurant.
$$ Lekkerwijn, R45, just before the junction with the R310 to Stellenbosch, T021-874 1122, www.lekkerwijn.com. A fine B&B in fine park-like gardens with peacocks and guinea fowl, wih 6 rooms plus a self-catering cottage suitable for a family of 4. The bedroom wing was designed by Herbert Baker and is arranged around a private pillared courtyard, tastefully furnished lounge and swimming pool.

Paarl Winelands
p103 maps p92 and p104
In town
$$$$ Grande Roche, Plantasie St, T021-863 5100, www.granderoche.co.za. A T-shaped manor house dating to 1707 which has established itself as one of the top hotels in South Africa, with 35 luxury a/c suites set in a collection of restored farm buildings in peaceful gardens surrounded by vineyards, 2 floodlit tennis courts, 2 swimming pools, gym. **Bosman's** restaurant is regarded as one of the best in the country (see Restaurants, page 112).
$$$ Pontac Manor Hotel, 16 Zion St, T021-872 0445, www.pontac.com. Elegant Victorian manor house with manicured gardens full of oak trees that are home to an army of squirrels. 22 spacious a/c rooms with antiques and fine fabrics, some with kitchenettes. Smart bar, comfortable lounges with fireplaces and a quaint daytime café (see Cafés, page 113).
$$ Lemoenkloof Guest House, 396a Main St, T021-872 3782, www.lemoenkloof.co.za. Country house on northern edge of town, with 30 a/c rooms with floral fabrics, fresh flowers and black-and-white tiled bathrooms, grouped in several historical buildings dating to the early 1800s. Pleasant gardens, palm-shaded pool and sunny breakfast room.
$$ Zomerlust Guest House, 193 Main St, T021-872 2117, www.zomerlust.co.za. A restored historic house in the centre of town with 14 rooms, some in converted

stables. Courtyard, terrace, swimming pool, library, wine cellar and cosy restaurant for breakfasts as well as lunch and dinner on request.

Out of town
$$$ Eben-Haëzer Country Manor, Sonstraal Rd, 4 km from town centre, T021-862 7420, www.eben-haezer.co.za. Original Cape Dutch homestead, with 6 large luxury rooms, Victorian-style bathrooms, plus 1 very private honeymoon cottage with its own splash pool. Breakfast served under oak trees in the tea garden or in the 18th-century dining room, beautiful whitewashed chapel for weddings.
$$$ Palmiet Valley Estate, 1 km north of junction 62 on the N1, T021-862 7741, www.palmiet.co.za. A restored 1642 historic Cape Dutch homestead located on a wine estate with 10 spacious doubles and 1 honeymoon suite, each decorated with antiques, private balconies or terraces, neat garden, swimming pool, massages available, very good food served in the dining room or on the terrace.
$ Berg River Resort, 5 km out of town towards Franschhoek on the R45, south side of the N1, T021-863 1650, www.berg riverresort.co.za. Self-catering chalets of varying comfort sleeping 2-6, caravan and camping sites with electric points, pool, mini-golf, petting farmyard, canoes, tractor rides, kiosk for snacks and drinks, nice spot next to the river and ideal for families.

Wellington district *p107, map p92*
$$$-$$ Diemersfontein Wine and Country Estate, Van Riebeck Drive, off the R303, T021-864 5050, www.diemersfontein. co.za. A classic country house set in beautifully tended gardens on a wine estate, with 30 rooms, either in the main house or in restored farm buildings, some with kitchenettes, traditional, plush furnishings, elegant teak-panelled lounge, swimming pool, very good restaurant (see Restaurants, page 113) and horse riding.

❷ Restaurants

Strand and Somerset West
p93, map p92

$$$-$ La Vigna, Lord Charles Hotel (see Where to stay, page 107). Open 1200-2200. Refreshing minimalist decor, lovely garden terrace and you can visit the wine cellar. Long and varied menu including oysters, Indian curries, oriental stir-fries, barbecues and lavish desserts. Also an excellent spot for afternoon teas.

$$ 96 Winery Road, at The Country Guesthouse (see Where to stay, page 107), T021-842 2020, www.96wineryroad.co.za. Open 1200-1500, 1900-2200, closed Sun evening. Pleasant restaurant in an informal farmhouse setting with tables set under oak trees. Very good grills and some fish such as Norwegian salmon, and specials like guinea fowl or duck and cherry pie. Picnics can be pre-booked to enjoy in the gardens next to the farm dam.

Stellenbosch and around
p95, maps p92 and p96

As well as the restaurants in town, eating at a wine estate is especially nice for lazy lunches in a picturesque setting. Many of these are listed separately under details of the individual estates on the Stellenbosch wine route (page 98).

$$$ Moyo, Spier, on the R310, T021-8091133, www.moyo.co.za. Open 1130-2300. Superb restaurant in a beautiful location and a highlight of a trip to South Africa. Arranged in Bedouin tents with outside tables in delightful tree houses or wrought-iron gazebos lit by candles. The vast buffet has just about everything imaginable from hot mussels to fine cheese and pan-African food. Each table is entertained by women who decorate your face with traditional Xhosa white paint, Zimbabwean musicians, jazz bands and township opera singers.

$$$ Volkskombuis, Aan de Wagen Rd, T021-887 2121, www.volkskombuis.co.za.

Open 1200-1430, 1830-2130, closed Sun during winter. High standards of food and service, with a focus on traditional Cape cooking. Try the braised oxtail or home-made chicken pies. Housed in a restored Herbert Baker Cape Dutch homestead, with views across the Eerste River.

$$ The Big Easy, 95 Dorp St, T021-887 3462, www.thebigeasyrestaurant.co.za. Mon-Fri 0730-1000, 1200-2200. Brasserie-style restaurant owned by successful South African golfer Ernie Els featuring memorabilia and photos, set in a historic building dating from 1798. Farm breakfasts, tapas like oysters and game carpaccio, and mains including seared tuna and steaks, more than 170 Stellenbosch wines on the wine list.

$$-$ Jan Cats, at the Stellenbosch Hotel, see Where to stay, page 108. Open 0700-2200. Casual hotel restaurant with cosy interior and street-side terrace on Dorp St, with good-value pub-style meals like steak chips plus local favourites like West Coast mussels or Cape Malay curry.

$$-$ Wijnhuis, corner Church and Andringa streets, T021-887 5844, www.wijnhuis.co.za. Open 0800-2300. Bustling wine bar and wine shop in characterful historic building, pretty outside eating in a courtyard. Breakfasts served until noon, and menu offers steak, some seafood and venison, delicately presented, and over 20 wines available by the glass.

Cafés

Dorp Street Deli, 56 Dorp St, T021-886 8807, www.dorpstrdeli.co.za. Mon-Sat 0700-2300. Delicious range of breakfasts, creative sandwiches and light lunches such as quiche and pasta. The deli sells imported cheese and ham and freshly baked bread and pastries. Open late and is licensed.

Franschhoek Valley
p100 maps p92 and p100

Franschhoek is dubbed 'gourmet capital of South Africa', and for good reason.

Booking ahead, especially at the weekends, is advised. For a full list of more than 40 restaurants in the area, visit www.franschhoek.org.za/franschhoek-restaurants.

$$$ La Petite Ferme, on Franschhoek Pass Rd, T021-876 3016, www.lapetiteferme.co.za. Daily for lunch 1200-1600. Spectacular views over the Franschhoek Valley from this smart 'boutique' winery. Well known for its wholesome country fare like baby chicken with lemon stuffing, or hearty braised rabbit with parsnips.

$$$ Mange Tout, Dassenberg Rd, T021-876 2770, www.montrochelle.co.za. Open 1200-1500, 1900-2130. Small, formal restaurant based at the ultra-smart **Mont Rochelle Hotel**. Perfect setting overlooking the vineyards, excellent gourmet menu with a contemporary French theme, also arranges picnics, long wine list.

$$$ Monneaux, at Franschhoek Country House (see Where to stay, page 107). Open 0800-1000, 1200-1430, 1900-2100. Highly rated, serving contemporary fusion cuisine, attractive outdoor terrace and cosy dining room. To whet your appetite consider bacon-wrapped fish with almond cream or chicken breast marinated in ginger and beetroot.

$$$ Reuben's, 19 Huguenot Rd, T021-876 3772, www.reubens.co.za. Open 1200-1500, 1800-2200. Franschhoek's top restaurant run by South Africa's best-known celebrity chef, there's another branch in Cape Town's **One&Only** luxury hotel (page 54). A faultless experience with sculptured cuisine that is presented like works of art. To whet the appetite think double-baked gruyère soufflé with honey truffle dressing or herb-buttered mussels with celery purée and bouillabaisse sauce. Book at least 2 weeks in advance.

$$$ The Tasting Room, at Le Quartier Français (see Where to stay, page 109). Tue-Sat 1900-until meal ends. Consistently rated as one of the best restaurants in South Africa run by an award-winning Relais & Chateaux Grande Chef. Formal 8-course gourmet dinners are a taste-sensation and a theatrical experience and take about 3½ hrs. Justifiably, advance bookings are essential.

$$ The French Connection Bistro, 48 Huguenot Rd, T021-8764056, www.frenchconnection.co.za. Open 1200-1530, 1830-2145. French bistro serving refreshingly unfussy food such as steamed mussels, steak frites or Toulouse sausages and mash. Good food and generous portions at sensible prices.

Cafés

Café des Arts, 7 Reservoir St, T021-876 2952, www.cafedesarts.co.za. Tue-Sat 0800-1700, Wed, Fri-Sat 1830-2100. A small art gallery and cosy informal place with log fire, open kitchen, garden tables, and a daily changing chalkboard menu for breakfast and lunch, and on some nights dinner. Well-liked for its hearty-style plates – Franschhoek is more often associated with haute cuisine.

Paarl Winelands
p103 maps p92 and p104

$$$ Bosman's, at the **Grande Roche Hotel**, Where to stay, page 107). Open 0700-1030, 1200-1400, 1830-2100. Award-winning international cuisine in a grand vineyard-fringed setting. Popular 3-course set lunch, but the real treat is the celebrated 5-course menus (R580), offering superbly created Cape cuisine. A sommelier talks you through the wine.

$$ Harvest at Laborie, Taillefer St, off the R45 south of town, T021-807 3095, www.harvestatlaborie.co.za. Daily 1200-1530, Wed-Sun 1830-2130. Relaxed and family-friendly restaurant on wine estate with pleasant seating under giant oak trees. Delicious Mediterranean dishes, as well as Cape specialities like bobotie and Karoo lamb burgers, and uses vegetables and herbs from the estate's own gardens.

$$ Noop, 127 Main St, T021-863 3925, www.noop.co.za. Mon-Sat 1100-2300. Set in a restored heritage building with outside tables on the stoep, this unpretentious restaurant has a varied menu from local

venison burgers to prawn tempura. Make room for the traditional malva pudding.
$$ Wilderer's, Wilderer's Distillery, 3 km outside Paarl on R45 on the south side of the N1, T021-863 3555, www.wilderer.co.za. Tue-Sun 1100-1700. Relaxed lunchtime continental restaurant in a schnapps distillery. The speciality is *lammkuchen*, a type of pizza from Strasbourg, and they also serve pasta, veal and fish dishes. Finish off with a shot of their pear or fynbos schnapps. Live jazz on the 1st Sun of the month.
$$-$ The Goatshed, Fairview (see page 106), T021-863 3609, www.goatshed. co.za. Open 0900-1700. At the popular wine and cheese farm, which can sometimes be overrun with tour groups, but don't let that put you off as the food is excellent. Cheese platters with freshly baked bread are the highlight, but the mains of duck, lamb, veal and trout will appeal to the hungrier. Naturally the baked cheesecake is superb.

Cafés
Café du Pontac, Pontac Manor Hotel, see Where to stay, page 107. Open 0700-1700. Old-fashioned tearoom with quaint sideboards, high back chairs, chandeliers and tables on the pretty veranda of this 17th-century manor house. Breakfast buffets (0700-1000), filled baguettes, salads, pastas and high teas.
Proviant Kaapse Tafel en Spens, 54-56 Main Rd, T021-863 0949. Tue-Sun 0800-1700. Traditional Afrikaans roadside café and farmstall with outside tables on the stoep and views of Paarl Mountain. The menu features South African dishes like babotie, oxtail and frikkadels, served with mealie pot bread and home-made ginger beer.

Wellington district *p107, map p92*
$$ Seasons, at the Diemersfontein Wine and Country Estate (see Where to stay, page 107). Open 0800-1100, 1215-1530, 1830-2100. Contemporary restaurant with

tables overlooking the farm dam and mountains. Light lunches such as tomato and goat's cheese tart or warm trout salad, and heavier dishes for dinner such as crusted salmon or pork belly.
$$-$ Oude Wellington, R301, Bain's Kloof Pass, 5 km east of town, T021-873 1008, www.oudewellingtonrestaurant.co.za. Open 0800-2000. Lovely spot on a wine and brandy estate in an old whitewashed farmstead dating to 1795 with outside seating in the grounds with dogs, peacocks and ostriches roaming around. Wholesome country-style cooking using produce from the farm.

🎧 Bars and clubs

Stellenbosch *p95, map p96*
Dros, corner of Bird and Alexander streets, T021-886 4856, www.dros.co.za. Open 0800-2400. A large bar-cum-restaurant serving standard pub fare such as burgers, steaks, ribs and pizza and the noisy bar livens up with students later.
Fandango, Shop 11, Drostdy Centre, T021-887 7506, www.fandango.co.za. Open 0930-0100. Café and bar with a good value all-day food menu, internet access, tables outside on the square, popular for after-work cocktails, occasional live music. Also rents out bicycles.
Osetra Tapas & Champagne Lounge, 7 Eikenhof Building, Church St, T021-886 5115, www.osetra-lounge.com. Tue-Sun 1600-2400. Fashionable spot with smart leather couches, wooden floors and stylish lighting, serving wine and champagne by the glass, inventive cocktails and tasty tapas platters to share.
$ Brazen Head, 62 Andringa St, T021-882 9672, www.brazenhead.co.za. Open 1100-late. Friendly, informal Irish-themed pub and restaurant with beer garden, Guinness and Kilkenny on tap, Irish whiskies, long varied menu including a 1-kg steak, seafood platter and traditional Irish stew.

🎭 Entertainment

Stellenbosch *p95, map p96*
Theatre

Endler & Fismer Hall, at the university, Victoria St, T021-808 2340, www.sun.ac.za/music. As part of the university music faculty, this shows classical, choral and chamber music productions at lunchtime and in the evening.

Oude Libertas Amphitheatre, on the wine estate of the same name, 4 km west of the centre off the R310, T021-808 7473, www.oudelibertas.co.za. Outdoor events from Nov-Mar in an attractive outdoor amphitheatre surrounded by lawns where patrons can have a picnic and bottle of wine beforehand. There's a farmers market here every Sat 0900-1400.

✳ Festivals

Stellenbosch *p95, map p96*
Aug Stellenbosch Wine Festival, www.wineroute.co.za, in the 1st week of Aug. An annual event to promote local award-winning wines along with traditional rural cuisine and wine and food pairing events in the restaurants, music and arts.

Franschhoek *p100, map p100*
Jul Franschhoek Bastille Festival, www.franschhoekbastille.co.za, usually the 2nd week of Jul. There's the opportunity to don a beret and join Franschhoek's residents to celebrate Bastille Day, with a food and wine marquee, barrel rolling and chefs and waiter races, a French film festival and a masked ball.

🛍 Shopping

Strand and Somerset West
p93, map p92

Somerset Mall, junction of N2 and R44, T021-852 7114, www.somersetmall.co.za. Mon-Sat 0900-1800, Sun 0900-1600. The largest shopping mall serving the Winelands

with all the usual facilities including restaurants, a bowling alley and cinema.

Stellenbosch *p95, map p96*
Stellenbosch's most famous shop and a tourist attraction in its own right is **Oom Samie se Winkel** (page 97).

Stellenbosch Antiques, 17 Andringa St, T021-883 3917, www.stellenboschantiques. co.za. Mon-Fri 0900-1700, Sat 0900-1300. A 30-year-old shop and a relative treasure trove of antiques and collectables, including oriental carpets, jewellery, silver and copper ware, ceramics and Victorian and art deco furniture.

Simonsberg Cheese Shop, Stoffel Smit St, Plankenbrug Industria, to the east of town across the railway line, T021-809 1017, www.simonsbergcheeselovers.com. Mon-Fri 0900-1700, 0900-1300. This popular brand of cheese is found in all South African supermarkets. You can sample and buy here and it also sells preserves to compliment the cheese.

Franschhoek *p100, map p100*
African Art Gallery, 42 Huguenot Rd, T021-876 2165, www.africanartgallery. co.za. Open 0900-1730. Series of rooms on 2 storeys selling local arts and crafts, including antique furniture, Massai jewellery, woven baskets, fabrics and batiks.

Huguenot Chocolates, 62 Huguenot St (next to the tourist office), T021-876 4096, www.huguenotchocolates.com. Mon-Fri 0800-1730, Sat-Sun 0930-1700. A chocolaterie making fine Belgian chocolates, sold in elegant boxes tied up with ribbon. You can watch them being made and the aromas are irresistible.

The Treasure House, 3 Bordeaux St, T021-876 2167, www.treasurehouse.co.za. Tue-Sun 1000-1700. With over 10,000 rare, antiquated, out-of-print and contemporary books, as well as paintings and vinyl records, this is worth a browse and they can organize international shipping.

⚙ What to do

Stellenbosch p95, map p96
Bicycle hire
Cycling between the wine estates is a pleasurable way of exploring the Winelands. Expect to pay about R150 per day for bike and helmet hire.

Adventure Shop, 36 Market St, next to the tourist office, T021-882 8112, www. adventureshop.co.za. They'll drop off bikes at hotels or you can arrange to pick them up at the office.

Fandango, see Bars and clubs, page 113. This bar also rents out bicycles.

Horse riding
Equine Sport Centre, 4 km north of Stellenbosch on the R44, T082-463 3139, www.equinesportcentre.co.za. Horse trails go through the wine farms on the R44 between Stellenbosch and Klapmuts including Delvera, Warwick, Remhoogte, Morgenhof and Knorhoek. Short rides start from R150, with wine tasting from R250-595 depending on how many estates are visited and if a picnic is supplied. Beginners welcome, children over 8.

Wine tours
As well as below, many Cape Town tour operators organize day trips to the Winelands, see page 68.

Vine Hopper, T021-882 8112, www. vinehopper.co.za, or book through the Adventure Shop (above). A useful hop-on, hop-off bus that tours between some estates and the tourist office in town, costing R200 per person for a 1-day ticket and R360 for a 2-day ticket, pickups 0900-1630. There are 2 routes – 1 to the north and 1 to the south – of town and 6 estates on each are visited. Allow an additional R20-30 or so for wine tasting at each estate.

Franschhoek Valley p100, map p100
Bicycle hire
Franschhoek Cycles, Mont View Building, Fabriek St, T021-876 4956, www. franschhoekcycles.co.za. Mon-Fri 0830-1730, Sat 0830-1300. A range of bikes for hire for self tours of the village and wine farms including mountain bikes, hybrids, a tandem, children's bikes and bikes with baby seats. Rates start from R150 for 1-4 hrs to R540 for 3 days, can also arrange guided tours.

Horse riding
Paradise Stables, outside the village on the Robertsvlei Rd, T021-876 2160, www.paradisestables.co.za. Guided trails through the vineyards with stops at 2 estates for wine tasting for R650 (including tastings) or hourly rides for R200. Beginners welcome, children over 12.

Paarl Winelands
p103, maps p92 and p104
Horse riding
Wine Valley Horse Trails, at Rhebokskloof Wine Estate (page 107), T021-869 8687, www.horsetrails-sa.co.za. Rides through the vineyards on the estate and into the Paarl Nature Reserve, from R350 for 1 hr to R750 for half a day with wine tasting. Quad-bikes and carriage rides for non-riders are also on offer. Beginners welcome, children over 8.

⊖ Transport

Bus
Local The Winelands is generally not well serviced by public transport. Apart from private taxis, the best and cheapest option to get from Cape Town International Airport to the Winelands towns is by shuttle transfer bus; see page 21 for more details of these services, and all accommodation in the Winelands can pre-book an airport transfer. Transfers for 1-2 people (the cost goes down with more) are in the region of R300 from the airport to **Somerset West** and **Strand** (32 km); R400 to **Stellenbosch** (40 km); R550

to **Franschhoek** (70 km); R450 to **Paarl** (60 km); and R500 to **Wellington** (70 km).
Long distance Long-distance bus passengers will have to make their own way to/from Somerset West from the other Winelands towns.

The **Baz Bus** stops in Somerset West at the BP service station next to the Lord Charles Hotel (page 107) on the corner of Main Rd and the R44. From Cape Town it arrives 0900-0915, and from Port Elizabeth 2015-2030. For more information see page 8.

Greyhound, **Intercape** and **Translux** all stop at the Total service station at Somerset Mall (page 114) on the N2 in Somerset West on the Cape Town–Durban route. Times are roughly 1 hr before or after Cape Town.

Bus companies
Baz Bus, www.bazbus.com. **Greyhound**, www.greyhound.co.za. **Intercape**, www.intercape.co.za. **Translux**, www.translux.co.za.

Train
Local **Metrorail** (see box, page 22) runs from central Cape Town to Somerset West and Strand, and to Wellington via Stellenbosch and Paarl, though these are not advised for visitors as petty theft can be a real concern.

❶ Directory

Strand and Somerset West
p93, map p92
Medical services Medi-Clinic, Main Rd, T021-850 9000, www.mediclinic.co.za.

Stellenbosch *p95, map p96*
Medical services Medi-Clinic, corner Saffraan and Rokewood avenues, off the R44 south of town, T021-861 2095, www.mediclinic.co.za.

Paarl *p103, map p104*
Medical services Medi-Clinic, Berlyn St, Paarl North, T021-807 8000, www.mediclinic.co.za.

Contents

Footprint features

Whale Coast & Garden Route

Whale Coast

The evocatively named Whale Coast lives up to its title from July to November, when large numbers of whales seek out the sheltered bays along the coast for breeding. Whales can be seen close to the shore from False Bay all the way east to Mossel Bay, but by far the best place for whale spotting is Hermanus as the whales favour the sheltered Walker Bay, and daily sightings are guaranteed in August and September.

The most beautiful and exhilarating stretch of this coast is between Gordon's Bay and Hermanus, where the mountains plunge into the ocean forming a coastline of steep cliffs, dangerous headlands and natural harbours. This route is often compared to the spectacular Chapman's Peak Drive on the Cape Peninsula, and rightly so. This is an area of much beauty and also botanical significance and, along with Table Mountain National Park, is part of the UNESCO-declared Cape Floral Kingdom. It's known for its fynbos and over 1700 plant species have been recorded here. Elsewhere along the coast there are opportunities to see the fearsome great white shark, and the seaside towns feature miles of sandy beaches and rock pools. The region makes both an interesting day trip from Cape Town and an ideal stopover to and from the Garden Route.

Arriving on the Whale Coast → *For listings, see pages 127-130.*

It's easiest to rent a car and self-drive from Cape Town south along the Whale Coast. It takes about 1½ hours to drive the 122 km inland route from Cape Town to Hermanus via the N2 and then the R43 from Bot River. But the more pleasurable alternative is along the R44 that leaves the N2 at Somerset West at the base of Sir Lowry's Pass and follows the headland at the eastern end of False Bay. It goes via the coastal villages in the lee of the Hottentots Holland Mountains and joins the R43 after Kleinmond. This route is just over 140 km from Cape Town to Hermanus and takes a leisurely 2½ hours.

None of the three major coach companies runs a coastal service via Hermanus, although the hop-on hop-off **Baz Bus** (www.bazbus.com, see page 8) runs along the N2 and stops at Bot River, which is 23 km from Hermanus.

If you don't have a car, the Baz Bus comes into its own when you head further east along the Garden Route (see page 131) as the N2 hugs the coast, collecting and dropping off passengers at their chosen hostel.

Whale Coast

Where to stay 🛏
Blue Gum
  Country Estate **1**
Buçaco Sud **6**
Great White House **7**

Grootbos Private
  Nature Reserve **8**
Moonstruck on
  Pringle Bay **9**

Restaurants 🍴
Hook, Line & Sinker **3**
Mariana's **4**
Mogg's Country
  Cookhouse **6**

Gordon's Bay, Rooiels and Pringle Bay

After leaving the N2 at Somerset West, the first town immediately on the R44 is Gordon's Bay, a popular family seaside resort with two sandy beaches, **Bikini** (which has been awarded Blue Flag status) and **Main**, both of which are safe for swimmers. The rocky shoreline, a short walk from the seafront, is popular for fishing. The most likely catch includes mackerel, steenbras and kabeljou. The beach road is lined with a number of seafood restaurants and this is a popular lunch spot at the weekends for people from Cape Town.

Following the R44 south, the next coastal resort after Gordon's Bay is **Rooiels** (19 km), a cluster of holiday homes at the mouth of a small river. The beach has a strong backwash, so be wary if children are swimming. There's a large troop of chacma baboons in this region that move between Rooiels and Betty's Bay and they can sometimes be seen on the beach. Continuing towards Hermanus, the road leaves its precipitous course and climbs the hills inland. After 5 km turn right to **Pringle Bay**, which is dominated by a large rock outcrop known as the Hangklip, 454 m. This is the rock you see when standing by the lighthouse at Cape Point looking across False Bay. Hangklip was formerly known as 'Cabo Falso' ('false cape'), because of its resemblance to Cape Point. It prompted sailors from the east to turn north earlier than they should have done into what is now known as False Bay. The gravel loop road around **Cape Hangklip** is a scenic distraction; another track leads to Hangklip. The road rejoins the R44 just before Silver Sands.

Betty's Bay

This small holiday village, midway between Somerset West and Hermanus, is known for its penguin colony and botanical garden. The community was named after Betty Youlden, the daughter of a local businessman who had plans to develop the Cape Hangklip area in the 1930s. Fortunately little came of the idea and today the village remains an untidy collection of holiday homes in a beautiful location. At Stony Point there is a **reserve** ⓘ *0900-1700, R10 per person*, to protect a small breeding colony of African penguins, one of the few places where you are guaranteed to see these birds breeding on the mainland. A boardwalk allows visitors good views of the penguins without disturbing them. Also here are the remains of a whaling station plus the hulk of a whaler, the *Balena*. Behind the village are the well-known **Harold Porter Botanic Gardens**, worth a visit if time permits. Along the main beach is another area of protected land, the **HF Verwoerd Coastal Reserve**. There is safe swimming close to the kelp beds, and the dunes above Silver Sands are a popular spot for sandboarding.

Harold Porter Botanic Gardens

ⓘ *Off the R44, T028-272 9311, www.sanbi.org, Mon-Fri 0800-1630, Sat-Sun 0800-1700, R20, children (6-16) R12, under 5s free, Leopard's Kloof Restaurant and gift shop, 0900-1630.*

This garden, lying between mountains and coast, was originally acquired in 1938 by Harold Porter, a keen conservationist. In his will he bequeathed the grounds to the nation. There are 10 ha of cultivated fynbos garden and a further 191 ha of natural fynbos which has been allowed to flourish undisturbed. [Fynbos is the term given to a type of vegetation that is dominated by shrubs and comprises species unique to South Africa's southwestern and southern Cape.] The reserve incorporates the whole catchment area of the Dawidskraal River. The garden has many fynbos species, including proteas, ericas, legumes, buchus and brunias. Another draw is the chance of seeing red disa flowering in its natural habitat – this usually occurs from late December to late January. More than 88 species of bird have been identified; of special interest are the orange-breasted sunbird and the rare protea canary, which is only seen in fynbos environments.

Kleinmond, Vermont and Onrus

Kleinmond is a popular summer resort in Sandown Bay that has been frequented by the wheat farmers of the interior since 1861 and is today a sizeable resort. Exercise caution when swimming at Kleinmond as the sandy beach is steep; children should be watched at all times. The name Kleinmond refers to the 'small mouth' of the Bot River lagoon. The settlement is overlooked by the magnificent Kogelberg Mountains which in the spring are full of flowering proteas. Information is available from the helpful **Hangklip-Kleinmond Tourism Bureau** ① *signposted, 14 Harbour Rd, just off the R44, T028-271 5657, www.ecoscape.org.za, Mon-Fri 0830-1700, Sat 0900-1400, Sun 1000-1400.* To the east of the town is the Bot River Lagoon, a popular sailing and canoeing area. Where the Bot River meets the sea is a large marsh which is home to thousands of waterfowl, especially at low tide. The more common species are spoonbills, herons, pelicans, gulls, terns, kingfishers and geese and a pair of fish eagles breed at the lagoon. There is also a small herd of wild horses that roam the marshlands; after several attempts to cull them in the 1950s, they are now protected.

After Kleinmond the R44 joins the R43, which then continues along the coast to the next sizeable settlements of Vermont and Onrus, these days more or less suburbs of Hermanus, before arriving in Hermanus proper. **Vermont**, named after the American state, was founded by CJ Krige who became the first speaker of the South African parliament. The beach here is sheltered by high dunes and is safe for children. **Onrus**, meaning 'restless', lying on the east bank of the mouth of the Onrus River, was named by the first European settlers because of the perpetual noise made by the waves along the rocky coastline. The Onrus River forms a small lagoon with a short sandy beach which is also safe for children to swim from. The beach is popular with surfers too.

Hermanus and around → *For listings, see pages 127-130.*

Hermanus has grown from a rustic fishing village to a much-visited tourist resort famed for its superb whale watching. It is the self-proclaimed world's best land-based whale-watching site, and indeed Walker Bay is host to impressive numbers of whales during the calving season (July to November). However, don't expect any private viewings – Hermanus is very popular and has a steady flow of binocular-clutching visitors. While this means it can get very busy, there is also a good range of accommodation and restaurants, and while you may find it far too crowded at Christmas or during the whale season, at other times it reverts to its small-town calm.

Hermanus Tourism ① *Old Station Building, Mitchell St, T028-312 2629, www. hermanus.co.za, Mon-Fri 0800-1800, Sat 0900-1700, Sun 0900-1500 (shorter hours in winter),* is extremely helpful and has lots of information on the surrounding area, plus an accommodation booking service.

Background

The town is named after Hermanus Pieters, an old soldier who set up camp in the bay while looking for better pastures for his animals during the hot summer months. The presence of a freshwater spring persuaded him to spend the summer here. Soon other farmers arrived with their families from the interior. Almost by accident it became a holiday destination – the herds required little attention, so the men turned their attention to fishing while the women and children enjoyed themselves on the sandy beaches. When the farmers returned inland to the winter pastures, it was the fishermen who remained and settled here.

In the 1920s the town gained a reputation as an excellent location for convalescing, and even doctors from Harley Street in London were recommending the 'champagne air' of Hermanus. As it became popular with the gentry, so suitably smart hotels were built to accommodate them. After the Second World War the construction of a new harbour stimulated the expansion of the fishing industry and there are now three canning factories in Walker Bay.

Places in Hermanus

The **Old Harbour** is a national monument and a focal point for tourist activities. A ramp leads down the cliff to the attractive old jetty and a group of restored fishermen's cottages, including the **Old Harbour Museum** ⓘ *T028-312 1475, www.old-harbour-museum.co.za, Mon-Sat 0900-1300, 1400-1700, R15, children (under 12) R10.* The displays are based on thelocal fishing industry and include models of fish, a whale skeleton, some shark jaws, fish tanks and early fishing equipment. One of the most interesting features is the recordings of calls between whales. There are also telescopes to watch the whales further out. An information plaque helps identify what you see. Outside the

Hermanus

Where to stay 🛏
Auberge Burgundy 1
Hermanus Backpackers 13
Marine 7
Misty Waves 11
Mitchell St Village 12
Quarters 2
Windsor 10
Zoete Inval 3

Restaurants 🍴
Annie se Kombuis 6

Bientang's Cave 1
Burgundy 2
Fisherman's Cottage 4
Mogg's Country
  Cookhouse 7
Pavilion 3

Whale watching

The WWF acknowledges Hermanus as one of the 12 best places in the world to view whales. It is the ideal destination if you wish to see whales from land without bobbing around in a boat. The town promotes itself as the 'heart of the Whale Coast', and during the season most visitors should not be disappointed. The town's advantage is that whales can come very close to the shore. The combination of low cliffs and deep water at the base of the cliffs means that you are able to look down from above into clear water and see the outlines of whales from as close as 10 m.

To add to the excitement there is a whale crier who between 1000 and 1600 during September and October strolls around the town centre blowing a kelp horn to announce the arrival of each whale in Walker Bay. The whale crier is easily identified: he wears a giant Bavarian-style hat and carries a sandwich board which records the daily sightings of whales from different vantage points around Walker Bay.

The first southern right whales start to appear in Walker Bay from June onwards. By the end of December most have returned to the southern oceans. The whales migrate north to escape heavy winter storms in the oceans around Antarctica. In August and September most of the calves are born in the calm sheltered bays, where the cows then stay with their young for a further two months. They can travel up to 2000 km to and from Antarctica on this continuous annual cycle. Out of an estimated world population of only 7000 southern right whales, up to 80 have been recorded mating and calving in Walker Bay. The best months are September and October when daily sightings are almost guaranteed. You would be unlucky not to see some sign of whale action during this period, though of course they are just as likely to be in the middle of the bay as up close to one of the vantage points along the cliff path.

The southern right whale is distinguished from other whales by its V-shaped 'blow', produced by a pair of blowholes, and callosities which appear randomly on and around the oval head. The callosities are growths of tough skin in patterns which help to identify individuals. Southern right whales are basically black with occasional streaks of grey or white on the back. Their flippers are short, broad and almost square. They are thought to live for up to 100 years, and a fully grown adult can weigh as much as 80 metric tonnes.

They are so-named because they were regarded as the 'right' whale to catch. The carcass yielded large quantities of oil and baleen, and the task of collecting the booty was made all the more easy by the fact that the whale floated in the water when killed. The northern right whale is virtually extinct, and the southern right has shown only a slight increase in numbers since international legislation was introduced to protect the species. The South African coastline is the most likely place in the world to see them in coastal waters.

museum on the harbour ramp is a collection of small restored fishing boats, the earliest dating from 1855. Also on show are the drying racks for small fish and cement tables which were once used for gutting fish.

The **De Wet's Huis Photo Museum** ① *Market Sq, T028-313 0418, Mon-Fri 0900-1300, 1400-1700, Sat 0800-1300, 1400-1600, entry fee to the Old Harbour Museum covers this, and you can also pay the fee here*, houses an interesting collection of photography depicting the historical development of Hermanus. The building is interesting in itself as it was a Sunday school next to the Dutch Reformed Church, and it was carefully dismantled stone by stone and re-erected in Market Square.

Outside the old harbour is a memorial to those who died in the First World War. Set in the stonework is a barometer and the words "to help to protect the lives of present and future fishermen". Either side of the beehive-shaped monument are two ship's cannons. The new harbour, to the west of the old harbour in Westcliff, is still a busy fishing port. It's a great idea to head down to the dockside to buy fresh crayfish, mussels or line-caught fish from the fish shop. The staff will be happy to advise you on how best to cook your selection.

Walks around Hermanus

The excellent **Cliff Path** starts at the new harbour in Westcliff in the west and follows the shore all the way round Walker Bay to the mouth of the Klein River in the east, a distance of just over 10 km. Between cliffs the path goes through stands of milkwood trees and takes you around the sandy beaches. The most popular viewpoints are Dreunkrans, Fick's Pool, Gearing's Point, the Old Harbour, Die Gang, Siever's Punt, Kwaaiwater and Platbank. On an ideal day allow at least a morning for the walk. Bench seats are provided at the prime viewpoints, which make them good spots for a picnic.

Beaches

There are some good beaches a short distance in either direction from the town centre. The best beaches to the west are found at Onrus and Vermont (see page 121). Heading east towards Stanford and Gansbaai, there are long, open beaches or secluded coves with patches of sand and rock pools. **Grotto Beach** is the largest, best developed and most popular for swimming and is one of South Africa's many Blue Flag beaches. The fine white sands stretch beyond the Klein River Lagoon, and there are changing facilities, a restaurant and a beach shop. Slightly closer to the town centre is **Voëlklip Beach**, a little run down, but with well-kept lawns behind the sand. Conditions are good for swimming and surfing. The most popular spot for surfers is **Kammabaai** next door to Voëlklip beach. There are braai facilities under the shade of some milkwood trees.

Fernkloof Nature Reserve

ⓘ *T028-313 8100, www.fernkloof.com, 24 hrs, free. The visitor centre, 500 m from the entrance, has a display of the most common plants you are likely to see when walking in the reserve. All the hiking trails start from here.*

Set in the hills behind Hermanus, the reserve has a 60-km network of trails through an area rich in protea and coastal fynbos. Access is from the east end of Hermanus – just before the Main Road crosses Mossel River, turn up Fir Street. The reserve gates are just beyond the botanical society buildings. The diversity of plants in the reserve is due to the long period it has been under protection, plus its range of elevation from 60 to 850 m. With such a varied plant population, there is also a wide range of bird and animal species including mongoose, dassie and baboon. Higher up in the mountains, look out for breeding black eagles. Small patches of indigenous forest remain in some of the moist ravines.

Hermanus wine route

Hidden away in the **Hemel-en-Aarde Valley** behind Hermanus are a few vineyards producing some surprisingly good wines, mostly Burgundy varieties based around Pinot Noir and Chardonnay grapes. Rarely crowded, there are several vineyards open to the public and have tastings in their cellars. Most are along the R320, and their details and a map can be found at www.hermanuswineroute.com. **Hamilton Russell Vineyards** ① *T028-312 3595, www.hamiltonrussellvineyards.com, sales and tastings: Mon-Fri 0900-1700, Sat 0900-1300,* is the oldest and one of the more picturesque estates along the route and dubs itself both the most southerly wine estate in Africa and the closest to the sea. The cellar and tasting room are set beside a small trout lake. To get there follow the R43 out of Hermanus towards Cape Town, after 2 km turn towards Caledon, R320, then turn right 5 km along this gravel road. For those short of time, **Wine Village** ① *at the entrance to the Hemel-en-Aarde Valley, the corner of the R43 and the R320, T028-316 3988, www.wine-village.co.za, Mon-Fri 0900-1800, Sat 0900-1700, Sun 1000-1500,* offers tastings and sells wine from over 600 Cape estates and is very informative about cultivators and blends. It can also organize international shipping.

Hermanus to Gansbaai → *For listings, see pages 127-130.*

Stanford

The next town along the R43 17 km east of Hermanus, Stanford is a peaceful Victorian village set inland from the Atlantic, which has become a popular centre for artists and craftsmen. It is an attractive spot, with some well-restored Victorian thatched cottages and a beautiful setting on the Klein River. **Stanford Tourism** ① *13 Queen Victoria St, T028-341 0340, www.stanfordinfo.co.za, Mon-Fri 0830-1630, Sat 0900-1600, Sun 1000-1300,* is in the courtyard of the old Stanford Hotel. Some of the more notable buildings include **Bachelor's Hope** at 19 Morton Street, which was built in 1902. In the 1930s it was dubbed Bachelor's Hope because it was home to the village's lady teachers and many a local bachelor found his wife there. The **Anglican Church** on the corner of Longmarket and Morton streets dates from 1872. The **Dutch Reformed Church** on the corner of Queen Victoria and Church streets was built in 1926 but was replaced in the 1960s by the present hall. However, the original church tower, clock and organ remain and have been restored.

Just out of the village off the R326 towards Caledon, the **Birkenhead Brewery** ① *T028-341 0013, www.walkerbayestate.com, Wed-Sun 1100-1700, tours at 1100 and 1500, R20,* is worth a stop and six beers are brewed and sold. The tastiest is Birkenhead Premium Lager, a slow-brewed beer using rich malted two-rowed barley and aromatic Hallertau and Saaz hop cones. Many of the ingredients are grown on the site and you can take a tour of the hop garden before a tasting and perhaps a meal in the pub.

Klein River Cheese ① *T028-341 0693, www.kleinrivercheese.co.za, Mon-Fri 0900-1700, Sat 0900-1300, picnics mid-Sep to mid-May, 1100-1500,* is another popular place to stop. The factory specializes in making Gruyère and other cheeses using Jersey and Friesland milk. Visitors can watch cheese being made, taste the produce in the shop, or enjoy a delicious picnic lunch on the banks of the Klein River. To get here from the R43, take the left turn onto the R326 opposite the turning to Stanford and follow the signposts.

Shark-cage diving

Offshore from Gansbaai, Dyer Island is named after Samson Dyer, a black American who lived on the island collecting guano around 1806. The Portuguese first named it Isla de Fera ('Island of Wild Animals') and the name is still applicable. Today the island is an important breeding spot for African penguins and many other sea birds. On nearby Geyser Island there is a breeding Cape Fur seal population thought to number 50,000. Both are protected by Cape Nature and you are not allowed on to the islands. The area between the two islands is known as Shark Alley, as great white sharks are attracted to the breeding seals. One of the most popular activi-ties here is cage diving to see the sharks, and viewing a great white at such close quarters is certainly an amazing experience. Several companies offer trips, and people with a diving certificate can see them from an underwater cage. However, non-divers can still do it; they can also enter the cage at the top with snorkelling equipment, or alternatively dive by first spending a day doing a course. Most boats depart from the harbour in Gansbaai and trips last 3-7 hours, and long shark-diving day trips can be organised from Cape Town. Expect to pay in the region of R1350 including a light breakfast and lunch, plus around R300-400 for transfers to and from Cape Town, and R350 for a DVD. Children under 12 are not permitted in the cage. Shark Diving Unlimited, T082-441 4555, www.sharkdivingunlimited.com. Shark Lady, T028-313 2306, www.sharklady.co.za. White Shark Adventures, T028-384 1380, www.whitesharkadventures.com. White Shark Diving Co, T082-559 6858, www.sharkcagediving.co.za.

Gansbaai

The R43 reaches Gansbaai 22 km south of Stanford. This popular fishing bay dates back over a century and was named by fishermen who used it for protection against large storms. The original name gansgat ('goose hole') refers to the colony of Egyptian geese, which used to nest in the reeds that surrounded a natural spring in the bay. These days the village is a prosperous fishing harbour with a modern deep-water wharf and several fish-canning factories. It has, however, managed to retain the character of a small community and busy fishing harbour, albeit with strong ties to the tourist industry. It is the principal base for shark-cage diving and a number of Capetonians have second houses along this coast. Like Hermanus, there are some excellent vantage points along the cliffs and beaches for whale watching. **Gansbaai Tourism** ① *Gateway Centre, Kapokblom St, T028-384 1439, www.gansbaaiinfo.com, Mon-Fri 0900-1730, Sat 0900-1600, Sun 1000-1600*, has information on the shark-cage diving operators and maps of the coastline showing the area's walking routes.

To the southwest of Gansbaai, a gravel road runs 8 km along the rugged coast to the most southerly point of Walker Bay marked by the 18-m tall **Danger Point Lighthouse** ① *Mon-Fri 1000-1500, R14, children (under 12) R7*, is an octagonal white masonry tower and the lighthouse keeper will give visitors a tour . In May 1852 the *HMS Birkenhead* sank offshore here with a loss of 445 lives, though every woman and child on the ship escaped unharmed in the lifeboats and this is where the phrase 'women and children first' was thought to be originated. It took the sinking of a further 20 ships before the lighthouse came into operation in 1895.

Whale Coast listings

For hotel and restaurant price codes and other relevant information, see pages 10-13.

🛏 Where to stay

Gordon's Bay *p120*
$$ Celtic Manor, 22 Suikerbossie Drive, T021-856 1907, www.celticmanor.co.za. High up on the hill above Gordon'sBay with sweeping views of False Bay, boutique guesthouse with 6 rooms and 1 self-catering apartment sleeping 4, guests share dinner around a large dining table, comfortable lounge and bar, pool and spa treatment room.

Pringle Bay *p120*
$$ Moonstruck on Pringle Bay, 264 Hangklip Rd, T028-273 8162, www.moonstruck.co.za. Intimate guesthouse with large windows overlooking the ocean and mountains, 4 spacious rooms, stylish decor, balconies and fireplaces, pool with wooden deck, 100 m from the beach reached by a private path through the fynbos.

Betty's Bay *p120*
$$ Buçaço Sud, Clarence Drive, T028-272 9750, www.bucacosud.co.za. Spanish-style villa with 6 tastefully decorated rooms, terracotta tiles, fireplaces in public areas, all rooms have either mountain or coastal views, breakfast served in attractive courtyard with pool.

Hermanus *p121, map p122*
There are dozens of accommodation options in Hermanus; these are just a few. For a full listing, **Hermanus Tourism** runs an accommodation booking service; www.hermanusaccommodation.co.za. Be sure to book well ahead during whale season and school holidays, when room rates are also at their highest.
$$$$ The Marine, Marine Drive, T028-313 1000, www.collectionmcgrath.com/marine. A historic hotel and one of the finest in the country with 42 luxurious rooms, some with stunning ocean views, all with exceptionally fine furnishings – silk curtains, plush carpets, 4-poster beds and marble bathrooms. Also has a spa, heated pool, shop, restaurants and bars.
$$$ Quarters, 5 Harbour Rd, T028-313 7700, www.quarters.co.za. Contemporary boutique hotel overlooking the old harbour and ocean, 18 smart rooms with a/c, Wi-Fi and DSTV, most with balconies and some with kitchenettes, rooftop wooden deck and pool, spa treatments in rooms, breakfast and an easy stroll to restaurants.
$$$-$$ Auberge Burgundy, 16 Harbour Rd, T028-313 1201, www.auberge.co.za. Provençal-style villa in the heart of Hermanus. 17 rooms with private terraces or balconies, some with fine views across Walker Bay, the penthouse can sleep 6, all set around a sumptuous inner courtyard with a pool.
$$$-$$ Misty Waves, 21 Marine Drive, T028-313 8460, www.hermanusmistybeach.co.za. Spacious modern 4-star hotel on 2 levels with ample decks and roof terraces, suites have ocean views and spa baths, pool, restaurant, the annex next door offers elegant B&B accommodation with 4-poster beds and chandeliers.
$$ Mitchell St Village, 56-60 Mitchell St, T028-312 4560, www.56mitchellstreet.co.za. A block back from the sea with 11 individually decorated rooms, some have private courtyards or balconies and fireplaces, 2 swimming pools, attractive lounge with honesty bar, spa treatment facilities, short walk to restaurants.
$$ Windsor Hotel, 49 Marine Drive, T028-312 3727, www.windsorhotel.co.za. Large and popular, this is Hermanus's oldest hotel built in 1896, set on cliffs overlooking the ocean, with 70 rooms with TV, pay more for the ones with sea views. Excellent views across Walker Bay from the glazed lounge, though a slightly plain restaurant. Frequently used by tour groups.

$ Hermanus Backpackers, 26 Flower St, T028-312 4293, www.hermanusbackpackers. co.za. Well positioned behind Main Rd, dorms, doubles/twins with or without bathrooms, vibey atmosphere, bar with pool table, TV lounge with DVD library, nightly braai, pickup from Baz Bus for a small fee, will book all activities and give out maps of the area.

$ Zoete Inval, 23 Main Rd, T028-312 1242, www.zoeteinval.co.za. Friendly budget choice with 9 B&B double and family rooms, and dorms in a converted loft, self-catering facilities, pleasant TV lounge, sunny deck with jacuzzi. Will meet the Baz Bus at Bot River Hotel for a small fee.

Hermanus to Gansbaai *p125*

$$$$ Grootbos Private Nature Reserve, off the R43, 13 km south of Stanford, T028-384 8000, www.grootbos.com. There are 2 luxury lodges on this 1750 ha private reserve: **Forest Lodge** has 16 free-standing steel and glass suites set in a milkwood forest with stunning views over Walker Bay, the **Garden Lodge** has 11 stone and thatch rooms set on a hillside surrounded by fynbos. Facilities include restaurants, bars, pool and spa, guided beach and flower walks and horse riding.

$$$-$$ Blue Gum Country Estate, 7 km from Stanford on the R326, T028-341 0116, www.bluegum.co.za. Set on a working farm which the Klein River runs through, the 12 rooms are in the manor house or garden cottages with colonial decor, wooden floors, DSTV, 4-poster beds and private verandas, restaurant, lots of walks around the farm and a pool.

$$-$ The Great White House, 5 Geelbek St, Gansbaai, T028-384 3273, www.thegreat whitehouse.co.za. Across the road from the harbour, thatched house with 3 cottage-style rooms that sleep 2-4, fireplaces and wooden floors, good restaurant and pub (see Restaurants, page 129) used by the shark dive companies to do their briefings, and there's a tidal pool opposite for those brave enough to swim in the Atlantic.

🍴 Restaurants

Gordon's Bay *p120*

$$$-$$ Harbour Lights, Old Harbour, Beach Rd, T021-856 1830. Open 1200-1500, 1800-2200. Popular place, especially with families in the holidays, with great views of the yacht basin at night, serving linefish and seafood platters, plus there's a sushi bar, a good wine list and a collection of rare whiskies.

$$-$ Bertie's Moorings, Harbour Island, T021-856 3343, www.berties.co.za. Sun-Thu 1000-2200, Fri-Sat 1000-2400. Lively pub serving light meals and good seafood on the waterfront, also a venue for local live bands at the weekends, the furniture and the bar are made from wine barrels.

Pringle Bay *p120*

$$ Hook, Line & Sinker, 382 Crescent Rd, T028-273 8688, www.hooklineandsinker. co.za. Tue-Sun, lunch 1200, dinner 1900. Lunch is beer-battered hake and chips wrapped in newspaper, while dinner is a chalkboard menu of seafood cooked by charismatic owner and chef Stephan in the open-plan kitchen. On Wed and Sun nights he also cooks steak. Only seats 26 people and very popular with Cape Town people so reservations are essential.

Hermanus *p121, map p122*

$$$ The Burgundy, Market Sq, Marine Drive, T028-312 2800, www.burgundy restaurant.co.za. Open 0830-1700, 1900-2200. Restored rural cottage set back from the old harbour. One of the top restaurants in town but relaxed, with tables spilling onto a shady terrace outside. Excellent seafood including superb grilled crayfish and good poultry too like chicken stuffed with dates or duck with orange sauce.

$$$ The Pavilion at the Marine (see page 127). Tue-Sat 1900-2130. Superb award-winning establishment with a glamorous monochrome interior and sweeping views over Walker Bay. The menu offers gourmet seafood including crayfish and scallops, as well as quail, duck, venison and prime beef. The wine list is excellent and includes plenty of fish-friendly whites.

$$ Annie se Kombuis, Warrington Arcade, 8 Harbour Rd, T028-313 1350, www. anniesekombuis.co.za. Lunch Tue-Sun 1100-1430, dinner Mon-Sat 1800-2130. A great place to try traditional South African dishes like *smoorsnoek* pâté with crusty farm bread, *waterblommetjie*, babotie, oxtail, chicken pie, ostrich, venison and seafood, served up in a homely atmosphere with farm-style furnishings.

$$ Bientang's Cave, access is via steps from the car park on Marine Drive, between Market Sq and The Marine, T028-312 3454, www.bientangscave.com. Open 0900-1600, whale season (Jul-Nov) 1900-2130. The name doesn't lie, it's an actual cave with an extended deck overlooking the waves. Superb spot for whale watching during season. Excellent seafood buffets and famous bouillabaisse soup, simple wood benches and long tables. Very popular, book ahead.

$$ Fisherman's Cottage, corner Harbour and Main roads, T028-312 3642. Mon-Sat 1000-2100. Tiny place set in a charming old thatched cottage with thick whitewashed walls and run by a Belgium chef. Try the seafood bouillabassie or steak tartare with capers and save room for the very good crème brûlée and brandy tart.

$$-$ Mogg's Country Cookhouse, Hemel-en-Aarde Valley, 11 km from Hermanus off the R320 towards Caledon, T076-314 0671, www.moggscookhouse.com. Wed-Sun 1230-1400. Lovely rustic setting in an old farm labourer's cottage and great spot for lunch if you're visiting the vineyards. Every dish is home made using herbs and veggies from the garden and likely choices include barley and oxtail soup, kudu pie with pumpkin fritters, or parmesan, artichoke and spinach tart.

Stanford *p125*
$ Mariana's, 12 Du Toit St, T028-341 0272. Thu-Sun 0900-1600. Deli stocked with local products, cheeses, stuffed olives and chutneys. Also serves bistro-style meals on the vine-shaded stoep. The cheese soufflé or mussels are particularly good. Much of the produce is grown in the vegetable and herb garden.

Gansbaai *p126*
$ The Great White House (see Where to stay, page 128). Open 0800-2000. Serves filling breakfasts, light lunches and snacks, in a historic cottage with a skeleton of a southern right whale hanging from the ceiling or on the veranda overlooking the harbour. This is where sea-shaken cage-shark divers warm up in front of the fireplace after their excursion.

❸ Festivals

Hermanus *p121, map p122*
August Hermanus Food and Wine Festival, www.hermanuswineandfood.co.za. Wine tasting from over 70 vineyards, plus cheese, olives and sushi in the gourmet food tent, and a coffee and brandy tasting lounge.
September Hermanus Whale Festival, T028-313 0928, www.whalefestival.co.za. Primarily an arts festival which attracts theatre and singing acts along with children's events and a craft market, and also the best time of the year to spot whales in Walker Bay.

❍ Shopping

Hermanus *p121, map p122*
As befits a popular tourist town there are plenty of curio shops and speciality boutiques. Market Square has a small, daily craft, curio and clothes market.
Village Square, T028-312 2761, www. village-square.co.za. Mon-Sat 0900-1700, Sun 1000-1500. Right in the heart of things and adjacent to Market Square and Marine Drive, 60 shops, plus restaurants, most of which have outdoor seating with views of Walker Bay.

❶ What to do

Hermanus *p121, map p122*

Boat trips

Hermanus Whale Cruises, office at the New Harbour, T028-313 2722, www.hermanus-whale-cruises.co.za. 2-hr whale-watching cruises in season (Jun-Dec), at 0900, 1200, 1400 and 1600, R650, children (6-13) R250, under 5s free, including snacks and soft drinks. For a small extra fee will pick up from hotels. As a permit holder, they are allowed to get the boat within 50 m of the whales.

Southern Right Charters, office at the New Harbour, T082-353 0550, www.southern rightcharters.co.za. Again boat-based 2-hr whale watching Jun-Dec, 0900, 1200 and 1500, and also permitted to get within 50 m of the whales.

Walker Bay Adventures, office at the Old Harbour, T082-739 0159, www.walker bayadventures.co.za. 2-hr sea-kayaking trips from the old harbour for R350, but it is prohibited to get closer than 300 m to whales. Also organizes canoe trips on the Klein River Lagoon; the 5-hr trip, R450 including lunch, is good for birdwatching and there are more than 130 species around the lagoon, while the 3-hr 'wine tour', R500, stops at **Mosaic Private Sanctuary** for snacks and wine tasting.

Diving

Scuba Africa, New Harbour, T028-316 2362, www.scubaafrica.com. Equipment hire, dive courses (NAUI) and daily organized dives

from R450. In addition to coral reef and kelp forest dives, there are 3 stimulating wreck dives between Hermanus and Arniston.

Golf

Hermanus Golf Club, Main Rd, Eastcliff, T028-312 1954, www.hgc.co.za. A beautiful 18-hole par-73 course in the lee of the mountains with heather-lined fairways, some holes have sea views, visitors welcome, green fees from R47.

Swimming

Below the Marine Hotel (see page 127) is the **Marine Tidal Pool**, which always has plenty of sealife and fish. Along Westcliff Rd is a smaller pool known as **Fick's Pool**, which is a sheltered spot and has the bonus of a sandy bottom.

Gansbaai *p126*

For details of shark-cage diving see box, page 126.

Dyer Island Cruises, T082-801 8014, www.whalewatchsa.com. 2½-hr boat trips to Dyer and Geyser Islands to see penguins and seals. All cruises depart from Kleinbaai harbour near Gansbaai and, during the season, whales and sharks may be spotted too, R900, children (6-12) R600, under 5s free.

❶ Directory

Hermanus Medi-Clinic, Hospital St, T028-313 0168, www.mediclinic.co.za.

Garden Route

The Garden Route is probably South Africa's most celebrated area, a stretch of coast heralded as one of the country's highlights. The publicity it receives has made it hugely popular and few visitors to Cape Town miss it. The area is undeniably beautiful: a 200-km stretch of rugged coast separated from the interior by the Tsitsikamma and Outeniqua mountains, with long stretches of sand, nature reserves, leafy forests and tourist-friendly seaside towns. Officially the route runs from Heidelberg in the west to the Tsitsikamma Forest in the east, though most visitors drive from Cape Town along the N2 highway over the Hottentots Holland Mountains and through the Overberg to Mossel Bay and beyond. In contrast to the dry and treeless area of the Karoo on the interior side of the mountains, the ocean-facing slopes along the Garden Route are covered with luxuriant greenery, and it is this dramatic change in landscape, which occurs over a distance of no more than 20 km, that prompted the name.

The larger towns, such as Plettenberg Bay and Knysna, are highly developed tourist resorts, while other areas offer untouched wilderness and wonderful hikes, including one of the most famous in the country, the Otter Trail. If hiking isn't your scene, the beaches are stunning, offering a mix of peaceful seaside villages and livelier surfer spots, and there are various attractions hugging the N2 to distract the motorist. Finally, the Garden Route is coming into its own as an adventure destination and there are numerous activities on offer from bungee jumping to mountain biking.

Touring the Garden Route

There are a number of organized tours for exploring the Garden Route which start and finish in Cape Town. For those on a budget and short of time, the **Bok Bus**, T082-3201979, www.bokbus.com, offers comprehensive three- to seven-day budget tours of all the major attractions along the Garden Route. Accommodation is in hostels or you can upgrade to a guesthouse. Prices start at R3850 for the standard five-day tour and includes breakfasts, most dinners and entrance fees. There are numerous other coach and minibus operators running short scheduled tours from Cape Town along the Garden Route that appeal to a wide range of age groups and offer a variety of accommodation alternatives depending on budget. These include: **African Eagle**, T021-464 4266, www.daytours.co.za. **Cape Rainbow**, T021-551 5465, www.caperainbow.com. **Hylton Ross**, T021-506 2575, www.hyltonross.co.za. **Springbok Atlas**, T021-460 4700, www.springbokatlas.co.za.

Arriving on the Garden Route

Getting there

The Garden Route is served by George Airport (page 139) at the western end and Port Elizabeth Airport at the eastern end. Flights link both these with Cape Town and Johannesburg. The options here are to fly into one, hire a car to explore the Garden Route and return the car to the other. Alternatively, drive there from Cape Town and drop off a car in Port Elizabeth and fly back or onwards from there.

By road, the most direct route from Cape Town to the Garden Route is along the N2; it's an easy 385-km drive to Mossel Bay via the Overberg and you can break your journey for lunch in the attractive town of Swellendam. Alternatively, if you have the extra time there is the option of travelling from (or back to) Cape Town either via the Whale Coast (page 118) or along Breede River Valley/Route 62.

Getting around

To get the most out of the Garden Route you really need a car, and whilst it's quite easy to drive the full length of the Garden Route in a day, most visitors either choose a base for exploring the area, or spend a day or two in several places of interest along the way. Many of the attractions are in between the major resorts so it's good to have the flexibility to stop when you want. The **Baz Bus** offers a very adequate service and drops and picks up at Garden Route backpackers' hostels every day. Mainline buses also operate a daily service, but most departures and arrivals are in the middle of the night and it's not as economical as the **Baz Bus**.

Best time to visit

The area's popularity means that good-value accommodation is difficult to find, and gets booked up months in advance, especially during peak season. It is advisable to avoid the area during the two weeks over Christmas and the New Year, and at Easter. For the rest of the school holidays most of the self-catering accommodation might be fully booked, but hotels and bed and breakfasts should have a free room – call in advance to be sure. For more information about the Garden Route visit www.gardenroute.co.za. The regional towns have tourist offices, and the branches of Cape Town Tourism can provide comprehensive information (see page 24).

Overberg → *For listings, see pages 161-180.*

Having climbed the spectacular Sir Lowry's Pass from Somerset West into the Hottentots Holland Mountains, the N2 highway cuts east across the interior of the Overberg towards Mossel Bay. In the early days of settlement, people would refer to the area beyond the Hottentots Hollands as 'over the berg'. The landscape is immediately very different on this side of the mountains – the road passes through forested hills before opening onto endless dry, orange plains. Most of the towns en route are quiet farming centres, and were some of the first areas settled by white farmers as they ventured east of Cape Town. It is easy to pass quickly through the region without taking much in, and if you are keen to get to the Garden Route, Mossel Bay can be reached in three hours; but there are several sights worth lingering over on the way.

East to Caledon

Some 10 km from Sir Lowry's Pass is a turning signposted Villiersdorp, R321. This takes you back into the heart of the Winelands, or north to the Breede River Valley. A short loop takes you to the undistinguished twin towns of Grabouw and Elgin, although Grabouw has the notoriety of being the centre of South Africa's apple industry and is where the popular fizzy drink Appletizer is made. Regional information is available from **Elgin Valley and Grabouw Tourism** ① *T021-848 9838, www.elginvalley.co.za, 0900-1700*, at the Peregrine Farm Stall on the N2; worth a stop for refreshment at the charming Red Tractor Café and a farm stall has been here since the 1960s. Continuing east, the N2 crosses the Houhoek Pass and then reaches Bot River where there is the turning for Hermanus (35 km). It is a further 23 km on the N2 to Caledon.

Caledon

The regional capital of the Overberg, 120 km from Cape Town, lies just off the N2 at the foot of the Swartberg Mountains. It is a typical rural town – small and quiet, and the prosperity of the town and the region is based on agriculture. Look out for the endangered blue crane which is found on open farmland in the area – 75% of South Africa's blue cranes, the national bird, are found in the Overberg.

The town is famous for its hot springs, which produce over 800,000 litres per day. The water has a high ferrous carbonate content. Not surprisingly the first European settler, Ferdinandus Appel, sought to develop the springs. He was granted an 18-ha freehold, on the condition that he built baths and accommodation. Word of the water's healing powers spread quickly and distinguished guests from the Dutch East India Company frequented the springs. Today, the **Caledon Hotel** (see Where to stay, page 161), harnesses the springs, and day visitors can use the spa's facilities (1000-1900). The pool at the top is the hottest, with water temperatures averaging 40°C, and there are additional saunas, cold pool, steam room and a café.

Swellendam → *For listings, see pages 161-180.*

Founded in 1745, Swellendam is the third oldest European town in South Africa (after Cape Town and Stellenbosch), and it is also one of its most picturesque with an appealing, quiet atmosphere. The main centre bears witness to its age with an avenue of mature oak trees and whitewashed Cape Dutch homesteads. Combined with the rural setting and beautiful views, it's a very pleasant spot to spend a day or two, or at the very least pull in from the N2 for lunch given that it is roughly halfway between Cape Town and the Garden Route.

Tourist information is available at **Swellendam Tourism** ① *Oefeningshuis, Voortrek St, T028-514 2770, www.swellendamtourism.co.za, Mon-Fri 0900-1700, Sat 0900-1200*. This office produces a leaflet called Swellendam Treasures, which outlines the interesting Cape Dutch buildings still standing today.

Background

Swellendam started as a trading outpost for the Dutch East India Company. The new settlement was named after Governor Hendrik Swellengrebel and his wife, Ten Damme. Once established, all sorts of characters passed through looking for their fortunes or more land. One of the most successful was Joseph Barry who, in the 1800s, had a virtual monopoly on all trade between Cape Town and the new settlements in the Overberg and Little Karoo.

In 1795 a particularly strange event took place. Just at the point when British soldiers were bringing an end to Dutch rule in the Cape, the burghers of Swellendam declared themselves to be an independent republic, in a reaction to the mal-administration and corruption of the Dutch East India Company. Hermanus Steyn was president from 17 June to 4 November 1795 but, once the British had set up a new regime in Cape Town, the republic was quietly forgotten about. During the 19th century the town prospered and grew as the agricultural sector gradually expanded. This came to an abrupt halt in May 1865, when a fire that started in a baker's destroyed 40 of the town's finest old buildings. Even greater harm was caused by a prolonged drought and when, in 1866, the influential Barry Empire was declared bankrupt the whole region's fortunes declined. Today the town is a prosperous community, and many of the old buildings are still standing, or have been restored.

Places in Swellendam

Of all the old Cape buildings in town the **Drostdy Museum** ① *18 Swellengrebel St, T028-514 1138, www.drostdymuseum.com, Mon-Fri 0900-1645, Sat-Sun 1000-1500, R25, children (6-16) R5 under 6 free*, which covers entrance to a number of buildings, is the most impressive and is often described as one of the country's great architectural treasures. The main building dates from 1747, built as the official residence and seat for the local magistrate or landdrost. Originally built in the shape of a T, the addition of two wings changed the form to an H. Inside, some of the floors have been preserved; what was the lounge has a lime-sand floor, while the kitchen floor is made from cow dung, which helps keep the room cool. The museum concentrates on local history, with a well-preserved collection of 18th- and 19th-century furniture. Within the grounds is a restored Victorian cottage, Mayville, which has an antique rose garden plus the original gazebo and is today home to a coffee shop.

Close by is an open-air display, on the Crafts Green, of many of the early farm tools, charcoal burners, wagons and a horse-driven mill complete with threshing floor. Opposite the museum is the Old Gaol, which housed both prisoners and local government officials, including the jailer who was also the postmaster. In the middle of all the cells was one without windows, known as the 'black hole'. Today, this is a local arts and crafts centre, with a good café.

Not far from the town centre are more restored buildings from the town's early days. The Oefeningshuis (1838) first served as a place for the religious instruction of freed slaves; it now houses the tourist office. Note the painted plaster clock face, which reads 1215, set above a working clock. This was designed for illiterate churchgoers – if the painted face was the same as the clock's, it was time for service. Worth a look is the fine, domineering Dutch Reformed Church. This large whitewashed building has a tall central clock tower and a mix of architectural styles. Just next to the church, on Church Square, are some fine examples of early two-storey town houses built by wealthy farmers who used to visit the town for holy communion. The square had to be large enough to hold their ox wagons. Another grand town house is the Auld House dating from 1802 which for many years was the family home for the Overberg trader, Joseph Barry. Inside is some furniture, originally fitted on a steamer which used to sail between Cape Town and Port Beaufort. Also worth a visit is the small Church of St Luke built in 1865. Finally, look out for the shop Buirski & Co, built in 1880. It has one of the finest examples of Victorian wrought-iron balconies and fittings in the town.

Bontebok National Park

① *6 km from Swellendam, the turning off the N2 is clearly signposted, on the Mossel Bay side of Swellendam and there is a 5-km gravel road from the highway to the entrance, T028-514 2735, www.sanparks.org, Oct-Apr 0700-1900, May-Sep 0700-1800, R60, children (under 16) R30. Shop selling snacks, drinks and curios.*

This park can be visited for a few hours or there is accommodation (see page 161), and is a good place to spot several species of antelope in a pleasant setting on the Breede River. There are two loop roads for drives, and some short walking trails from the rest camp where there is also a swimming spot in the river.

At the beginning of the 20th century the bontebok was the rarest species of antelope in Africa. It had been hunted and driven off its natural habitat by the early settlers in the Overberg. Fortunately, something even scarcer came to their rescue – a group of local conservation-minded farmers, who recognized the need to set up a protected area to save the remaining animals (rumoured to be fewer than 20). In 1931 the first reserve was established, but it was not until the herd was moved to a more suitable environment beside the Breede River in 1960 that the numbers started to recover significantly. This has proved to be a success but, although no longer endangered, there are still not many places where the bontebok can be seen in the wild. Today, there are about 200 bontebok in the park and other antelope indigenous to the Overberg have been introduced to the reserve, including red hartebeest, steenbok and duiker plus the rare Cape mountain zebra. Furthermore, the Breede River provides a perfect setting for the Cape clawless otter. Bird species number about 200, and include blue crane, spurwing goose, secretary bird, Stanley's buzzard, and sunbirds and cuckoos may be seen around the office and rest camp.

Heidelberg to Albertinia

Continuing east from Swellendam along the N2, the road passes several small agricultural towns. Heidelberg, 58 km from Swellendam, is dominated by its Dutch Reformed church on the banks of the Duivenhoks River, and was named Heidelberg after the city in Germany in 1855. After another 34 km, Riversdale is a small farming centre based around wheat, wool and potatoes. The small **Julius Gordon Africana Museum** ① *Long St, T028-713 8053, Mon-Fri 0800-1300, free,* outlines the lives of several local characters and is home to some paintings by Thomas Baines and Peter Wenning. Around the town are no fewer than 15 stone churches, the oldest being the St Matthew's Anglican Church, built in 1856.

The **Tourist office** ① *T028-713 1996, www.riversdale.co.za, Mon-Fri 0830-1730, Sat 0900-1200*, is on the N2 as you drive through.

Abertinia is another 39 km along the N2 and has a pretty backdrop formed by the smooth foothills and sharp peaks of the Langeberg Mountains. An product collected around Albertinia is the juice from aloe plants, *Aloe ferox*, which is an important ingredient in medicine and cosmetics. You can visit the **Alcare Aloe Factory** ① *T028-735 1454, www.alcare.co.za, 0900-1700*, on the N2 just outside town. They conduct free tours and sell a variety of aloe skincare products and there's a coffee shop. Mossel Bay is 53 km from Albertina.

Garden Route Game Lodge ① *7 km east of Albertinia off the N2, T028-735 1200, www.grgamelodge.co.za, day visitors 0730-1630, 2-hr game drives 1100 and 1400, R385, children (3-12) R175, under 3s free*, is a private game lodge that has been stocked with a number of species of large game including giraffe, white rhino, lion, elephant, kudu, zebra, wildebeest and buffalo. It's a popular excursion from Cape Town and one of the nearest places to the city for wildlife viewing. Transfers from Cape Town can be arranged. There is luxurious accommodation (see page 162), and day visitors are welcome for game drives, which must be pre-booked, and breakfast and lunch are available in the à la carte restaurant for extra. There is also a cheetah-breeding centre and reptile encounters are on offer where the resident herpetologist (reptile man) will share his knowledge of snakes, crocodiles and other coldblooded creatures.

Mossel Bay

Where to stay ▭	Point **9**	Restaurants ❼
1 Point Village Guest House **3**	Protea Mossel Bay **6**	Bahia dos Vaqueiros **8**
Diaz Strand **2**	Santos Express Train	Café Gannet **4**
Mossel Bay Backpackers **4**	Lodge **8**	Café Havana **1**

Mossel Bay → *For listings, see pages 161-180.*

Built along a rocky peninsula which provides sheltered swimming and mooring in the bay, Mossel Bay is one of the larger and less appealing seaside towns along the Garden Route. Nevertheless, during the school holidays, the town is packed with domestic visitors. A fact often overlooked in promotional literature is that since the discovery of offshore oil deposits, Mossel Bay is also the home of the ugly Mossgas natural gas refinery and a multitude of oil storage tanks. The town has a number of Portuguese flags and names dotted around, thanks to the first European to anchor in the bay – Bartolomeu Dias, who landed in February 1488, followed by Vasco da Gama, who moored in the bay in 1497. The bay's safe anchorage and freshwater spring ensured that it became a regular stopping-off point for other seafarers, and today many of the local attractions relate to the sea and reflect the bay's importance to the early explorers. The town was named by a Dutch trader, Cornelis de Houtman, who in 1595 found a pile of mussel shells in a cave below the present lighthouse.

Arriving in Mossel Bay
Getting there All mainline buses stop at the Shell Truckpoort at Voorbaai, on the N2 7 km from Mossel Bay. The **Baz Bus** is the only service that goes right into town.

Kaai 4 **2**
Pavilion **7**
Sea Gypsy Café **3**

Tourist information Mossel Bay Tourism Bureau ⓘ *corner of Church and Market streets, T044-691 1067, www.visitmosselbay. co.za, Mon-Fri 0800-1800, Sat-Sun 0900-1600*, provides information and acts as a central reservations office for accommodation.

Places in Mossel Bay
Bartolomeu Dias Museum Complex ⓘ *T044-691 1067, www.diasmuseum. co.za, Mon-Fri 0900-1645, Sat-Sun 0900-1545, R20, children (6-18) R5, under 5s free.* Here you'll find the Culture Museum, the Shell Museum, an Aquarium, the Maritime Museum, some Malay graves, and the original freshwater spring that attracted the early sailors and which still flows into a small dam. There's also a tea shop on site in a restored 1830s cottage. The displays in the Maritime Museum are arranged around a full-size replica of Bartolomeu Dias's caravel (which you can climb aboard for an extra fee; R20, children R5). Also here is a tree with a fascinating past, the **Post Office Tree**, a giant milkwood situated close to the freshwater spring. History relates that in 1500 a letter was left under the tree by a ship's captain. A year later it was retrieved

by the commander of the Third East India Fleet en route to India. Messages were also left carved in rocks and left in old boots tied to the branches. The tree has been declared a national monument and it is still possible to send a postcard home from here – all mail dispatched from the Post Office Tree is franked with a special commemorative stamp and makes a great souvenir.

In the middle of the bay is **Seal Island** which can be visited by cruises departing from the harbour. The island is inhabited by colonies of African penguins and Cape fur seals (the best month to see seal pups is November). Between September and November the warm waters of the bay are often visited by southern right, humpback and Brydes whales while calving. Another vantage point for viewing whales and dolphins is **The Point** at the end of Marsh Street. Close by is the 20-m-high **Cape St Blaize Lighthouse** ① *Montague St, T044-690 3015, Mon-Fri 1000-1500, R14, children (under 12) R7*, built in 1864, one of only two remaining continuously manned lighthouses in South Africa.

St Blaize Trail

The St Blaize Trail is a perfect introduction to the stunning coastline that you are likely to encounter along the Garden Route. This is a 13.5-km walk along the cliffs and rocky coast west from Mossel Bay. The official trail starts from Bats Cave, just below the lighthouse; the path is marked by the white image of a bird in flight. As you walk further from the town the scenery becomes more and more spectacular. You can leave the coast at Pinnacle Point, and follow a path inland to Essenhout Street. This cuts about 5 km off the walk. The path ends by a group of houses in Dana Bay. From here you will have to organize your own transport back into town, so it helps to have a mobile phone to call a taxi from Mossel Bay. A helpful map is available from the tourism office. You are rightly warned to be careful in places during strong winds, as there are some precipitous and unprotected drops from the cliff tops.

Botlierskop Private Game Reserve

① *T044-696 6055, www.botlierskop.co.za. To get there turn off the N2 on to the R401 to the northeast of Mossel Bay, the Klein Brakrivier turn-off, and follow signs for 25 km.*
This private reserve is situated on a 2400-ha game farm, which is home to 24 different species of animals and a wide variety of birds. A former farm, the land has been restocked and wildlife includes the rare black impala, rhino, elephant, lion, buffalo, giraffe, mountain zebra and eland. Activities include game drives, nature walks, picnics and horse riding. The most exciting activity is elephant riding, which costs from R450, children (under 12) R225, no children under six. There is luxurious accommodation available (see Where to stay, page 162) or you can visit for the day, though booking is essential. Check out the website for prices and programmes.

George and around → *For listings, see pages 161-180.*

Often referred to as the capital of, the Garden Route, George owes this status to the fact that it has an airport. It is also an important junction between the N2 coastal highway and the N12 passing through the Outeniqua Pass into the Karoo. It lies in the shadow of the Outeniqua Mountains, but unlike the majority of towns along the Garden Route, it is not by the sea. The town itself is a mostly modern grid of streets interspersed with some attractive old buildings and churches. While it is pleasant enough, it has little appeal compared to other towns along the coast; the main reason overseas visitors come here is en route to

Oudtshoorn, the capital of the Little Karoo, known for its ostrich farms and the Cango Caves (see page 144), and to play golf. George has several outstanding golf courses and has previously hosted the President's Cup.

Arriving in George

Getting there   George Airport ⓘ *T044-876 9310, www.acsa.co.za,* is 10 km southeast of the town centre. It has ATMs, restaurants and car rental desks (see Transport, page 178). George is on the N12, 6 km north of the N2, and 55 km south of Oudtshoorn over the Outeniqua Pass. The N2 continues from George to Wilderness, but the alternative route back from the Garden Route to Cape Town is from Oudtshoorn via the scenic Route 62 east to Worcester and then the N1; a distance of roughly 450 km. If you're short of time, or not returning to Cape Town, the easiest access to Oudtshoorn for a day or two of exploring before returning to the Garden Route is from George.

Tourist information   George and Wilderness Tourism ⓘ *124 York St, T044-801 9103, www.visitgeorge.co.za, Mon-Fri 0800-1700, Sat 0900-1300,* has a wide range of information on the Garden Route.

Background

The first settlement appeared here in 1778 as a forestry post to process wood from the surrounding forests. In 1811 it was formally declared a town, and named after King George III. It was at this time that its wide tree-lined streets – Courtenay, York and Meade – were laid out. For the next 80 years the town remained the centre for a voracious timber industry. Much of the indigenous forest was destroyed supplying wood for wagons, railway sleepers and mine props. Some of the trees, which are endemic to South Africa, came to be known as **stinkwoods** because of their odour when freshly cut. Few remain today, although they are slow growing back.

Places in George

Within the town itself there are only a few sights of interest. On the corner of Cathedral and York streets, **St Mark's Cathedral,** consecrated in 1850, has an unusually large number of stained-glass windows for its size; many were designed by overseas artists of limited fame. In 1911 a bible and royal prayer book were given to the church by King George V. The interior of the **Dutch Reformed Mother Church** at the north end of Meade Street reflects the town's early history as a centre for the timber industry. The pulpit is carved out of stinkwood and took over a year to create. The ceiling was built from yellowwood, and six yellowwood trunks were used as pillars. The mountains create an impressive backdrop to the church when viewed from the corner of Courtenay and Meade streets.

The small 12-ha **Garden Route Botanical Garden and Southern Cape Herbarium** ⓘ *49 Caledon St, T044-874 1558, www.botanicalgarden.org.za, Sep-Apr 0700-1900, May-Aug 0730-1800, free, tea garden Mon-Fri 1000-1600,* has a wide variety of indigenous trees, flowerbeds, fynbos and succulent plants with the Outeniqua Mountains as a backdrop. It was established on land where two dams were built in the 1800s to send water down into George via a series of stone-lined furrows. The dams are still there: one has become a shallow wetland while the other is a lovely stretch of open water' both attract a number of birds.

In front of the tourist office, housed in the King Edward VII library, is an ancient oak tree known as the **Slave Tree**. It is one of the original trees planted by Adrianus van Kervel in the early 1800s and has been declared a national monument. The tree acquired its name because of the chain embedded in the trunk with a lock attached to it. The story of the chain can be traced back to when a public tennis court was in use next to the library (now the information office), and the court roller was secured to the tree to prevent playful children from rolling it down the street. Housed in the old Drostdy, the **George Museum** ① *Courtenay St, T044-702 3523, Mon-Fri 0900-1630, Sat 0900-1230, entry by donation*, has displays on the timber industry as well as musical instruments and a collection of old printing presses. In the Sayer's Wing is an exhibition devoted to former President PW Botha, who was a member of parliament for George for 38 years. The **Outeniqua Transport Museum** ① *2 Mission Rd, just off Knysna Rd, T044-801 8289, Sep-Apr, Mon-Sat 0800-1700, May-Aug, Mon-Fri 0800-1600, Sat 0800-1400, R20, children (4-12) R10, under 3s free*, has an interesting display outlining the history of steam train travel including 13 steam locomotives, a 1947 Royal Mail coach, and a room dedicated to model railways, as well as a collection of vintage cars and flight memorabilia.

Victoria Bay

If you are based in George and wish to spend a quiet day by the sea, this small resort is only 9 km or 15 minutes' drive away. Victoria Bay, 2 km off the N2, is an excellent place to surf during the winter. It has a narrow cove with a broad sandy beach, a grassy sunbathing area, and a safe tidal pool for children. There's only one row of houses with some of the best-positioned guesthouses in the region.

Oudtshoorn → *For listings, see pages 161-180.*

By far the largest settlement in the Little Karoo, this is a pleasant administrative centre which still retains much of the calm of its early days. It is a major tourist centre and the two major reasons for coming here are the countless ostrich farms that surround the town and the superb Cango Caves. There are also several nature reserves and scenic drives, which are introductions to the diversity of the landscape. Oudtshoorn itself is appealing, with broad streets, smart sandstone Victorian houses, many of which are now B&Bs, and a good choice of restaurants.

Arriving in Oudtshoorn

Getting there and moving on Oudtshoorn is 55 km north of George and the junction with the N2 coastal road. The quickest route from the Garden Route is to drive from George and head north over the Outeniqua Pass (N12), but another route goes from Mossel Bay over the Robinson Pass (R328). Alternatively, Cape Town is roughly 450 km from Oudtshoorn via the scenic Route 62 east to Worcester and then the N1. **Greyhound** and **Intercape** buses stop at Oudtshoorn daily on the route between Mossel Bay and Johannesburg via Bloemfontein.

The centre of town is compact and it is easy to find your way about on foot, but you'll need transport to see the outlying sights such as the Cango Caves and ostrich farms.

Oudtshoorn Tourist Bureau ① *Baron van Rheede St, T044-279 2532, www. oudtshoorn.com, Mon-Fri 0800-1800, Sat 0830-1300*, has a well-informed, enthusiastic and helpful team and is worth a visit for details on accommodation and the less well-known sights of the Karoo.

Background

In 1838 a small church was inaugurated on the Hartebeestrivier Farm to serve the farmers who had settled along the banks of the Olifants and Grobbelaars rivers. Nine years later the village of Oudtshoorn was founded when land was subdivided and sold by the surveyor J Ford. The town was named after Baron Van Rheede van Oudtshoorn, who died on his way to the Cape to take up the post of governor in 1773. In 1858 the first group of British immigrants settled in the village.

When visiting during the dry season it is easy to see how for many years the supply of water to the new settlement restricted its growth. A severe drought in 1865 persuaded many established farmers to move on and most made the long trek to the Transvaal. In its early days, water was brought to the town in barrels and then sold to households at sixpence a bucket. But the local farmers learnt to cope with this handicap and many of South Africa's early irrigation experts came from the region. When you cross the Grobbelaars River in the centre of town during the dry season, all the bridges and culverts seem redundant but they provide ample evidence of how much water can pass through

Oudtshoorn

To 3, Wilgewandel Holiday Farm, Cango Ostrich Farm, Cango Wildlife Ranch, Cango Caves & Swartberg Pass

To Highgate, Safari Ostrich Farms & Calitzdorp (61 km)

Klein Karoo Medi-Clinic

Oakdene

Mimosa Lodge

Gottland House

Suspension Bridge

Pinehurst

Catholic Cathedral

Bushman Curios

Le Roux Town House

CP Nel Museum

To 1, Railway Station & George (55 km)

Park · Buitekant · Jan van Riebeeck · Grobbelaars River · R328 · High St · Victoria · Adderley · Van der Riet · Hope · Church · St Saviour · Voortrekker · R62 · Vrede · N12 · St John · High St · Church · St George · Oxford · Jubilee · Rand · Baron van Rheede St

300 metres
300 yards

Where to stay
Backpacker's Paradise **2**
Karoo Soul **1**
Protea Hotel Riempie Estate **3**
Queen's **11**
Rosenhof Country House **12**

Turnberry Boutique Hotel **5**   Paljas **5**

Restaurants
Café Brûlée **2**
Colony **3**
Headlines **4**
Kalinka **1**

Whale Coast & Garden Route Garden Route ● 141

when it rains. If you have time, walk across the Victorian **Suspension Bridge** where Church Street crosses the river; this is now a protected national monument.

It was the advent of two ostrich-feather booms (1865-1870 and 1900-1914) that truly established the town, and led to the erection of the fine sandstone buildings and 'ostrich palaces' that now line Oudtshoorn's streets. For a period of almost 40 years it was the most important settlement east of Cape Town. At the peak of its fortunes, ostrich feathers were selling for more than their weight in gold – little wonder that so many birds were bred. While ostrich farming no longer brings in as much wealth, it remains an important business in the Karoo. Today, it is the production of specialized agricultural seed which contributes most to the region's wealth.

Places in Oudtshoorn

Within the town limits there is little to see aside from appreciating the sandstone Victorian buildings. There are several **ostrich palaces** in town, which unfortunately are not open to the public, but are still worth a look from the outside for their ornate exteriors. Most examples are in the old part of town on the west bank of the Grobbelaars River. Look out for **Pinehurst**, on St John Street, designed by a Dutch architect, and **Gottland House**, built in 1903 with an octagonal tower. Other buildings of note include **Mimosa Lodge**, **Oakdene** and **Rus in Urbe**. Unfortunately, many fine Victorian buildings were demolished in the 1950s.

The **Catholic Cathedral**, on Baron von Rheede Street, is a fascinating modern cruciform building with splendid stained-glass windows and a chapel beneath the main altar. The cathedral houses two notable works of art: the first is a painting given by Princess Eugenie in memory of her brother – the last of the Bonapartes, who died fighting with the British against the Boers. The second is a replica of a Polish icon incorporating childhood items from refugee children sent to Oudtshoorn during the Second World War; the children returned bearing the gift to celebrate the 50th anniversary of their evacuation.

In the centre of town, the **CP Nel Museum** ① *3 Baron van Rheede St, T044-272 7306, www.cpnelmuseum.co.za, Mon-Fri 0800-1700, Sat 0900-1300, R20, children (under 16) R5,* is a fine sandstone building with a prominent clock tower and was originally built as a boys' high school. The masons who designed the building had been brought to Oudtshoorn by the 'feather barons' to build their grand mansions. The displays include a reconstructed trading store, synagogue and chemist, plus an interesting section on the history of the ostrich boom and the characters involved. The rest of the collection of historic objects was bequeathed to the town by CP Nel, a local businessman. A short walk away is **Le Roux Town House** ① *146 High St,* which is part of the CP Nel Museum and the entry fee covers both. This classic town house was built in 1908 and provides a real feel for how the wealthy lived in the fine ostrich palaces of Oudtshoorn. The interior and furnishings are in art nouveau style and the furniture was shipped from Europe between 1900 and 1920. During the summer, teas are served in the garden. **Arbeidsgenot** ① *Jan van Riebeeck Rd,* is the former home of Senator Cornelius Langenhoven, a leading figure in the history of the Afrikaans language who wrote the old national anthem of South Africa.

Around Oudtshoorn → For listings, see pages 161-180.

Visiting an ostrich farm in the area can be great fun, although the appeal of riding ostriches, feeding ostriches, buying ostrich eggs and leather, or eating ostrich-egg omelette can fade quickly. To keep visitors for longer, some farms have introduced different species. Visiting the farms or the Cango Caves without your own transport can be surprisingly tricky. There are no tour companies that organize daily trips, although it is possible to find a guide through the tourist office. Otherwise, you might want to hire a car for the day.

Cango Ostrich Farm ① *in the Shoemanshoek Valley along the R328 towards Cango Caves, 14 km from Oudtshoorn, T044-272 4623, www.cangoostrich.co.za, 0800-1630, R75, children R40, 45-min tours depart every 20 mins*, is one of the several attractions on the way to and from the Cango Caves. The farm attractions are also within walking distance of each other. You can interact directly with the birds, sit on or ride them, buy local curios and sample Karoo wines and cheeses.

Wilgewandel Holiday Farm ① *in the Shoemanshoek Valley along the R328 towards Cango Caves, 25 km from Oudtshoorn, T044-272 0878, www.wilgewandel.co.za, 0800-1500, camel rides R45, children (3-13) R30, other activities R5-10 per person*, offers you the chance to ride a camel around the farm – a pleasant change from all those ostriches. There are also lots of attractions for children such as farmyard animals, a pet area, trampolines, bumper boats, donkey cart rides, and a restaurant serving anything from tea and scones to crocodile and ostrich steaks.

Highgate Ostrich Farm ① *10 km from Oudtshoorn off the R328 towards Mossel Bay, T044-272 7115, www.highgate.co.za, 0800-1700, R110, children (under 16) R65, 1½-hr tours depart every hour, on the hour*, a very popular show farm named after the London suburb of Highgate, has been owned by the Hooper family since the 1850s and opened its gates to visitors in 1938. You will learn everything there is to know about the bird, and can then try your hand at riding (or even racing) them. Snacks and drinks are served on the porch of the homestead.

Safari Ostrich Farm ① *6 km from Oudtshoorn off the R328 towards Mossel Bay road, T044-272 7311, www.safariostrich.co.za, 0730-1700, adults R80, children (under 16) R40, 1-hr tours depart every hour, on the hour*, has the usual array of ostrich rides, educational exhibits and curio shops. There is also a smart homestead known as Welgeluk. The house was built in 1910, and is a perfectly preserved example of an ostrich palace. There are roof tiles from Belgium, teak from Burma and expanses of marble floors, proof of the wealth and influence the short-lived boom brought to Oudtshoorn families. Unfortunately, the house is closed to visitors; the closest you can get is the main gate.

Cango Wildlife Ranch ① *in the Shoemanshoek Valley along the R328 towards Cango Caves, 3 km from Oudtshoorn, T044-272 5593, www.cango.co.za, 0800-1700, R130, children (4-15) R85, under 4s free*, provokes mixed opinions as it is, in effect, a zoo which stocks animals including white lions, leopards, cheetahs and, oddly, jaguars, pumas and rare white Bengal tigers. There is even an albino python. However, the ranch is a leading player in conservation and breeding, particularly with cheetah and wild dog, and the enclosures are very spacious. After walking safely above the animals, you have the choice of paying a little more to pet a cheetah, or you can visit the restaurant. A new attraction here is the **Valley of the Ancients**, a well-forested string of lakes and enclosures connected by boardwalks that are home to a number of unusual animals. The pools are home to Nile crocodiles, pygmy hippos, monitor lizards and otters, while birds include flamingos and marabou storks. You can watch the crocodiles being fed by hand and this is probably the only place in the world that offers cage diving with crocodiles (R330; children must be over 10).

Following the R328 north, the road passes several ostrich farms and then follows the Grobbelaars River Valley towards the Cango Caves (see below). The little village of **Schoemanshoek**, 15 km from Oudtshoorn, is in a lush valley with small farms and homesteads and has some good places to stay.

Cango Caves

① *On the R328 29 km north of Oudtshoorn, T044-272 7410, www.cangocaves.co.za. 0900-1700, standard 1-hr tour departs every hour on the hour last tour 1600, R80, children (5-15) R45, under 5s free, 1½-hr adventure tour, half past every hour 0930-1530, R100, children (6-15; minimum age is 6) R60, restaurant, curio shop.*

Tucked away in the foothills of the Swartberg Mountains 29 km from Oudtshoorn, the Cango Caves are a magnificent network of calcite caves, recognized as among the world's finest dripstone caverns. In 1938 they were made a national monument. Despite being seriously hyped and very touristy, they are well worth a visit. Allow a morning for a round trip if based locally; if you have a car it is possible to visit them and Oudtshoorn on a day trip from towns along the Garden Route such as Mossel Bay, George and Wilderness.

The only access to the caves is on a guided tour. The standard one-hour tour is a good introduction to the caves and allows you to see the most impressive formations. It is, however, aimed at tour groups, so visitors with a special interest may find it rather simplistic. During the tour, each section is lit up and the guide points out interesting formations and their given names. Although one small chamber is lit in gaudy colours, the rest are illuminated with white light to best show off the formations. These are turned off behind you as you progress further into the system as research has shown that continued exposure to light causes damage to the caves. The adventure tour lasts for 1½ hours, is over 1 km long and there are over 400 stairs. This can be disturbing for some people, since it involves crawling along narrow tunnels, and at the very end climbing up the Devil's Chimney, a narrow vertical shaft. It leads up for 3.5 m and is only 45 cm wide in parts – definitely not for broad people. If at any stage you feel you can't go on, inform the guide who will arrange for you to be led out. Although strenuous, this tour allows you to see most of the caves, and gives a real feeling of exploration. The caves are usually around 20°C, so a T-shirt and shorts will be fine. Wear shoes with reasonable grip, as after rain the floors can become a little slippery. During the holidays it gets very crowded and nearly 200,000 people pass through the caves each year. Each tour has a maximum number of people, so you may have to wait an hour or more. It's a good idea to get here early in the morning to avoid queues, or alternatively pre-book.

Wilderness and around → *For listings, see pages 161-180.*

This appealing little town is an ideal base for exploring the Garden Route and has a superb swathe of sandy beach. Check locally for demarcated areas for swimming and surfing.

Children should be supervised in the sea as there are strong rip currents. One of the safest spots for swimming is in the Touw River mouth. Except for the few hectic weeks at Christmas and New Year, Wilderness is generally very relaxed and has an excellent range of accommodation. The highlight is the Wilderness Section of the Garden Route National Park, a quiet, well-managed area of the park, with three levels of self-catering accommodation and a campsite.

The town itself doesn't have much of a centre, but stretches instead up the lush foothills of the Outeniqua Mountains and along leafy streets by the lake and river. The supermarket, restaurants, post office and tourist office are by the petrol station, where the N2 crosses the Serpentine channel.

Arriving in Wilderness
Wilderness Tourism ① *Leila's Lane, T044-877 0045, www.wildernessinfo.org, Mon-Fri 0800-1700, Sat 0900-1300,* is a very helpful office, especially when it comes to finding good-value accommodation during the peak season.

Background
The first European to settle in the district was a farmer, Van der Bergh, who built himself a simple farmhouse in the 1850s. But it was in 1877 that the name was first used, when a young man from Cape Town, George Bennet, was granted the hand of his sweetheart only on condition that he took her to live in the wilderness. He purchased some land where the present-day **Wilderness Hotel** stands and promptly named it 'wilderness' (of dense bush and forest) to appease his new father-in-law. At this time the only road access was from the Seven Passes Road between George and Knysna, and Bennet cut a track from this road to his new farmhouse. In 1905 the homestead was converted it into a boarding house, and when the property changed hands in 1921, the farmhouse/boarding house underwent further alterations and the Wilderness Hotel came into being.

Garden Route National Park (Wilderness Section)
① *Off the N2, 4 km east of Wilderness, reception, T044-877 1197, www.sanparks.org, 0700-2000, R96, children (2-11) R48. There are two rest camps and the nearest supermarkets and restaurants are in Wilderness.*
This section of the Garden Route National Park stretches from the Touw Rivermouth to the Swartvlei Estuary, covers 2612 ha and incorporates five rivers and four lakes as well as a 28-km stretch of the coastline. The four lakes are known as Island, Langvlei, Rondevlei and Swartvlei, and are situated between the Outeniqua foothills and sand dunes which back onto a beautiful, long sandy beach. The main attractions are the dense hardwood forest, the water and the birdlife in the reed beds affording the opportunity to encounter the brilliantly coloured Knysna lourie, or one of the five kingfisher species that occur here. During spring, a carpet of flowers on the forest floor further enhances the verdant beauty of the park.

There are two ways in which to enjoy the surroundings; on foot or in a canoe. You can cover more ground by walking, but canoeing is ideal for seeing birds. There are five trails in the park from 2-10 km. The longest is the **Pied Kingfisher Trail**, a 10-km circular route, which can be completed in three or four hours and goes via Wilderness village. It follows the river in one direction and the beach on your return. The other walks are also forest walks, except for the 3-km **Dune Molerat Trail**, which takes you through dune fynbos where you may see proteas in flower in season. Maps are available at reception.

The rest camps have canoes for hire – these should be arranged through **Eden Adventures** (see page 176) who have an office at reception. One of the more interesting short routes is to continue up the Touw River past the Ebb and Flow Camps. This quickly becomes a narrow stream and you have to leave your canoe. A path continues along the bank of the stream through some beautiful riverine forest and a 2-km boardwalk takes you to a waterfall where you can swim. Eden Adventures also have mountain bikes, some with child seats, to rent out for use on the trails in the park.

Sedgefield and around → *For listings, see pages 161-180.*

Unless you turn off the N2, all that can be seen of Sedgefield is a collection of curio shops, supermarkets and snack bars. Between the main road and the beach is the **Swartvlei Lagoon**, South Africa's largest natural inland saltwater lake, most of which lies on the inland side of the N2. The lake is a popular spot for watersports and birdwatching, although the two pastimes don't always go well together. Around Sedgefield's lakes and forests look out for the secretive starred robin, the blue mantle flycatcher, the difficult-to-see Victorian warbler and the rare African finfoot.

The village itself is of little interest, but the country around the lakes is spectacular and very peaceful. On the Knysna side of Sedgefield is another lake, **Groenvlei**, a freshwater lake lying within the Goukamma Nature Reserve. **Sedgefield Tourism** ① *30 Main Rd, T044-343 2658, www.visitsedgefield.com, Mon-Fri 0800-1700, Sat 0830-1300*, has good information on accommodation.

Goukamma Nature Reserve
① *T044-802 5310, www.capenature.co.za, 0800-1800, entry for day visitors R40, children (2-13) R20. For information on accommodation, see page 165.*
The reserve was established to protect 2230 ha of the hinterland between Sedgefield and Buffalo Bay. This includes Groenvlei or Lake Pleasant, a large freshwater lake, and a 13-km sandy beach with some magnificent sand dunes covered in fynbos and patches of forest containing milkwood trees. The **Goukamma River** estuary in the eastern part of the reserve has been cut off from the sea by the large sand dunes. The lake is now fed by natural drainage and springs, and is surrounded by reed beds which are excellent for birdwatching; more than 75 species have been identified. To get there, look out for the Buffalo Bay signpost where the N2 crosses the Goukamma River, and the railway crosses the N2. Follow the Buffalo Bay road for 8 km and turn right to the office. There are six hiking trails within the reserve from 4.2 km to 15 km and maps are available at the office. The circular 6.5-km **Bush Pig Trail** starts from the office and takes about two or three hours. It runs along a fynbos-covered ridge of dunes, with fine views of the ocean and lakes, and returns via a milkwood forest. Other trails follow the beach. On any of the walks in the reserve, always carry plenty of drinking water and keep an eye out for snakes, especially among the sand dunes.

Knysna and around → *For listings, see pages 161-180.*

Knysna (the 'K' is silent) is the self-proclaimed heart of the Garden Route. It is no longer the sleepy lagoon-side village it once was – far from it – but is nevertheless a pleasant spot to spend a day or two. The town itself is fully geared up for tourists, which means a lot of choice in accommodation and restaurants, as well as overcrowding and high prices. It remains quite an arty place, though, and many of the craftspeople who have gravitated to the region display their products in craft shops and galleries. Nevertheless, development is continually booming and has set the pace for Knysna to become the Garden Route's most popular residential and lifestyle destination. A number of years ago a slick waterfront complex complete with glitzy shops and restaurants known as the **Knysna Quays** was developed around the old harbour, while more recently an extensive marina has been built on Thesen's Island with apartments and hotels, man-made beaches, sports fields and other recreational activities and is linked to the mainland by a causeway. If you're trying to choose between Knysna and Plettenberg Bay as a base, Knysna offers more amenities and activities, while Plett is far more relaxed and has the better beach. Both get very busy during high season.

Arriving in Knysna
Getting there and around Knysna can easily be accessed by road as it lies on the N2 between Cape Town (500 km) and Port Elizabeth (260 km). **Baz Bus** has a daily service between Cape Town and Port Elizabeth, from where it continues to Durban five times a week. Mainline buses stop at Knysna daily on the route between Cape Town and Durban.

1 Knysna

➡ **Knysna maps**
1 Knysna, page 147
2 Knysna Lagoon, page 149

Where to stay 🛏	Restaurants 🍴	Raasoie 5
Knysna Backpackers 1	34' South 9	Thai Kitchen 8
Protea Knysna Quays 3	Anchorage 1	
Rex 4	Cruise Café 4	**Bars & clubs** 🍸
Wayside Inn 13	JJ's 2	Zanzibar 2
Yellowwood Lodge 14	Mon Petit Pain 3	

Translux has a service between Knysna and Johannesburg and Tshwane (Pretoria) via Bloemfontein. The centre of town is compact and it is easy to find your way about on foot, but you'll need transport to see the outlying sights.

Tourist information **Knysna Tourism** ① *40 Main St, T044-382 5510, www.visitknysna. co.za, Mon-Fri 0800-1700, Sat 0830-1300, hours extended in high season*, can make reservations for accommodation, tours and public transport. It's a helpful and professional office, well clued-up on the region.

Background

The Hottentots named a local river in the area by a word that sounded like Knysna to the early Europeans, and it's generally believed to mean a place of wood or leaves. In 1804 George Rex, a timber merchant, purchased the farm Melkhoutkraal, effectively taking ownership of all the land surrounding the lagoon. It was rumoured he was the first and illegitimate son of England's King George III. By 1817 the Knysna Lagoon was being used by ships to bring in supplies, and later to take away timber. The vast, indigenous forests just outside Knysna became an invaluable source of timber for buildings, ships and wagons. In 1870, Arnt Leonard Thesen and his family moved from Norway to Knysna and set up the first trading store and counting house, and by 1881 the settlements of Melville and Newhaven united to form the new town of Knysna. The timber industry continued well into the 20th century and unfortunately wiped out much of the natural forest on the coast, so whilst there are still tracts of Knysna forest with yellowwoods and stinkwoods towering over forest ferns, much of the region has been given over to pine plantations and looks very different to what it did 150 years ago.

Places in Knysna

Although there are a couple of sights and museums in the town, Knysna's highlights are its natural attractions. The **Knysna National Lakes**, a broad largely undefined region of protected areas, is wonderful to explore, comprising lakes, islands, seashore and beach.

Along with Wilderness and Tsitsikamma, the area is now administered by SANParks as part of the newly proclaimed Garden Route National Park, and is now referred to as the **Knysna Lakes Section**. The most accessible area, and the main feature of the town is the **lagoon**, around which much of Knysna life revolves. **The Heads**, the rocky promontories that lead from the lagoon to the open sea, are quite stunning. More than 280 species of bird are listed in the area and the tidal lagoon and open estuary of the Knysna River provides an excellent place to view waders in the summer months, and plovers, gulls, cormorants and sandpipers are common. Large species like African fish eagle and osprey should also be watched out for.

The area also incorporates the remaining tract of Knysna forests on the southern slopes of the Outeniqua Mountains behind Knysna, which first attracted white settlers to the region. No longer a single expanse, the patches go under a variety of names and include Diepwalle Forest (page 151) and Goudveld Forest (page 151). They are noteworthy for the variety of birdlife and their magnificent trees. Species of special interest include the yellowwood, assegai, stinkwood, red alder, white alder and the Cape chestnut. A variety of short walks has been laid out in the forests. In some areas horse riding and mountain biking is allowed.

One of the striking features of Knysna is the location of the sprawling township, which is at the top of the hills above the town. From a boat trip on the lagoon you can look back at the town; all the sleek modern and luxurious development in the foreground and, quite by contrast, the tight cluster of shacks at the very top of the hill.

The **Knysna Museum** ① *Queen St, T044-302 6320, Mon-Fri 0930-1630, Sat 0930-1230, free but donations accepted*, is housed in the Old Gaol – the first public building erected by the colonial government in the 1870s. Most of the collection focuses on fishing methods used along the coast, with a variety of nets and tackle on display. Unless you are a devoted angler this is not going to take up too much of your time. The highlight is in fact a fish, or to be more precise, a coelacanth. This is a prehistoric fish that was believed to be extinct, but a live specimen was famously caught by a fisherman in 1938. There is also an art gallery, tearoom and gift shop.

Millwood House ① *T044-302 6320, Mon-Fri 0930-1630, Sat 0930-1230, free but donations accepted*, is a single-storey wooden building similar to those that once made up the gold-mining community of Millwood (see page 151). The house was originally built in sections and re-erected here. It is now a national monument and houses the local history museum, including a display depicting the goldrush days. Next door is **Parkes Cottage**, a similar wooden house, which was moved three times before arriving at its present site.

② Knysna Lagoon

Where to stay 🛏
Belvidere Manor **2**
Knysna Houseboats **3**
Leisure Isle Boutique
  Lodge **6**
Pezula Resort Hotel & Spa **3**
Phantom Forest
  Eco-Reserve **1**

The Turbine Boutique
  Hotel & Spa **4**
Under Milkwood **10**

Restaurants 🍴
East Head Café **3**
Ile de Pain Bread & Café **4**
Knysna Oyster Co **5**

O'Pescador **2**

Bars & clubs 🍸
Bosun's Pub & Grill **6**

→ Knysna maps
1 Knysna, page 147
2 Knysna Lagoon,
  page 149

Originally erected in Millwood village, it was moved into Knysna when the gold ran out. In 1905 it was moved to Rawson Street, and then finally in 1992 it was moved to its present site.

There are two **St George's** churches in Knysna, the old and the new. Both ran into financial difficulties during construction. To complete the old church the Bishop of the Cape Colony, Robert Gray, persuaded six local businessmen to come up with the necessary £150. The church was consecrated in October 1855. The interior has a timbered ceiling and a fine yellowwood floor. In the 1920s it was decided that a second church needed to be built to accommodate the local congregation. It was 11 years between the foundation stone being laid and the church being consecrated by Bishop Gwyer of George in April 1937. Construction had been delayed due to lack of funds. The community was very proud of the fact that all the materials used in the construction were local – the stone for the walls was quarried from the other side of the lagoon in the Brenton hills. Most of the interior fittings are made from stinkwood, and commemorate local worthies.

Mitchell's Brewery ① *Arend St, Knysna Industria, T044-382 4685, www.mitchellsbrewing. com, Mon-Fri 0830-1630, tours 1100, 1230 and 1430, R80, tasting only R50.* This produces a range of home-made lagers and bitters (the latter being very rare in South Africa), and visitors can take a tour of the fermentation cellars, which includes tasting of up to seven beers plus a pint of your choice at the end, and the brews are also available from many hotels and restaurants along the Garden Route. The most popular are the Forester's Draught pilsner-type lager, the Bosun's Best Bitter, and the heavily spiced Scottish-type traditional ale known as Ninety Shilling.

Featherbed Nature Reserve ① *T044-382 1693, www.knysnafeatherbed.com, daily 1000, R450, children (11-15) R215 (4-10) R100, under 4s free (including lunch), 1430, R320/110/50 (without lunch), additional times in season,* is a private nature reserve in the unspoilt western side of the **Knysna Heads**. It can only be reached by the **Featherbed Co** ferry which runs from the John Benn Jetty, at the Knysna Quays. The reserve is home to South Africa's largest breeding herd of blue duiker (*Cephalophus monticola*), an endangered species. Also of interest is a cave once inhabited by the Khoi, which has been declared a national heritage site. This four-hour excursion includes return ferry trip, 4WD vehicle ride up the western promontory of the Knysna Heads and an optional 2-km guided nature walk through the forest, onto the cliffs, into the caves and along the spectacular coastline. It ends with a buffet lunch under some milkwood trees before returning to Knysna. This is an excellent family excursion. The Featherbed Co also offers 1½-hour cruises around the lagoon on the double-storey *John Benn* (which has a cash bar) at 1230 and 1800 (1700 in winter) for R140, children (4-15) R65, and on a paddle cruiser at 1230 for R185, children (4-15) R90, or a dinner cruise at 1800 (1700 in winter), which includes a three-course buffet dinner, R420, children (11-15) R215 (4-10) R120. In addition, they run the **Cruise Café** at the boat departure point at the Knysna Quays (see Restaurants, page 171).

West of Knysna → *For listings, see pages 161-180.*

Belvidere, Brenton and Brenton-on-Sea

These villages, 12-14 km from town on the western shores of the lagoon, are now smart suburbs of Knysna. Belvidere lies on the banks of the river where it enters the lagoon, and the small village church, **Belvidere Church**, is a miniature replica of a Norman church. It was built in 1855 from local stone and timber, with picturesque stained-glass windows and stinkwood fittings. The rose window on the west side was installed in 1955. Further along the road is the seaside resort of Brenton-on-Sea, where the great attraction is the nearest sandy beach to Knysna, making it very popular during the school holidays. There is a fine hotel and a limited selection of seaside cottages.

Goudveld Forest

About 30 km northwest of Knysna, in the **Goudveld Forest**, are the remains of an old mining town, **Millwood** ① *open sunrise-sunset*. Take the Phantom Pass road out of Knysna, just before the village of Rheenendal take a right turn, signposted to Millwood, and pass through the SANParks boom gate into the forest. This was the site of a minor goldrush in the 1880s, just before the gold was discovered at Pilgrim's Rest and Johannesburg. The first gold was discovered here in 1876 when a local farmer picked up a nugget in the Karatara River. This triggered the usual manic influx, and by 1887 Millwood had a court building, three banks, 32 stores, six hotels and three newspapers. By 1900 most people had left as the reefs became too difficult to mine. Today only one building survives, along with some mining machinery which has remained untouched for over 60 years. There are a few picnic spots and short paths leading into the forest; you only have to walk a few metres before being completely enveloped by trees.

East of Knysna → *For listings, see pages 161-180.*

Diepwalle Forest and Elephant Trail

① *From Knysna, follow the N2 towards Plettenberg Bay, after 7 km turn onto the R339 and the Diepwalle forest station is about 16 km on a gravel road. The R339 passes through the middle of the forest en route to Uniondale via the Prince Alfred's Pass. Open 0600-1800, no charge but you must sign in at the forest station where maps are on offer.*

Starting from the Diepwalle forest station is the 20-km Elephant Walk, an easy-going, level hike that gives a clear insight into the forest environment. The trail is marked by elephant silhouettes and takes around seven hours to complete. The hike is made up of three loops, but it is possible to shorten the walk by completing only one or two loops. The three paths are simply known as Routes I, II and III, and are 9, 8 and 6 km long, respectively. Apart from the (very slim) possibility of spying the rare Knysna elephant (see box, page 152), the main attractions are the giant forest trees, particularly the Outeniqua yellowwood. There are eight such trees along the full trail – the largest, at 46 m, is known as the **King Edward VII Tree**, and stands just off the R339 by the Diepwalle picnic spot at the end of Route I and the start of Route II. The end of the **Outeniqua Trail** meets with Route III.

Knysna Elephant Park

① *On the N2, 20 km from Knysna and 10 km before Plettenberg Bay, T044-532 7732, www. knysnaelephantpark.co.za, 0830-1630, 1-hr tours depart every 30 mins, R230, children (5-12) R100, under 5s free, bookings not required; elephant riding 0930, 1030, 1500, 1600, R885, children (6-12) R425, children under 6 not permitted, booking essential.*

This small park is a refuge for orphaned elephants. Visitors are taken on tours around the forest area and are allowed to touch and play with the little elephants. Although the animals are 'free range' they are very used to human contact, making it a wonderful experience for children. Longer walks with the elephants can also be arranged and the elephant riding is a two-hour excursion through the bush ending with refreshments. Sleeping with the elephants is also on offer, and six rooms have been built above the elephants' boma where they sleep at night (see Where to stay, page 166). This is also the only realistic chance you'll have of seeing elephants in the area – the fabled indigenous

Invisible elephants

No guide to Knysna would be complete without a mention of the fabled Knysna elephants. Their rumoured existence has come to represent the last stand of wildlife against man in the region. Reputedly the elephants live deep in the forest but few people have ever seen them, and little is known about their numbers or their characteristics. In 1876, several hundred elephants were recorded in the region, but under heavy pressure of ivory hunters they were reduced to 20 to 30 individuals by 1908. In 1970 the Knysna elephant population was estimated at 11, and by 1994, only one Knysna elephant was known to survive, an elderly female. In the same year, two young elephants from the Kruger National Park were introduced into the range of the elderly female in an effort to increase numbers. But they only joined up with the elderly female for short periods before choosing to spend 80% of their time in mountainous fynbos habitat beyond the Knysna forest. In 1999 they were recaptured and relocated to a private game reserve in the Eastern Cape. Since then, and although researchers claimed to have found spoor in 2007, no elephants have been seen. But the myth continues so happy hiking – you may just see more than the Knysna lourie.

ones are far too elusive (see box, above). The restaurant serves breakfast, light lunches and afternoon teas. There's another similar elephant experience at **The Elephant Sanctuary** further along the N2 at The Crags, 19 km east of Plettenberg Bay (see page 156).

Plettenberg Bay → *For listings, see pages 161-180.*

Plettenberg Bay, or 'Plett', as it is commonly known, is one of the most appealing resorts on the Garden Route. Although it is modern and has little of historical interest, the compact centre is attractive and the main beach beautiful. Plett has now become fashionable and, during the Christmas season, the town is transformed. Wealthy families descend from Johannesburg and the pace can get quite frenetic – expect busy beaches and long queues for restaurant tables. For the rest of the year it is calmer and the resort becomes just another sleepy seaside town. There are three beaches that are good for swimming, and a number of attractions along the N2 to the east of 'Plett', particularly around the settlement of The Crags, where visitors could easily spend a full day visiting the wildlife sancturies.

Arriving in Plettenberg Bay
Getting there For short trips to other towns along the Garden Route the **Baz Bus** represents the best value and most convenient schedule and has a daily service in either direction between Cape Town and Port Elizabeth. Mainline buses stop at the Shell Ultra City out of town on the N2.

Tourist information Plettenberg Bay Tourism ⓘ *Melville's Corner shopping centre, Main St, T044-533 4065, www.plettenbergbay.co.za, Mon-Fri 0900-1700, Sat 0900-1300, slightly longer hours during the peak summer season,* is a helpful office with quite a detailed website.

Pletternberg Bay

To N2, Keurboom River Nature Reserve, Nature's Valley & Garden Route National Park
(Tsitsikamma Section), Goose Valley Golf Estate & Plettenberg Bay Game Reserve

Where to stay 🛏

Albergo For
  Backpackers **1**
Beacon Island **2**
Grand Café & Rooms **8**
Hunter's Country House
  & Tsala Treetop Lodge **7**
Plettenberg **5**

Plettenberg Park Hotel
  & Spa **10**
Robberg Beach Lodge **6**
Stone Cottages **9**
Whalesong **11**

Restaurants 🍴

Cornuti **1**

Le Fournil de Plett Bakery
  & Café **2**
The Lookout Deck **5**
Nguni **6**
Zinzi **3**

Background

In 1630 a Portuguese vessel, the *San Gonzalez*, was wrecked in the bay. This was 20 years before Jan van Riebeeck's arrival at the Cape. The survivors stayed here for eight months, during which time they built two smaller boats out of the wreckage, and one of the boats managed to sail up the coast to Mozambique. The survivors were eventually returned home to Lisbon, but they left behind a sandstone plaque on which they had inscribed the name *Baia Formosa*. Today a replica can be seen in Plett in the same place that the first was left by the sailors. (The original is now on show in the South African Museum in Cape Town.) The Portuguese had a number of names for the bay, but none stuck for very long. Later the Dutch also gave the bay several different names, such as Content Bay and Pisang River Bay; it was only in 1778 when Governor Joachim van Plettenberg opened a timber post on the shores of the bay, and named it after himself, that a name stuck.

Plettenberg remained an important timber port until the early 1800s when the Dutch decided to move operations to Knysna since it was a safer harbour. For a period the bay became famous as a whaling station but all that remains is a blubber cauldron and slipway near the **Beacon Island Hotel**.

Places in Plettenberg Bay

While there are a few old buildings still standing which represent a little of the town's earlier history, including the remains of the Old Timber Store (1787), the Old Rectory (1776) and the Dutch Reformed Church (1834), most of the buildings were destroyed in a fire in 1914, and today the main streets are just a collection of modern shopping malls and restaurants. The real attraction of this area is the sea and the outdoors. Aside from the three beaches, **Robberg**, **Central** and **Lookout**, there is excellent deep-sea fishing and, in season, good opportunities to spot whales and dolphins, particularly southern right whales from June to October. Plett climbs up a fairly steep hill; there are many elevated land-based vantage points as well as regular boat tours offering closer encounters with the marine life. The nearby **Keurbooms River lagoon** is a safe area for bathing and other watersports, and the dunes around the lagoon are now part of the **Keurbooms River Nature Reserve** (see page 155).

The **Milkwood Trail** is a 3-km circular trail in and around the town. Follow the yellow footprints. You can start the walk anywhere along the route and it takes you via Piesangs River lagoon, Central Beach, and Lookout Rocks, and in the centre of town, past some of the historic buildings.

There are also some recommended walks in the **Robberg Nature Reserve** ① *8 km south from Plett on Robberg Rd, T044-533 2125, www.capenature.co.za, Feb-Nov 0700-1700, Dec and Jan 0700-2000, R40, children (2-13) R20*. There are three possibilities ranging from 2-9 km on this loop along the Robberg Peninsula which forms the western boundary of Plettenberg Bay. Follow the 'seal' markers. Walking is easy thanks to boardwalks, and there are plenty of prominent viewpoints from which it is possible to see whales, seals and dolphins in the bay, but beware of freak waves along the coastal paths. Allow at least four hours for the full route. **Eden Adventures** based in Wilderness (see page 176) can also arrange 45-m abseiling in the reserve.

Plettenberg Bay Game Reserve

① *12 km north of Plett, leave town on the N2 east and turn on the R340 to Uplands, T044-535 0000, www.plettenbergbaygamereserve.com, 2-hr game drives May-Sep 1100 and 1500, Oct-Apr 0830, 1000, 1100, 1230, 1500 and 1600, R425 per person 2-hr horse safaris 1000 and 1500, R425 per person (no children under 12).*

This private reserve is located on 2200 ha spread across the hills above the Garden Route coastline with good views of Plettenberg Bay and offers open 4WD safaris or guided horse-riding trails. The reserve boasts a diversity of natural biomes, including fynbos, grasslands and indigenous forests, and on the property is the natural confluence of the Keurbooms and Palmiet Rivers. The reserve has been stocked with over 35 species of game, including lion, rhino, giraffe, hippo, crocodile, buffalo and a large variety of antelope, and 101 species of bird have been recorded. Accommodation is in a luxury lodge (see Where to stay, page 167) or visit for a game drive/horse ride followed by a drink and light meal in the bar.

East of Plettenberg Bay → *For listings, see pages 161-180.*

The N2 continues east from Plettenberg Bay, but don't expect to travel too fast as there are a number of attractions and sights in rapid succession that are worth stopping for.

Keurbooms River Nature Reserve
ⓘ *On the east side of the Keurbooms River Bridge on the N2, 7 km east of Plett, T044-533 2125, www.capenature.co.za, 0800-1800, R40, children (2-13) R20, canoe hire R55 per day, if you just want to picnic next to the river at the reserve entrance near the bridge it's R5 per person.*
First up is the 750-ha Keurbooms River Nature Reserve. The headwaters of the Keurbooms River come from the Langkloof, north of the main Tsitsikamma mountain range. Its gorge is spectacular and well worth a voyage upstream to enjoy the unspoilt, unpolluted beauty. A variety of habitats are conserved, including the relatively unspoilt riverine gorge, patches of Knysna forest along the flood banks and in protected kloofs, coastal fynbos, and dune fields. The reserve is named after the Western Keurboom (*Virgilia oroboides*) or choice tree, which grows in the coastal forest edges. The environment attracts a number of birds; look out for the Knysna lourie, malachite and giant kingfisher, Narina trogon fish eagle, white-breasted cormorant and various sunbirds. You can hire canoes from the **Cape Nature office**, but taking a sailing trip upstream on the **Keurbooms River Ferry** (see What to do, page 177, for further details) is the best way to spend a few hours. You are ferried 5 km along the river through a spectacular gorge overhung by indigenous trees and other flora.

Monkeyland and Birds of Eden
ⓘ *The Crags, 16 km east of Plett, turn off at the signpost on the N2 at the Forest Hall turning, Monkeyland and Birds of Eden are a further 2 km down the road, T044-534 8906, www. monkeyland.co.za, www.birdsofeden.co.za, 0800-1700 (1800 in summer), 1-hr guided tours of Monkeyland depart every 30 mins, each attraction costs R150, children (3-12) R75; a combo ticket for both is R240, children R120.*
As the name suggests, **Monkeyland** is a primate reserve with lemurs, apes and monkeys from several continents where the animals are free to move about in the living indigenous forest. Most are rescued pets. Visitors are advised to join a guided tour which takes in various waterholes in the forest. Guides have a keen eye for spotting animals. One of the highlights here is the Indiana Jones-style rope bridge that spans 118 m across a canyon, offering glimpses of species that spend their entire lives in the upper reaches of the forest. The primates themselves also use this bridge (supposedly the longest of its kind in the southern hemisphere). If you don't wish to join a tour, the day centre has a good viewpoint and the restaurant serves a tasty lunch. Great for kids. **Birds of Eden** is a 2.3-ha mesh dome spanning more of the same forest with 2 km of walkways, 900 m of which is elevated, that go past waterfalls and dams. Along the same principal as Monkeyland, previously caged

birds have been released into a natural environment and visitors, who are permitted to wander around without a guide, can get a bird's eye view of macaws, cockatoos, parrots and louries.

The Elephant Sanctuary Plettenberg Bay

ⓘ *Directly adjacent to Monkeyland and Birds of Eden, T044-534 8145, www.elephantsanctuary. co.za, daily programmes start at 0800, 1000 and 1400, 'trunk-in-hand' R425, children (4-14) R195, elephant ride R435, children (8-14) R325.*

This offers a similar experience to the Knysna Elephant Park on the N2 west of Plettenberg Bay (page 151). Guests can interact with the six tame elephants and ride them. There is no need to book for the one-hour 'trunk-in-hand' option, when guides explain about elephant behaviour and you can feed and walk with them. This is followed by an optional 10-minute ride, but booking ahead for this is recommended in high season. There are other options to 'brush down' the elephants first thing in the morning or before they go to bed in their 'stables'; check the website for programmes, and there's luxury accommodation (**$$$**).

Tenikwa Wildlife Awareness Centre

ⓘ *Before Monkeyland and Birds of Eden take the signposted left road for 2 km, T044-534 8170, www.tenikwa.co.za, 1-hr Wildcat Experience; tours depart every 30 mins 0900-1630, R185 children (6-13) R95, under 6s free, bookings not required; 1½-hr Cheetah Walk; 0730 and 1630, R580 per person, no under 16s or under 1.5 m min height, booking essential.*

At the same turn-off to Monkeyland and Birds of Eden is this centre for orphaned, abandoned and injured wildlife, which it endeavours to rehabilitate and return to the wild whenever possible. Many of the animals are brought to the centre by **Cape Nature** from their protected reserves along the Garden Route, and when released are returned to these sites, while some are introduced back into the wild on some of the private game reserves in the Eastern Cape. In accordance with Cape Nature's regulations, the public cannot interact with any of the animals scheduled to be rereleased as this would reduce their chances of rehabilitation. But the centre has some resident species which can be viewed at close quarters. The one-hour **Wildcat Experience** starts with a visit to the educational centre before a short walk to meet servals, caracals, leopards, African wildcats, black-footed cats and cheetahs in enclosures. The **Cheetah Walk** takes visitors for a walk with two semi-tame cheetahs through large tracts of fynbos and indigenous forest at either sunrise or sunset when they are exercised. The experience lasts around 1½ hours and includes refreshments; it can be combined with the Wildcat Experience (at a discounted rate). Other animals on display include meerkats and tortoises, and birds such as marabou storks and blue cranes (South Africa's national bird). African penguins can be seen through glass in the penguin pool; many of them have been washed ashore by strong currents from colonies on the islands along the Garden Route, and after they are stabilized, they are returned to sea. There's a pleasant tea garden on site.

Nature's Valley

If you are in a hurry, stay on the N2 – this is a good stretch of road, although there is a toll of around R10. The more spectacular route is via the village of Nature's Valley along the old R102 that branches off the N2 just after The Crags, about 30 km east of Plettenberg Bay. This approach by road is particularly spectacular. The R102, dropping 223 m to sea level via the narrow Kalanderkloof Gorge, twists and turns through lush green coastal forest. Look out for ververt monkeys in the trees. At the bottom is a lagoon formed by the sand dunes blocking the estuary of the **Groot River**. A right turn leads into the village, which is surrounded on three sides by the western section of the **Garden Route National Park (Tsitsikamma Section)** (see below), and is made up of a collection of holiday cottages and the **Nature's Valley Restaurant & Trading Store**, an all-in-one shop, restaurant, bar, takeaway and **tourist information bureau** ① *T044-270 6833, www.natures-valley.com, 0830-1700.* Note that there are no banks in Nature's Valley. There are several braai spots on the sandy beach, but be warned that swimming in the sea is not safe. Canoes, rowing boats and yachts can all be used on the Groot River and lagoon, but powerboats are prohibited.

Groot River and Bloukrans Passes

As the road starts to climb out of the Groot Valley on the Groot River Pass, built in 1880 by Thomas Bain, it passes the **Nature's Valley Rest Camp** on the right. This is the only camp at the western end of the Garden Route National Park (Tsitsikamma Section) (see page 158 for booking details). Many visitors will find themselves here because it is one end of the Garden Route's most spectacular hiking trails, the **Otter Trail** (see box, page 159). From the top of the Groot River Pass the road continues for 6 km before crossing a second river valley, the Bloukrans Pass. Here it descends 183 m into the narrow gorge before crossing the river and climbing up again. The R102 rejoins the N2 highway 10 km further on and crosses the **Bloukrans Bridge**, built in 1984, 217 m above the Bloukrans River, and reputedly the highest single-span arch bridge in Africa. Just after the bridge is a turning to the left that leads to a viewpoint at the top of the Bloukrans Gorge.

The main reason for stopping here is the **Bloukrans Bungee Jump** ① *40 km from Plett, T042-281 1458, www.faceadrenalin.com, 0900-1700, booking not essential but recommended, bungee jump R750, which includes the bridge walk, bridge walk only R100, DVDs and T-shirts available.* At 216 m this is the highest commercial bungee in the world. The first rebound is longer than the previous holder of the record, the 111-m bungee jump at Victoria Falls. It's a hugely exhilarating experience and the free fall once you've leapt from the bridge lasts seven seconds, travelling over 170 kph before you reach the maximum length of the bungee cord. The minimum age is 14 and there is no upper age limit; a 96-year-old has previously jumped. If you cannot muster the courage to jump, you can go on a guided bridge walk, which involves walking out to the bungee platform along the caged walkway underneath the road surface of the bridge, where a guide tells you how the bridge was built and a little bit about the surrounding area. This is not for anyone who suffers from vertigo, but if you want to support a mate who's doing a jump, it's a great way to feel some of the fear they are experiencing when standing on the lip of the bungee platform. Also at the top of the gorge is the **Tsitsikamma Forest Village Market**, a sustainable initiative to help local people make and sell curios to the many passing tourists. Shops are in a collection of attractive reed Khosian huts, and you can buy items such as candles or home-made paper.

Garden Route National Park (Tsitsikamma Section) → *For listings, see pages 161-180.*

Tsitsikamma is a khoi word meaning 'place of abundant or sparkling water', and this section of the Garden Route National Park consists of a beautiful 80-km stretch of lush coastal forest between Nature's Valley and Ouobosstrand. At the western end, where the Otter Trail (see box, page 159) reaches the Groot River estuary, the park boundary extends 3 km inland, but for most of its length it is no more than 500 m wide, though the park boundaries reach out to sea for more than 5 km in parts. The main administrative office is at Storms River Mouth Rest Camp, which is almost the midpoint of the park.

Arriving in the Garden Route National Park

Getting there The Tsitsikamma Section is 68 km from Plettenberg Bay and 195 km from Nelson Mandela Bay (Port Elizabeth). There are two access points into the park depending on which rest camp you are staying in, although day visitors generally enter through the Storms River Mouth entrance, where there are better facilities for those on day trips. The turn-off for **Storms River Mouth Rest Camp** is on a straight stretch of the N2, about 20 km after Bloukrans Bridge, and 4 km before the Storms River Village. A surfaced road leads down to the reception centre on the coast. The last part of this drive is a beautiful, steep descent through lush rainforest, a marked contrast to the coniferous plantations along the N2 toll road.

The **Nature's Valley Rest Camp** is 40 km west of Storms River Mouth and can only be reached from the R102; when approaching from Knysna take the Nature's Valley turning at Kurland (R102). If you miss this turning you cannot turn off the N2 toll road until it meets with the other end of the R102, at which point you are only 8 km from the turning for Storms River Camp. When approaching from Port Elizabeth look out for signs for Nature's Valley, R102. Nature's Valley Rest Camp is clearly signposted 3 km outside the village of the same name.

Best time to visit The best time to visit is between November and February. Bear in mind that, although this is midsummer, you can expect rain at any time. Annual rainfall is in excess of 1200 mm; June and July are the driest months, while May and October are the wettest.

Park information Gates 0600-1930, office 0730-1800, overnight visitors arriving after 1800 should arrange to pick up keys from the gate, T042-281 1607, www.sanparks.org, R120, children (2-11) R60. At the Storms River Mouth Rest Camp there's a shop, 0800-1800, which stocks gift items as well as groceries, wine and beer, and a restaurant, 0730-2130, and other facilities include a swimming pool, and short boat trips on the *Spirit of Tsitsikamma*, which runs every 45 minutes, 0900-1600, and goes up the Storms River Gorge from the jetty below the suspension bridge.

Vegetation and wildlife

A cross-section of the coastlands would reveal the Tsitsikamma Mountains (900-1600 m), whose slopes level off into a coastal plain or plateau at about 230 m, and then the forested cliffs which plunge 230 m into the ocean. The slope is only precipitous in a few places; elsewhere along the coast it is still very steep, but there is enough soil to support the rainforest which the park was in part created to protect. The rainforest is the last remnant of a forest which was once found right along this coast between the ocean and the mountains. The canopy ranges between 18 m and 30 m and is closed, which makes the paths nice and shady. The most common species of tree are milkwood, real yellowwood, stinkwood, Cape blackwood, forest elder, white pear and candlewood, plus the famous Outeniqua yellowwood, a forest giant. All are magnificent trees which combine with climbers such as wild grape, red saffron and milky rope to create an outstandingly beautiful forest.

Otter Trail

This is one of South Africa's best hiking trails, managed by **South African National Parks (SANParks)**, T012-426 5111, www.sanparks.org. The 42.5-km, five-day/four-night trail, marked with painted otter footprints and named after the Cape clawless otter that occurs in the region, runs between Storms River Mouth and Nature's Valley in the Tsitsikamma Section of the Garden Route National Park. Only 12 people can start the trail each day and groups must consist of a minimum of four, no under 12s and anyone over 65 needs a doctor's certificate to confirm fitness level. It costs R860 per person, which includes four nights in the hiking huts as well as the permit. Due to its popularity, bookings are open up to 13 months in advance.

None of the sectors is that long, but it is still fairly strenuous in parts since you have to cross 11 rivers and there are steep ascents and descents at each river crossing. The Bloukrans River crossing presents the most problems. Check tide tables; you will at least have to wade, or even swim across. Waterproofing for your rucksack is vital. If you are unable to cross the river, you can take the escape route, which branches to the right of the trail, where it climbs steeply to the top of the plateau and leads to the N2. At each overnight stop there are two log huts, each sleeping six people in bunk beds; mattresses and firewood are provided. Each hut has a braai place with a sturdy steel grill but hikers need to provide their own pots for cooking. There are numerous streams and springs throughout the length of the Otter Trail that are suitable for drinking. However, it may be wise to use purification tablets.

The trail traverses some spectacular landscape and never strays far from the coastline. Vegetation varies from fynbos plateaux to densely forested valleys and in parts goes along rocky cliffs and boulder-strewn beaches. Apart from the natural beauty and the birdlife, the trail passes some fine waterfalls and Strandloper caves. Look out for the fine old hardwood trees which have escaped the dreaded axe, and in spring, an abundance of wild flowers.

The mammal species that live in the park include caracal, bushbuck, blue duiker, grysbok, bushpig and the Cape clawless otter, but given the steep slopes and dense forest, sightings are very rare. Birdwatching, however, is very rewarding, and over 220 bird species have been identified. The most colourful bird in the forest is the Knysna lourie (*Tauraco corythaix*). Its call is a korr korr korr, and in flight it has a flash of deep red in its wings, with a green body and distinctive crest. In the vicinity of the Storms River and Groot River estuaries you will see an entirely different selection of birds: over 40 species of seabird have been recorded here. The most satisfying sighting is the rare African black oystercatcher, with its black plumage and red eyes, beak and legs.

Hiking in the park

There are four different trails in the vicinity of the Storms River Mouth Rest Camp. The most popular is a 1-km walk along a raised boardwalk from the restaurant to the mouth of the Storms River. The last part of the walk involves a steep descent – there is a solid handrail, but the wooden steps can be slippery after rains, as can other parts of the walk. At the bottom is the suspension bridge which appears in many pictures promoting the Garden Route. The views from this point are excellent, especially at midday when there is a clear view of the narrow river gorge extending back inland. The path continues on the other side of the bridge, and from here you can climb the hill for superb views; there are over 300 steps and the path is narrow and steep. Look out for identification labels on the trees as the path winds through the forest. This is a great opportunity to see the trees which a century ago were in great demand for household furniture and building projects – much of the reason for the extensive deforestation in the area. Allow at least an hour for the walk to the bridge and back.

The other trails close to the camp are the **Lourie Trail**, 1 km through the forested slopes behind the camp; the **Blue Duiker Trail**, 3.7 km further into the forest; and the **Waterfall Trail**, a 3-km walk along the first part of the Otter Trail (see box, page 159); hikers without a permit have to turn back at the waterfall.

In addition to the Otter Trail managed by SANParks is the **Dolphin Trail** ① *information and reservations T042-280 3588, www.dolphintrail.co.za*, a three-day guided trail to the east of Storms River Rest Camp. This is a far more upmarket hike – luggage is transported from one night stop to the next, accommodation is in luxurious lodges, all meals are included (pre-packed picnics for lunch), and the hike is professionally guided. This trail is R4990 per person for three days (no children under 12). For those without transport, transfer shuttles can be arranged from George or Port Elizabeth.

Storms River Village

Surrounded by the **Tsitsikamma Forest,** Storms River Village is 23 km from Bloukrans and 4 km east from the entrance to the Garden Route National Park (Tsitsikamma Section) and 1 km south of the N2. Administratively, this is the first settlement in the Eastern Cape Province, but it is also regarded as the first and last town along the Garden Route, hence its inclusion here. This small village of around 40 houses, some of them restored historical woodcutters cottages, has several accommodation options catering for visitors to the park and hikers wishing to head for the inland mountains. It's also a stop-off for the **Baz Bus** and the starting point for many of the adventure activities in the region. The small supermarket and liquor store are useful for those self-catering at Tsitsikamma. Note that the village is nowhere near the sea and is not to be confused with Storms River Mouth which is in the park. Another 5 km east of the village along the N2 is the Total Petroport **Tsitsikamma** next to the 120-m high bridge that spans the Storms River Gorge (again inland from the actual river mouth). A service station has been here since the bridge was built in 1956, and it remains a popular stopover with petrol pumps, curio shops, a restaurant and takeaways, and there's a viewing platform to look down into the river gorge. It's also an official stop for the mainline buses that travel along the Garden Route. From the Total Petroport, the N2 continues for another 165 km to Nelson Mandela Bay (Port Elizabeth).

Garden Route listings

For hotel and restaurant price codes and other relevant information, see pages 10-13.

Where to stay

East to Caledon *p133*

$$ Houw Hoek Inn, off N2 12 km past Grabouw, T021-284 9646, www.houwhoek inn.co.za. The oldest licensed hotel in South Africa on the site of Dutch East India Company toll gate; the oldest section dates from 1779, the upstairs was built in 1860, while there's a newer block of modern rooms. 50 rooms, restaurant in a converted farm building, and lovely gardens with pool dominated by large old oak and blue gum trees.

$$ Old MacDaddy, off N2 5 km after Grabouw, on the right and then 8 km on a gravel road, T021-844 0241, www.oldmac daddy.co.za. The rural retreat of the artistic hotels, **Grand Daddy**, and **Daddy Long Legs**, on Long St in Cape Town (see pages 51 and 52). Like the **Grand Daddy**, this also has a collection of 10 vintage Airstream trailers to sleep in with interiors themed and designed by an artist but in a farm environment in the Elgin Valley. Communal barn area with restaurant, bar, lounge with fireplace, pool and deck.

Caledon *p133*

$$$-$$ The Caledon Hotel, Spa & Casino, 1 Nerina Av, T028-214 5100, www.the caledoncasino.co.za, 1 km out of town just off the N2. Unattractive modern complex with 95 a/c rooms but with a good range of facilities based around the hot springs (see page 133). Flashy casino, 3 restaurants, pub, extensive gardens, a spa, and horse riding.

Swellendam *p133*

$$$ De Kloof, 8 Weltevreden St, T028-514 1303, www.dekloof.co.za. Elegant thatched Cape Dutch homestead (1801), 7 doubles and 1 family suite with contemporary African and Asian decor, bar and lounge

with fireplace, 12-m swimming pool, champagne breakfasts included and evening meals on request.

$$$ Shoone Oordt Country House, 1 Swellengrebel St, T028-514 1248, www. schooneoordt.co.za. A striking Victorian manor house with lattice balconies surrounded by landscaped gardens with pool, 10 rooms decorated with antiques, some with claw-foot baths and 4-poster beds, lovely conservatory restaurant serving 4-course dinners.

$$ Old Mill Guest House, 241 and 243 Voortrek St, T028-514 2790, www.oldmill. co.za. A beautiful listed building in a spacious garden with a stream flowing through, 6 characterful rooms set in outbuildings such as the old watermill, superb meals served in the restaurant.

$ Swellendam Backpackers, 5 Lichtenstein St, T028-514 2648, www.swellendam backpackers.co.za. Popular hostel with a dorm in the main house, plus individual double or triple Wendy houses in secluded corners around the garden, lots of camping space, internet, kitchen, home-cooked meals. Can arrange local tours, hiking in the mountains and visits to the nearby Bontebok National Park. **Baz Bus** stop.

Bontebok National Park *p135*

$$ Lang Elsie's Kraal Rest Camp, reservations through SANParks, T012-428 9111, www.sanparks.org. For cancellations and bookings under 72 hrs, and campsite reservations, contact reception, T028-514 2735. Pleasant location next to the Breede River, 10 self-catering chalets sleeping 4, 2 of which are wheelchair accessible, good views of the Langeberg Mountains from the outside terraces. Shady camping and caravan sites (**$**) along the river, some with electric points. Shop at reception sells snacks and drinks but stock up on fresh food in Swellendam.

Albertinia *p135*

$$$$-$$$ Garden Route Game Lodge
(see page 135), 7 km east of Albertinia off
the N2, T028-735 1200, www.grgamelodge.
co.za. Accommodation in main lodge or in
secluded thatched chalets, decorated with
an African theme, restaurant and bar with
wooden decks, spa, swimming pool, special
activities for children. Rates include game
drives and meals and transfers from Cape
Town can be arranged.

Mossel Bay *p137, map p137*

$$$ Diaz Strand, Santos Beach, T044-692
8400, www.diazbeach.co.za. Luxury hotel
in a commanding position on Santos
Beach overlooking the waves, 86 spacious
rooms, all with balconies and ocean views.
Facilities include outdoor rim-flow pool,
indoor heated pool and spa, a water theme
park with tubes and a lazy river, the Bahia
Dos Vaqueiros restaurant (see Restaurants,
page 168), a pizzeria and cocktail bar.
$$$ The Point, Point Rd, T044-691
3512, www.pointhotel.co.za. Large, ugly
construction but in an unbeatable location,
right on the rocks below the lighthouse.
All 52 rooms have sea views and balconies,
but could do with a refurb. The Lighthouse
restaurant and bar caters for most. The rock
pool just outside is good for swimming.
$$$-$$ Protea Hotel Mossel Bay, corner of
Church and Market St, T044-691 3738, www.
oldposttree.co.za, www.proteahotels.com.
This is part of the museum complex and
was formerly known as the Old Post Office
Tree Manor, with 31 comfortable rooms
in a smart manor house dating to 1846,
making it the third-oldest building in Mossel
Bay. Meals at Café Gannet, see Restaurants,
page 169, with views across the bay, small
swimming pool.
$$ 1 Point Village Guest House, Bland St
East, T044-690 7792, www.pointguesthouse.
co.za. Good location near the Point, neat
guesthouse with 7 rooms, some with
sea views, individually decorated in fresh
colours. Heated swimming pool in courtyard,

generous breakfasts, also rents out good-
value self-catering holiday cottages nearby.
$ Mossel Bay Backpackers, 1 Marsh St,
T044-691 3182, www.mosselbayhostel.co.za.
Dorms and doubles, breakfasts and dinners
available, kitchen, pool, convenient location
300 m from the beach and close to some
bars, travel centre can organize activities,
such as shark-cage diving. Baz Bus stop.
$ Santos Express Train Lodge, Santos
Beach, T044-691 1995, www.santosexpress.
co.za. A string of 5 train carriages set
30 m from the sea, with tiny but cheap
cabins sleeping 2-4 on bunks, shared hot
showers, sun deck and an onboard pub and
restaurant serving seafood, spit-roasts and
braais. Baz Bus stop.

Botlierskop Private Game Reserve
p138

$$$$ Botlierskop Private Game Reserve,
T044-696 6055, www.botlierskop.co.za.
19 luxury tented suites on wooden
platforms, good views over river and
mountains, some have private jetties
for fishing, decorated in a colonial theme
with 4-poster beds swathed in mosquito
nets. Rates include game drives, walks and
all meals.

George and around *p138*

$$$$ Fancourt Hotel and Country Club,
R404, 6 km north of George airport, T044-
804 0010, www.fancourt.com. An upmarket
resort and one of the world's leading golf
destinations, set on 500 ha, with 4 18-hole
golf courses, 2 of which were designed by
Gary Player. There are 150 rooms in the
19th-century manor house or garden
suites, spa, gym, tennis courts, 2 outdoor
pools, 1 indoor heated pool, and 3 superb
restaurants. Rates drop significantly in low
season (1 Apr-31 Aug).
$$ Oakhurst Hotel, corner of Meade and
Cathedral streets, T044-874 7130, www.
oakhursthotel.co.za. Centrally located
quality town inn in the design of a classic
Cape Dutch house with thatched roof,

25 smart, individually decorated rooms, large restaurant, lounge, bar and pool.

$$ Protea Hotel King George, King George Drive, T044-874 7659, www.proteahotels. com. Smart country hotel situated close to George Golf Course, with 109 comfortable a/c rooms set in a mock Victorian villa, some with balconies. Good **Fairway Restaurant** and wood-panelled **Rex Tavern** pub, 2 swimming pools in spacious grounds.

$ Outeniqua Backpackers, 115 Merriman St, T082-216 7720, www.outeniqua-backpackers.com. Good set up with dorms and doubles, braai area, breakfasts, DSTV and Wi-Fi. Rents out bikes and they'll drop you off at the top of Montagu Pass for the 15-km ride back down. **Baz Bus** stop and free pickups from George Airport.

Victoria Bay *p140*
$$-$ Sea Breeze, 300-m walk to the beach, T044-889 0098, www.seabreezecabanas. co.za. Modern development of 36 bright and airy self-catering 2- to 4-bed flats and chalets with DSTV and braai. The beach has a safe tidal pool, good for families.

Oudtshoorn *p140, map p141*
$$$ Queen's Hotel, 5 Baron van Rheede St, T044-272 2101, www.queenshotel.co.za. Elegant and historic central hotel (1880) next to the CP Nel Museum, with 40 a/c stylish and comfortable rooms, impressive marble foyer, excellent restaurant, café and deli (see Restaurants, page 170), bar, pool in courtyard.

$$$ Rosenhof Country House, 264 Baron van Rheede St, T044-272 2232, www. rosenhof.co.za. Victorian house (1852) with 12 a/c upmarket rooms, 2 suites have their own splash pools, beautiful rose garden, spa, gym, pool, fine food in the restaurant, pub, and cosy lounge with fireplaces decorated with valuable artwork.

$$ Protea Hotel Riempie Estate, Baron van Rheede St, 3 km north of town, T044-272 6161, www.proteahotels.com. Well-run Protea with easy access to the ostrich farms

on the R328. 29 a/c rooms in comfortable thatched rondavels opening up to the mature shady gardens, the restaurant offers tasty country cuisine, swimming pool.

$$ Turnberry Boutique Hotel, 130 St John St, T044-279 3268, www.turnberryhotel. co.za. Centrally located town hotel with 21 neat rooms, restaurant with outside patio, friendly tavern-style pub that's a focal point in town, and a courtyard splash pool. Short walk to sights on Baron von Rheede St.

$$-$ Karoo Soul, 1 Adderley St, T044-272 0330, www.karoosoul.com. Good-value budget lodge set in a mock-Tudor house with wide veranda and good views across town, doubles/twins, dorms and camping plus separate self-catering cottages sleeping 4, thatched bar, meals available. A peaceful option for families.

$ Backpacker's Paradise, 148 Baron van Rheede St, T044-272 3436, www.back packersparadise.hostel.com. Well-run lodge set over 4 houses, mix of dorms and en suite doubles, camping, volleyball court, kitchen, pub with pool table, nightly ostrich braais, splash pool, Wi-Fi, within walking distance of shops, free pickup from the Baz Bus in George. Plenty of activities can be organized from here including bike hire (see page 176).

Around Oudtshoorn *p143*
$$$ Altes Landhaus, 13 km north of Oudtshoorn towards the Cango Caves, T044-272 6112, www.alteslandhaus.co.za. Award-winning guesthouse in a Cape Dutch homestead that used to be a rectory, 10 spacious rooms, each has its own special character, evening meals with fine wines, salt pool in garden with pool bar.

$$ Oue Werf, 13 km north of Oudtshoorn off the road to Cango Caves, T044-272 8712, www.ouewerf.co.za. Old 1857 homestead with 13 comfortable B&B rooms in the farm house or in cottages decorated with antiques, and some have original reed ceilings. Pleasant gardens with pool and the **Orchard Deli and Coffee Shop** (Tue-Sun,

0800-1600) which also offers 4-course evening meals on request.

Wilderness and around *p144*

$$$ Dolphin Dunes, Buxton Close, approaching from George, turn right off the N2, 2.5 km after the Caltex petrol station T044-877 0204, www.dolphindunes.co.za. A fine upmarket purpose-built guesthouse with 9 tasteful rooms with ocean views, minibar and DSTV, some with wheelchair access, splash pool, private access to the beach on a boardwalk.

$$ Fairy Knowe, Dumbleton Rd, T044-877 1100, www.fairyknowe.co.za. A historic old hotel with 42 riverside rooms, recently refurbished, in a beautiful and peaceful forested location on the Touw River. Birdwatchers will enjoy regular visits from the Knysna lourie and there are a couple of resident Cape spotted eagle owls. Restaurant and bar with wooden deck, tennis courts, pool, and canoes and mountain bikes can be hired.

$$ Moontide Guest Lodge, Southside Rd, T044-877 0361, www.moontide.co.za. Award-winning guesthouse set under milkwood trees in a beautiful and tranquil garden right on the edge of the lagoon, with 8 delightful thatched cottages, one of them a honeymoon suite, each with tasteful decor with kilims and fine furniture. Easy access to the hiking trails in the national park, a short walk from the beach and a good spot for birdwatchers.

$$ Palms Wilderness Retreat, Waterside Rd, T044-877 1420, www.palms-wilderness. com. Thatched guesthouse with 11 spacious a/c rooms, lounge and bar, spa, swimming pool in intriguing garden with nooks and crannies under milkwood trees that are full of birds, gallery selling some carefully chosen African artifacts.

$ Fairy Knowe Backpackers, Dumbleton Rd, just off Waterside Rd, T044-877 1285, www.wildernessbackpackers.com. A great set-up in a farmhouse dating to 1874 with tight staircases and creaking wooden floors

surrounded by gardens, spotless dorms and doubles, camping space, bar, great breakfasts, nightly camp fires and braais. Can organize all activities. A very relaxing place to rest up for a few days. Baz Bus stops here.

Garden Route National Park (Wilderness Section) *p145*

$$-$ Ebb and Flow, turn right in the village to reception, reservations through SANParks, T012-428 9111, www.sanparks.org, for reservations under 72 hrs or cancellations contact the park reception directly, T044-877 1197. Accommodation is laid out in 2 camps (North and South) divided by the railway and the Touw River. Both have self-catering units sleeping up to 4 in cottages, log cabins, or cheaper forest cabins with shared kitchens, some with views of the river and reed beds. The nearest shop is in the village. **Camping** Both campsites are in beautiful locations on the banks of the river and have plenty of grass and shade, wash block, no communal kitchen but braais, some sites have electric points.

Sedgefield and around *p146*

$$$ Lake Pleasant, east of Sedgefield on the edge of Groenvlei, follow the Buffalo Bay signs from the N2, T044-349 2400, www. lakepleasantliving.co.za. Comfortable country hotel set right on the lake, 36 rooms opening onto gardens, cigar bar, restaurant, pool, tennis court, gym and spa. Rowing boats for hire and hides by the lake for birdwatching. **$$ Lake Pleasant Chalets and Lodges**, follow the Buffalo Bay signs from the N2, T044-343 1985, www.lake-pleasant.co.za. Self-catering timber chalets sleeping 2-6, with plenty of shade from milkwood trees. Peaceful location overlooking the lake, swimming pool, pub/restaurant, rents out mountain bikes, canoes and fishing tackle. **$$ Sedgefield Arms**, 3 Pelican Lane, off the N2 in the village centre, T044-343 1417, www.sedgefieldarms.co.za. Mix of self-catering cottages suitable for 2-6 people with patio and braai, or B&B. Attached restaurant and lively English theme pub, good spot for lunch on the lawn, pool, all set in leafy gardens.

Goukamma Nature Reserve p146
For reservations, T021-659 3500, www.capenature.org.za.
$$ There are 4 very comfortable self-catering houses, each sleeping 4, dotted around the reserve, plus the **Muvubu Bushcamp** which is a thatched house hidden away in a milkwood forest sleeping up to 8. Each house has a kitchen and braai area and is a short walk from the lake, where you can swim and watch the sunset; canoes are available at each house.

Knysna and around p146, maps p147 and p149
For something different, and especially recommended for families, **self-catering houseboats ($$$)** are available for hire on the Knysna Lagoon. All eating and sleeping equipment is included, 'valet parking' and room service from local restaurants is on offer from the mooring on Thesen's Island, and you can hire fishing tackle. They are very easy to operate and allow you to explore the lagoon at leisure, and you do not need to have any nautical experience, though potential 'captains' need to go through a navigational briefing first.
Knysna Houseboats, 34 Long St, Thesen's Island, T044-382 2802, www.knysnahouseboats.com.
$$$$ Pezula Resort Hotel & Spa, Lagoon View Drive, T044-302 3410, www.pezularesort.com. The Garden Route's most prestigious luxury resort with 83 suites spread across the clifftop overlooking the ocean, Knysna Heads or championship golf course (see page 176). **Zachary's** for gourmet food, cigar, champagne and whisky bars, award-winning spa, indoor and outdoor heated pools, and numerous sporting facilities. A shuttle bus takes guests to nearby Noetzie Beach.

$$$$-$$$ Phantom Forest Eco-Reserve, 7 km from Knysna on Phantom Pass Rd, T044-386 0046, www.phantomforest.com. Ultra-stylish accommodation in 14 luxurious and eco-friendly 'tree suites' connected by walkways, set in the forest high above the lagoon. Each has private terrace and luxurious bathroom – the showers and double baths are open to the trees, excellent restaurant, bar, spa and stunning pool on the edge of a wooden deck. The perfect place to experience the Knysna forest.
$$$ Leisure Isle Boutique Lodge, 87 Bayswater Drive, Leisure Isle, T044-384 0462, www.leisureislelodge.co.za. Award-winning luxury guesthouse, 11 spacious rooms with all-white luxurious decor and views across the lagoon, heated pool, spa, superb food in the elegant restaurant, canoes and mountain bikes available.
$$$ Protea Hotel Knysna Quays, Knysna Quays, T044-382 5005, www.proteahotels. com. Large state-of-the-art hotel, with 123 comfortable a/c rooms, pay more for views over the lagoon, cocktail bar, heated swimming pool. Great location next to the Knysna Quays where hotel guests can sign for meals to be charged to their room account.
$$$ Rex Hotel, 8 Grey St, T044-302 5900, www.rexhotel.co.za. Super stylish in an architectural gem of a modern building, with 30 spacious luxury rooms, in muted browns and creams, with kitchenettes and balconies. Breakfast included and it's a short walk to restaurants in the Knysna Quays.
$$$ The Turbine Boutique Hotel & Spa, 36 Sawtooth Lane, Thesen's island, T044-302 5745, www.turbinehotel.co.za. Hip and quirky, this luxury boutique hotel is built around an old power station and its turbines and has fantastic art hanging throughout. The 25 rooms have all mod cons and designer contemporary furnishings, most with lagoon views, and there's a tapas restaurant, café/bar and rim-flow pool.
$$$-$$ Under Milkwood, at the end of George Rex Drive, T044-384 0745, www. milkwood.co.za. 16 self-catering log chalets

sleeping 2-6 at Knysna Heads set in a grove of milkwood trees, though not all have views of the lagoon. Also has comfortable B&B rooms in the main building. Dec-Jan rates take a significant hike, as they do elsewhere in Knysna.

$$ Yellowwood Lodge, 18 Handel St, T044-382 5906, www.yellowwoodlodge.co.za. Attractive guesthouse in one of Knysna's older houses built in 1897, with 10 rooms, the upstairs ones have relaxing balconies with views of the lagoon and Heads. Generous buffet breakfasts, and immaculate garden with swimming pool.

$$-$ Wayside Inn, 48 Main St, T044-382 6011, www.waysideinn.co.za. Simple, friendly and one of the cheapest B&Bs in Knysna in a cottage right in the centre of town, with 15 neat rooms. Breakfast is served rather quaintly through a hatch in the rooms or on the patio and there are restaurants close by.

$ Knysna Backpackers, 42 Queen St, T044-382 2554, www.knysnabackpackers. co.za. Large dorms and some doubles, TV room, well-stocked kitchen, all meals on request, travel centre, set in a large rambling Victorian mansion in established gardens with space for camping and views across the lagoon, an easy stroll from the town centre. Baz Bus stop.

Belvidere *p150, map p149*
$$$ Belvidere Manor, 169 Duthie Drive, Belvidere, T044-387 1055, www.belvidere. co.za. Quiet location with 38 self-catering 1- to 3-bed cottages arranged around a pool in shady gardens. The manor house, from 1834, houses the elegant dining room, and The Bell pub is in an old farm cottage where you can see the wine cellar through a glass floor.

Knysna Elephant Park *p151*
$$$ Elephant Lodge, T044-532 7732, www.knysnaelephantpark.co.za. 5 twin rooms and 1 large family flat sleeping 6 over the boma where the elephants sleep,

so you can fall asleep to their nightly sounds (and smells!), and see them when they are out and about. Modern and comfortable with DSTV, a spacious thatched lounge with large picture windows for viewing. Dinner on request.

Plettenberg Bay *p152, map p153*
$$$$ Hunter's Country House and Tsala Treetop Lodge, Hunter's Estate, off the N2, the turning is 10 km towards Knysna, which is another 22 km, reservations T044-501 1111, www.hunterhotels.com. Sharing the same property, these 2 exclusive luxury hotels are members of the **Relais & Chateaux group**. The **Country House** has 21 thatched cottages with fireplace, antique furnishings and private patios in gardens full of wild flowers, while **Tsala** has 10 stunning wooden and glass suites with outdoor showers and splash pools built 6 m above ground in the tree canopy, plus 6 additional family villas. Each has swimming pools, restaurants, bars and shops, and gourmet picnics on the estate can be arranged.

$$$$ The Plettenberg, 40 Church St, Lookout Rocks, T044-533 2030, www.
collectionmcgrath.com/plett. A **Relais & Chateaux** property and everything you would expect of an exclusive top-class, 5-star hotel. Located on a headland overlooking the bay with 37 luxury a/c rooms with contemporary decor, though you pay much more for sea views, superb food and wine, rim-flow pool and spa.

$$$ Beacon Island, Beacon Island Cres, T044-533 1120, www.tsogosunhotels.com. Dubbed 'BI' by holidaymakers from Johannesburg, a multi-storey building dominating the bay, right on the water between 2 beaches, with 200 rooms, and a full range of facilities including 3 excellent restaurants, pool, tennis courts and gym. A superb location but an eyesore on Plett's sweeping beach.

$$$ The Grand Café & Rooms, 27 Main St, T044-533 3301, www.thegrand.co.za. Small and chic boutique hotel on Plett's main street with good bay views from the terrace, 8 designer rooms with oversized beds and extras like DVD players. Bistro-style restaurant (see page 172), shop selling contemporary African-inspired decor items, small splash pool, no children under 16.

$$$ Plettenberg Park Hotel & Spa, follow Robberg Rd from town and turn left after Robberg Nature Reserve, T044-533 9067, www.plettenbergpark.co.za. In an outstanding location perched right on a cliff-edge between Robberg Nature Reserve and the airport, and set in 200 ha with a private lake and network of walking trails, 10 spacious suites, 25-m infinity pool, restaurant and spa. Great for whale- and birdwatching but access to the beach is down the steep cliff.

$$$-$$ The Robberg Beach Lodge, 89 Beachyhead Drive, T044-533 0369, www.therobberg.co.za. A set of 4 upmarket guesthouses – **Beachy Head Villa**, **Robberg House**, **Cottage Pie** and **Cordovan Villa** – offering 29 stylish rooms in total. Shared facilities include 2 swimming pools, 2 lounges and bars, a rooftop viewing deck, and all are no more than 100 m from Robberg Beach.

$$$-$$ Whalesong Hotel, Marine Drive, at the junction of the N2, T044-533 5389, www.legendlodges.co.za. Above the town centre but handy for a late stop on the N2 and with sweeping ocean views, 24 comfortable thatched rooms with wooden decks and African ethnic decor, restaurant, bar, pool with sundeck, spa, travel desk for booking activities and Xhosa craft shop.

$$ Stone Cottages, corner of Harker and Odland streets, T044-533 1331, www.stonecottage.co.za. Group of rustic self-catering restored 19th-century cottages sleeping 2-5, with high ceilings and gleaming wooden floors, antiques and old photographs, panoramic views of the ocean, deck with jacuzzi overlooking the main beach. A good option for families or friends travelling together.

$ Albergo For Backpackers, 6 and 8 Church St, T044-533 4434, www.albergo.co.za. Centrally located hostel in 2 houses with sea views. Dorms, double rooms and camping area, garden with hammocks and bonfires, 2 kitchens, travel centre, TV room, bar and pool table, surfboards for hire. **Baz Bus** stop.

Plettenberg Bay Game Reserve *p154*
$$$ Baroness Safari Lodge, see page 154. Set in a restored homestead built in 1822, 10 spacious suites with verandas, antiques, 4-poster beds, and free-standing bathtubs with bush views, lounge and library, outside boma with fire, bar with a deck overlooking a waterhole, pool. Rates include meals and 1 game drive or horse ride.

East of Plettenberg Bay *p155*
$$$$ Hog Hollow Country Lodge, 18 km east of Plettenberg Bay at The Crags off the N2, T044-534 8879, www.hog-hollow. com. Set in a private nature reserve, with 15 suites, each with its own wooden deck with hammock overlooking the Matjies River gorge and Tsitsikamma Mountains. Good evening meals, swimming pool with stunning views, library/lounge, plenty of walks which are ideal for birdwatching,

$$$$-$$$ Kurland Hotel, 19 km east of Plettenberg Bay at The Crags off the N2, T044-534 8082, www.kurland.co.za. Set in expansive 1700-ha grounds, famous for its polo fields, with 12 Cape Dutch-style cottages, some with loft rooms for children, excellent food and wine, pool and spa, horse riding and quad-biking. Luxurious but family friendly with nannies and kids' activities.

$$ Forever Resorts Plettenberg, 6 km east of Plett on the Keurbooms River, T044-535 9309, www.foreverplettenberg.co.za. 30 neat self-catering chalets nestled along the riverbank, plus 112 camping and caravan spots (**$**) with excellent facilities, swimming pool, canoes and pedalos for hire, good all-round family option but gets busy during school holidays.

Nature's Valley *p156*

$$$-$$ Tranquility Lodge, 130 St Michaels Av, next to the Nature's Valley shop and pub, T044-531 6663, www.tranquilitylodge.co.za. Lovely reed-and-timber lodge in pretty gardens, 7 rooms with fireplaces, nicely decorated throughout with lots of lounging areas, good food, splash pool, each room gets its own double kayak to explore the lagoon and picnics can be arranged.

$$ Lily Pond Country Lodge, on the R102 3 km from the turn-off on the N2, T044-534 8767, www.lilypond.co.za. Set in 12 ha of lovely indigenous forest. 10 modern rooms with small patios, dining deck, and a jacuzzi and stunning black rim-flow pool surrounded by (as the name suggests) beautiful lily ponds which attract birds and butterflies.

**Garden Route National Park
(Tsitsikamma Section)** *p157*

Reservations, through **SANParks**, T012-428 9111, www.sanparks.org, for cancellations and reservations under 72 hrs contact **Storms River Mouth Rest Camp** directly, T042-281 1607.

$$-$ Storms River Mouth Rest Camp, off the N2 between the Storms River Bridge and Storms River village. This is the main camp on a narrow strip of land between the ocean and forested hills, and is one of the most beautiful settings of all the national parks. It's a real thrill to watch the waves crashing on the rocks right in front of you but it is exposed when the wind blows. There are a number of wooden fully equipped self-catering chalets sleeping up to 6, and basic forest cabins sleeping 2 and sharing communal kitchen and ablutions with campers. Swimming pool, shop selling some groceries and restaurant.

$ Nature's Valley Rest Camp, 40 km west of Storms River Mouth Rest Camp and accessed from the village of Nature's Valley. Set in an indigenous forest on the banks of the Groot River, with simple forest huts with 2 beds and electricity and campsites. Both of these share the wash block, but there's

no shop or restaurant, all supplies can be bought in Nature's Valley village, 3 km away.

Storms River Village *p160*

$$$-$$ Tsitsikamma Lodge, 2 km east of village along the N2, T042-280 3802, www.riverhotels.co.za/tsitsikamma. Country resort set in forested grounds with 32 log cabins, each with spa bath (perfect after a long hike) and braais, some with fireplaces and extra lofts for children. Restaurant serving buffet breakfasts and dinners, packed lunches available, swimming pool, can arrange transport to the start and from the end of the Otter Trail (see page 159).

$$ Tsitsikamma Village Inn, Darnell St, T042-281 1711, www.tsitsikammahotel. co.za. Central original Cape Dutch home-stead dating from 1845 with 49 rooms in the gardens in recreated colonial-style buildings; terraced Georgian cottages, woodcutter's log cabins, or a Drostdy (magistrate's house), for example. All have comfortable furnishings, many with brass beds and private stoeps. Good restaurant and the **Hunter's Pub** is the focal point of the village.

$ Tube 'n Axe, corner of Darnell and Saffron streets, T042-281 1757, www.tubenaxe. co.za. 4-bed dorms, doubles and 5 A-frame log cabins sleeping up to 4, set in a forested garden with plenty of room for camping and overland vehicles. The rustic bar has a pool table and braai pit. Breakfast and dinner available or self-catering kitchen. Shuttles to the Bloukrans Bridge Bungee, they rent out quad bikes and mountain bikes, and operate the popular **Blackwater Tubing** (see page 178). **Baz Bus** stop.

🍴 Restaurants

East to Caledon *p133*

$ Dassiesfontein, on the N2 halfway between Bot River and Caledon, T028-214 1475, www.dassies.co.za. Open 0830-1730. Country restaurant and farm stall selling home-made bread (they grind their own flour), cheese and biltong, tables in cottage decorated with antiques, local dishes such as bobotie and bredie, buffet lunch on Sun.

Swellendam *p133*

$$$ Herberg Roosjie van de Kaap, 5 Drostdy St, T028-514 3001, www.roosjevandekaap.com. Tue-Sun 1900-2130. Opposite the Old Drostdy and Swellendam's original inn, with cosy atmosphere in a candlelit room with thick walls and a low reed ceiling, superb gourmet South African fare, steaks and seafood. Also has 12 comfortable B&B rooms (**$$**) around a pool.

$$ Koornlands, 5 Voortrek St, T028-514 3567, www.koornlandsrestaurant.co.za. Mon, Wed-Sun 1200-2200. A historic Cape Dutch cottage serving local food such as crocodile steaks, ostrich fillets, loin of kudu, guinea fowl and freshwater trout. Desserts include a delicious Cape brandy tart.

Cafés

La Belle Alliance, 1 Swellengrebel St, T028-514 2252. Open 0800-1700. Under the trees by the Koornlands River, the building used to be Swellendam's Masonic Lodge, giant breakfasts, good sandwiches, and afternoon tea with Belgian chocolate cake and lemon meringue pie.

Old Gaol, Church Sq, Drostdy Museum, T028-514 3847, www.oldgaolrestaurant.co.za. Breakfasts, light meals such as bobotie or chicken pie, hot soup in winter, home-made lemonade, and best known for *melktert* cooked in a copper pan over coals.

Mossel Bay *p137, map p137*

$$$ Bahia Dos Vaqueiros, Diaz Strand, see Where to stay, page 162. Open 0700-1030, 1900-2200, and Sun lunch 1230-1500. Dominated by a giant frieze on the ceiling of the Portuguese landing on the coast and sweeping ocean views, an upmarket spot with cigar bar, walk-in wine cellar and attentive service. Interesting combinations of taste such as smoked ostrich with ginger chutney or lobster with figs.

$$ Café Gannet, Bartolomeu Dias Museum Complex (page 137), Market St, T044-691 1885, www.cafegannet.co.za. Open 0700-2300. Well-established seafood restaurant, popular all year round since the tour buses stop here, also grills and wood-fired pizzas, bay views from the shady outdoor terrace.

$$ Café Havana, 38 Marsh St, T044-690 4640, www.cafehavana.co.za. Open 1200-2200. Cuban-inspired decor, quirky mirrors and mosaic tables, long tapas and cocktail menu, and unusual mains such as Cuban pork and bean stew or steak with rum and cream. The lively bar stays open until late.

$$ Kaai 4, Quay 4, at the harbour, T084-258 1713, www.kaai4.co.za. Open 1200-1500, 1830-2200, but phone ahead as it's weather dependent. Open-air restaurant concept that first become popular on the West Coast, with rustic tables in the sand or under canvas on the harbour wall, with an excellent range of traditional South African food such as potbread, *potjiekos*, fish braais, lamb on the spit, and koeksisters for dessert.

$$-$ Sea Gypsy Café, Quay 4, at the harbour, T044-690 5496, www.seagypsy.co.za. Open 0900-2200. Some red meat and poultry dishes, but the seafood has literally just been pulled out of the sea on the dockside. Good-value platters and combos and excellent hake and sole and chips, crayfish in season. The quirky wooden deck decorated with fishing nets and buoys is perfect for sundowners.

$ Pavilion, Santos Beach, T044-690 4567. Open 1000-2300. Historic seaside pavilion built in 1916 and the ideal spot for lunch, just stroll up straight from the beach onto the old wooden veranda and enjoy a light lunch while watching the boats in the bay.

George and around *p138*

As well as the town restaurants, **Fancourt Hotel and Country Club** (page 162) has several superb top-range restaurants open to non-guests.

$$$-$$ La Locanda, 124 York St, T044-874 7803, www.la-locanda.co.za. Mon-Fri 1100-

2200, Sat 1700-2200. Home-style cooking from Italian chefs who make their own pasta and cure their own cold meats, and there's a long menu of over 60 dishes using well-researched recipes from Italy. South African and Italian wine.

$$ Kafé Serefé, 60 Courtenay St, T044-8742046 www.kafeserefe.co.za. Mon-Fri 1130-2230, Sat 1800-2230. Elegant interiors with Persian rugs and Arabic lamps, this Turkish restaurant serves a range of mezzes, some melt-in-the mouth kebabs and aged steaks, and for breakfast, bacon and egg shwarmas. Diners are entertained by a belly dancer on Wed and Sat nights.

$$ Old Town House, corner of Market and York streets, T044-874 3663. Mon-Fri 1200-1500, Mon-Sat 1800-late. Housed in one of George's oldest buildings (1848), which was the original town meeting hall, local specialities include springbok shank and kudu steak, plus seafood and grills, and excellent home-made desserts.

Oudtshoorn p140, map p141
$$$ Colony, Queen's Hotel, see Where to stay, page 163. Open 1800-2300. Excellent restaurant set in this historic hotel, local dishes include Karoo lamb, springbok steak and ostrich. Balcony overlooking the main street, good service, crisp white linen and bar with fireplace.

$$$ Kalinka, 93 Baron van Rheede St, T044-279 2596, www.kalinka.co.za. Tue-Sun 1800-2200. Award-winning restaurant in a cosy sandstone townhouse with a clutch of small dining rooms or at candlelit tables in the conservatory, ostrich features but also other dishes with an unusual twist such as caviar pancakes or stuffed quail.

$$ Headlines, 45 Baron van Rheede St, T044-272 3434. Mon-Sat 0830-1500, 1745-2300, Sun 1100-1500. Restaurant specializing in ostrich dishes of all kinds from ostrich-egg omelettes to ostrich-liver pâté. The Bushmen kebab is a favourite, with ostrich, venison, crocodile, pork/beef fillet and chicken all on one skewer.

$$ Paljas, 109 Baron van Rheede St, T044-272 0982. Open 1600-2200. Pan-African cuisine, a good selection of Cape Malay curries, Karoo roasts, West Coast seafood, and a few unusual Zulu and Xhosa dishes, a good place to try a 3-course meal with a lot of different flavours and interesting African-style decor.

Cafés
Café Brûlée, Queen's Hotel, see Where to stay, page 163. Open 0700-1700. Airy and elegant café with outside tables among potted palms, serving breakfasts, delicious and beautifully presented cakes. Wed-Fri there is a lunchtime table buffet priced by weight, the deli sells freshly baked bread, olive oil, jams and cook books.

Cango Caves p144
$$-$ Cango Caves Restaurant, at the Cango Caves, T044-272 7313. Open 0900-1700. Caters for tour groups but surprisingly good food and has terrace tables with views of the Swartberg Mountains. Breakfasts, light lunches, teas, the menu has a distinctive ostrich flavour – burgers, kebabs, steaks, or try the ostrich potjie with ginger and wild herbs or ostrich tempura with noodles.

Wilderness and around p144
$$$-$$ The Girls Restaurant, 1 George St, next to the Caltex petrol station at the N2 turn-off, T044-877 1648, www.thegirls.co.za. Tue-Sun 1800-2200. A simple brick building, but surprisingly warm and inviting inside and owner/chefs Roxanne and Cheri entertain in the open kitchen. Dinner only and expect Knysna oysters, prawns cooked in more than a dozen ways, excellent steaks and curries, and inventive vegetarian dishes.

$$-$ Pomodoro, George St, T044-877 1403. Open 0730-2230. Traditional Italian trattoria (look out for the big red tomato signs) with generous portions of antipasto, pastas, grills and seafood, specials like venison and tuna, classic desserts. Also serves breakfasts and has outside tables among ferns.

$ Zucchini, at the Timberlake Organic Village (see Shopping, page 173), on the N2, 7 km from both Wilderness and Sedgefield, T044-882 1240, www.zucchini.co.za. Mon, Wed and Sun 1100-1700, Thu-Sat 1100-2100. Wooden cabin decorated with local art, sunny outside deck, serving tasty organic light meals such as gourmet salads and sandwiches using free-range beef and poultry, milk and dairy products from local farms and home-grown produce.

Knysna and around

p146, maps p147 and p149

$$$ Anchorage, 11 Grey St, T044-382 2230, www.anchoragerestaurant.co.za. Open 1830-late, from 1200 in season. Established old-style seafood restaurant for platters and oysters, plus aged Angus steaks and a good choice for vegetarians, all accompanied by fine wines and excellent draught Mitchell's beer (to visit the brewery, see page 150).

$$$-$$ Cruise Café, 400 m west of the Knysna Quays, T044-382 1693. Mon-Sat 0800-2300, Sun 0800-1700. Great views of fishing boats on the lagoon, best known for seafood, plus good breakfasts and simple lunches such as fish and chips; more sophisticated and pricier menu in the evening such as prawn and crab risotto or roast duck; long wine and cocktail list.

$$ 34' South, Knysna Quays, T044-382 7268, www.34-south.com. Open 0830-2330. Snacks and meals daily in a deli-style seafood restaurant, try the sushi, seafood platter or paella, make up a meal from the packed fridges or buy takeaway items, including cookbooks, wine and home-made goodies, laid-back sunny deck overlooking the quays.

$$ JJ's, Knysna Quays, T044-382 3359, www.jjsrestaurant.co.za. Tue-Sun 1130-1530, daily 1830-late. Another good option at the Quays, still plenty of seafood but also game meat including crocodile, ostrich and kudu, and there's impromptu singing from the Xhosa staff. Look out for the framed money collection on the wall, which includes a

Zimbabwe 100-trillion dollar note and a 50-year-old British fiver.

$$ Knysna Oyster Co, Thesen's Island, T044-382 6942, www.knysnaoysters.co.za. Open 1000-2100, closes 1700 in off-season. Next to the oyster farm that has been in operation since 1949. The seafood restaurant is perhaps the best place to try a dozen of Knysna's famous raw or cooked oysters washed down with a glass of champagne. It's one of Kynsna's must-dos.

$$-$ Raasoie, 1 Memorial Sq, Main St, T044-382 1444. Mon-Sat 1130-1500, 1700-2200. Decorated with strings of fairy lights and some outside tables on the deck, this serves top-notch Indian food cooked by chefs from Mumbai and dished up in traditional copper bowls. Expansive choice for vegetarians and sells Cobra beer.

$ Thai Kitchen, 4 Memorial Sq, Main St, T044-382 1396. Mon-Sat 1100-2130. Cheap and cheerful, order at the counter, but delicious and authentic dishes, and you can watch the furiously sizzling woks in the open kitchen. The Phad Thai and Tom Yum soup are exceptional. Not licensed but BYO.

Cafés

East Head Café, 25 George Rex Drive, T044-384 0933, www.eastheadcafe.co.za. Open 0800-1600. Simple shack perched above the crashing waves, and you couldn't get a better view of The Heads unless you were on the water. Breakfasts, gourmet burgers, fish and chips (the battered hake is excellent) and, if the mood takes, washed down with a Pimm's or Bloody Mary.

Ile de Pain Bread & Café, The Boatshed, Thesen's Island, T044-302 5707, www.iledepain.co.za. Tue-Sat 0800-1500, Sun 0900-1330. Superb bakery and café emitting lovely warm smells of freshly baked goodies, such as croissants and pastries; they start baking at 0200. Excellent spot for brunch or light lunch and the baby chocolate brownies are to die for. **Mon Petit Pain**, Mon-Fri 0730-1500, Sat 0730-1300, is another outlet on the corner of Gordon and Grey streets.

Belvidere *p150, map p149*
$$$-$$ O'Pescador, Brenton Rd, Belvidere, T044-386 0036. Mon-Sat 1830-2230. Long-established and popular Portuguese restaurant, traditional cosy decor, Mozambique prawns or try the spicy fish dishes, peri peri chicken or grilled sardines. Portuguese wines, brandy and port.

Plettenberg Bay *p152, map p153*
$$$ Zinzi at Tsala Treetop Lodge, see Where to stay, page 166. Open 1230-1430, 1730-2230. Excellent gourmet food served in exquisite interior-designed dining room featuring lizard-print fabrics, pewter chandeliers and giant suede sofas. Expect the likes of local venison and seafood, plus global dishes including Moroccan lamb, Persian chicken or Szechuan tuna. The cellar has more than 3000 wines to choose from. Pricey but recommended for special occasions.
$$$-$ Nguni, 6 Crescent St, T044-533 6710, www.nguni-restaurant.co.za. Mon-Fri 1000-2200, Sat 1800-2200. Set in one of the oldest houses in Plett decorated with Nguni (cow) hides and historical photos, with well-presented dishes of South African gourmet cuisine such as springbok carpaccio, rib-eye game steaks, Karoo lamb chops and seared tuna.
$$ Cornuti, 1 Perestrella St, T044-533 1277, www.cornuti.co.za. Open 1200-2200. Stylish pizza restaurant with whitewashed walls and high ceilings, and busy cocktail and wine bar with ocean views. Unusual pizza toppings include tuna, ginger and wasabi or strawberries and chocolate sauce, plus standard Italian dishes and good grilled fish.
$$-$ The Grand Café & Rooms (see Where to stay page166. Open 0730-2200. Restaurant at this boutique hotel with shabby-chic decor of mismatched furniture, candelabras and gilt mirrors and excellent sea views from the deck. Small but sophisticated menu including seafood, Durban-style (spicy) curries and gourmet burgers.
$$-$ The Lookout Deck, perched on the Lookout Rocks, T044-533 1379,

www.lookout.co.za. Open 0900-2300. Popular family restaurant, excellent seafood, soups, salads and steaks, also has a busy bar, lively, bustling atmosphere. Perfect location; from the terrace you can watch surfers share a wave with a dolphin.

Cafés
Le Fournil de Plett Bakery and Café, Lookout Centre, Main St, T044-533 1390. Mon-Sat 0800-1600, Sun 0800-1300. French-style café and bistro with tree-covered patio, serving excellent baguettes and croissants, breakfasts and light meals, including open sandwiches, quiches and filled vol-au-vents.

East of Plettenberg Bay *p155*
$ Bramon Wine Estate, N2 18 km from Plett, 2 km before The Crags, T044-534 8007, www.bramonwines.co.za. Open 1100-1700. Wine estate best known for producing a Cap Classique sparkling wine, with garden restaurant that has good views of the Tsitsikamma Mountains and is close to the animal attractions at The Crags and overlooks the Elephant Sanctuary. Wines can be tasted, served with mezzes of cold meats, cheeses, oysters and olives and home-made bread.

Cafés
Peppermill Café, N2, 20 km from Plett, just before the entrance to Monkeyland, T044-534 8997. Open 0800-1700. At the Mill Centre mohair factory, serving breakfasts, light meals, including ploughman's lunch, cakes and fruit smoothies. The shop sells mohair blankets, scarves and luxurious soft socks, and there are a few Angora goats that children can pet.
Thyme and Again, N2, opposite the Keurboom River turning, T044-535 9432, www.thyme-and-again.co.za. Open 0800-1600. Great farm stall with tables on a vine-covered stoep, serving breakfasts and a delicious selection of still-warm breads, pies and pastries. Try the home-made ginger beer.

🎵 Bars and clubs

Knysna and around
p146, maps p147 and p149
Bosun's Pub & Grill, George Rex Drive, T044-382 6276, www.bosuns.co.za. Mon-Sat 1100-late, Sun 1100-1600. English-style pub serving ales on tap from Mitchell's Brewery (page 150, including Bosun's Bitter (bitter is hard to come by in South Africa). Pub grub like traditional bangers and mash or liver and onions, and a roast lunch on Sun. Hosts regular quiz nights and is a favourite spot for watching rugby and football.
Zanzibar, 5 Mellville Centre, Main Rd, T044-382 0386 www.zanzibarknysna.com. Open 1900-0200, 1200-0200 in season. Set in a converted theatre, with terraces overlooking Main Rd, dance floor and pool tables, tribal decor, occasional DJs, comedy and live music, and upstairs is a quieter cocktail lounge.

🎭 Entertainment

Mossel Bay *p137, map p137*
Theatre
Barnyard Theatre, 7 km west of Mossel Bay off the N2, T044-698 1022, www.thebarnyard.co.za. A rustic country theatre showing comedy, tribute bands and live music, and guests sit at wooden tables around the stage. You order food or take a picnic.

🎉 Festivals

Knysna *p146, map p147*
Jul Knysna Oyster Festival, Knysna, www.oysterfestival.co.za. Oyster braais, oyster tasting, oyster-eating competitions and other molluscular activities; there's live entertainment and lots of sporting events – cycling, running, canoeing, downhill racing and sailing.
Apr Pink Loerie Mardi Gras, Knysna, www.pinkloerie.com. A gay festival with parade and 4 days of non-stop entertainment for anyone who enjoys a

party. Most of Cape Town's gay community gravitates to Knysna for the weekend.

🛍 Shopping

Mossel Bay *p146, map p137*
Arts and crafts
Craft Art Workshop, Market St, next to the tourist office, T044-691 1761. Mon-Fri 0900-1700, Sat 0900-1500. Sells African curios from all over the continent and you can watch artists at work.

Shopping malls
Mossel Bay Mall, Louis Fourie Rd, T044-693 0965, www.mosselbaaimall.co.za. Mon-Fri 0900-1800, Sat 0900-1700, Sun 0900-14. Has a full range of shops, including a Checkers supermarket.

George and around *p138*
Arts and crafts
Strydom Gallery, Marklaan Centre, 79 Market St, T044-874 4027, www.artaffair. co.za. Mon-Sat 0900-1700. Pieces for sale from a cross section of South African artists and sculptors, organizes delivery worldwide.

Shopping malls
Garden Route Mall, out of town on the junction with the N2, T044-887 0044, www.gardenroutemall.co.za. Mon-Fri 0900-1800, Sat 0900-1700, Sun 0900-1500. A 125-store mall with all the usual South African chain stores, restaurants, and a multi-screen Ster-Kinekor cinema.

Oudtshoorn *p140, map p141*
Baron van Rheede St is lined with curio shops selling every ostrich by-product imaginable, from expensive leather purses to feather dusters and tacky enamelled eggs.

Wilderness and around *p144*
Food and drink
Timberlake Organic Village, off the N2 midway between Wilderness and

Sedgefield, 7 km to both, www.timberlake organic.co.za. Open 0900-1700. A collection of charming wooden cabins including a deli, cheese, wine and health-food shops, a café (great for cheesecake and chocolate cup cakes), a shack selling oysters and other seafood snacks, and the Zucchini restaurant (see Restaurants, page 171). All produce is organic, locally sourced, and the vegetables are grown in the on-site garden. Children will enjoy the jungle gym and trampoline, and exploring the enchanting Fairy Garden.

Sedgefield and around p146
Arts and crafts
Scarab Art and Craft Village, on the N2 next to the Engen petrol station, T044-343 2455, www.scarabvillage.co.za. Open 0900-1700. Well worth a stop for the interesting craft shops and stalls including one that demonstrates making handmade paper, and refreshments at the Café François.

Knysna and around p146, maps p147 and 149
Arts and crafts
Keeping in tune with Knysna's reputation as a cultural arts and crafts centre are a number of galleries and craft shops. Check at the tourist office for special exhibitions. There is a good African craft market on the side of the road as you enter Knysna on the N2 from George, with an extensive range of carvings, baskets, drums and curios. There is also a cluster of expensive curio shops and a daily fleamarket at the Knysna Quays.
Birds of Africa, 24 Main Rd, Industria, T044-382 5660 www.birdsofafrica.co.za. Mon-Fri 0830-1630. Unusual hand-carved and hand-painted wooden birds from local yellowwood and Mopani trees (though only from those that have been removed after collapse) and you can watch the artists at work.
Bitou Craft, Woodmill Lane Centre, Main St, T044-382 3251. Mon-Fri 0900-1800, Sat 0900-1330, Sun in season. Sells local arts and crafts including paintings, ceramics, rugs and wooden toys and they spin and dye

their own wool. There's another branch at Knysna Quays.

Shopping malls
Woodmill Lane Centre, corner Main and Long streets, T044-382 3045, www.wood millane.co.za. Mon-Fri 0830-1700, Sat 0830-1400, Sun 0900-1300. Knysna's nicest shopping mall, this is built around a restored Victorian timber mill constructed in 1919, for Geo Parkes & Sons, a Birmingham tool manufacturer, who was the first exporter of Knysna wood to England for the making of bobbins for the Midlands textile industry. They also manufactured wagon parts and a variety of tool handles. Today the centre has 75 shops, fountains and trees in the squares, and regular performing artists and buskers. There are several boutiques and arts and crafts shops and a branch of Pick 'n' Pay supermarket.

Plettenberg Bay p152, map p153
Arts and crafts
Lookout Art Gallery, Lookout Centre, Main St, T044-533 2210, www.lookout-art-gallery.co.za. Mon-Fri 0900-1700, Sat 0900-1330. Established gallery with antiques and artwork from local artists including paintings, sculptures, glassware and ceramics, and they can arrange to ship overseas.
Old Nick Village, N2, 3 km east of Plett, T044-533 1395, www.oldnickvillage. co.za. 1000-1700. Group of galleries, craft workshops and studios, and a weaving museum with working antique looms, set in restored 19th-century farm buildings. The Old Nick Shop is housed in the former Gansvlei General Dealers Store which traded from the 1890s to the 1960s – when its main (black) customer base was moved out of Plett to new townships during Apartheid. This is a pleasant stop with a restaurant, coffee shop and bakery with outside table in the indigenous garden where vervet monkeys may be spotted in the yellowwood trees, and there's a jungle gym on the lawns for children.

Food and drink
The Heath Farm Store, N2, 7 km towards Knysna, T044-532 7724, www.theheath. co.za. Open 0830-1700. Another interesting diversion when driving along the N2, with a clutch of quality craft and decor shops, a pretty garden with a boules court and hammocks, a kids' jungle gym and merry-go-round, a farm shop for excellent home-made bakes, organic produce, pickles and preserves, and Jade's Café for great coffee and more substantial meals.

⊙ What to do

Swellendam *p133*
Canoeing
Felix Unite River Adventures, T021-670 1300, www.felixunite.co.za. Runs trips from Cape Town for canoeing on the Breede River, with overnight stays in bush camps, restored Voortrekker ox wagons, or A-frame houses.
Umkulu, T021-853 7952, www.umkulu.co.za. Another operator that will take you to the Breede River from Cape Town for a day's float, some wine tasting, and an overnight stay at a local lodge.

Golf
Swellendam Golf Course, Andrew Whyte St, T028-514 1026, www.swellendamgolf course.co.za. 9-hole 72-par course in the lee of the Langeberg Mountains with views across town.

Mossel Bay *p137, map p137*
Boat trip
Romonza, from Vincent Jetty at the harbour, T044-690 3101, www.mosselbay.co.za/ romonza. Runs daily pleasure cruises, the most popular being outings to Seal Island in the bay. 1-hr boat trips depart on the hour 1000-1600, R140, children (under 12) R50; 2-hr sunset cruise (Nov-Apr) R150, children (under 12) R70 and there's a cash bar. Romonza also offers the only licensed boat-based whale watching in Mossel Bay (Jun-Oct), 3 hrs, R625, children (under 12) R400.

Diving
Electro Dive, Quay 4 at the harbour, T082-561 1259, www.electrodive.co.za. Can organize equipment hire and boat charters and offers PADI courses. Close to Santos Beach are 4 recognized dive sites that can be reached from the shore, and the Windvogel Reef is 800 m off Cape St Blaize.
White Shark Africa, Quay 4 at the harbour, T044-691 3796, www.whitesharkafrica.com. Offers cage diving and snorkelling in pursuit of a great white shark on a 15-m catamaran aptly named *Shark Warrior*. The trip costs R1350 and is 4-5 hrs long and includes lunch and drinks.

Fishing
Mossel Bay Deep Sea Adventures, Quay 4 at the harbour, T083-260 2222, www.deep seaadventures.co.za. Full- or half-day deep-sea fishing charters including all equipment, can take children from 8.

Surfing
Billeon, T044-691 3811, www.billeon.com. Offers 2-hr surfing lessons at The Point from R300 and rents out boards to experienced surfers.

George and around *p138*
Golf
Fancourt Hotel and Country Club, R404, 6 km north of George Airport, T044-804 0030, www.fancourt.com. 4 gold courses including the par 71, 5935-m, championship links course designed by Gary Player. The President's Cup was played here in 2003.
George Golf Club, Langenhoven St, T044-873 6116, www.georgegolfclub.co.za. Par 72, 18 holes, 5852-m course surrounded by trees. Visitors welcome except Wed and Sat afternoon.

Tour operators
Outeniqua Adventure Tours, T044-8711470, www.outeniquatours.co.za. Minibus tours to sights along the Garden Route or Klein Karoo, can also organize cycling tours.

Oudtshoorn *p140, map p141*
Backpacker's Paradise, www.
backpackersparadise.hostel.com, see Where
to stay, page 163. Plenty of activities can
be organized. Mountain biking to the
Swartberg Pass leaves daily at 0830; you
are driven to the top and enjoy the 15-km
long ride downhill. On the way back to
Oudtshoorn, you can stop at the Cango
Caves and all the other attractions along the
R328. They can also organize bus transfers
to the Cango Caves and ostrich farms.

Garden Route National Park (Wilderness Section) *p145*
Tour operators
Eden Adventures, at the Ebb and Flow
camps, T044-877 0179, www.eden.co.za
(page 164). Adventure operator that
organizes activities from their office at main
reception in the Wilderness section of the
park. Offer canoeing, kloofing, mountain
biking, abseiling and walking tours. The
guides are very knowledgeable about the
environment and are happy to answer
endless questions. They also offer abseiling in
Plettenberg Bay's Robberg Nature Reserve.

Sedgefield and around *p146*
Paragliding
Windmaster Paragliding, T072-152 6093,
www.paraglidingsa.com. There are many
thermic sites around Sedgefield and
Wilderness, which are perfect for paragliding
with amazing beach and lake views. Tandem
flights cost R350 for 10 mins; R550/20 mins;
R750/40 mins, DVDs and photos extra, can
arrange pickups from accommodation
between George and Knysna.

Knysna and around
p146, maps p147 and p149
Boat trips
For details of the hugely popular ferry
excursion to the Knysna Heads and
Featherbed Nature Reserve, see page 150.

Springtide Charters, Knysna Quays, T082-
470 6022, www.springtide.co.za. 3-hr sunset
cruises on a 50-ft sailing boat including a
stop for a swim, departs Dec-Jan 1700, Feb-
Apr and Oct-Nov 1600, May-Sep 1500, R750
including sushi and seafood snacks and
champagne. Can also arrange 4-hr lunch
excursions for R890 and the boat is available
to charter overnight for honeymooners to
stay in the lovely master cabin.

Diving
The 460-ton German ship, the *Paquita* struck
the Knysna Heads in 1903. The anchors are
still visible and the iron plates on the wreck
act as an artificial reef and make an unusual
dive. **Pro-Dive**, in the Beacon Island Hotel
in Plettenberg Bay (see page 177), can also
organize dives at Knysna.

Golf
Knysna Golf Club, George Rex Drive,
T044-384 1150, www.knysnagolfclub.com.
18-hole, par-73 course with good views of
the The Heads.
Pezula, at the Pezula Resort Hotel & Spa
(see Where to stay, page 165), T044-302
5310, www.pezulagolf.co.za. Immaculate
18-hole, par 72 championship course
covering 254 ha of Knysna's cliff-tops with
sweeping ocean views, considered the most
scenic in South Africa.

Tour operators
Knysna Forest Tours, T044-382 6130,
www.knysnaforesttours.co.za. Half- and full-
day guided hiking, from R350 per person in
the forests around Knysna and local nature
reserves, on trails of varied difficulty 3-16 km
long, plus canoeing on the Goukamma River
which is great for birdwatching.
Mountain Biking Africa, T082-783 8392,
www.mountainbikingafrica.co.za. Guided
mountain-bike trails around the forests in
the area, easy rides, lots of downhills, bikes
and refreshments included.

Plettenberg Bay *p152, map p153*
Diving and snorkelling
There are not many tropical fish but due to an abundance of planktonic matter there is a colourful reef life, and there is a good chance of seeing parrotfish, ragged-tooth sharks and steenbras. For those who enjoy snorkelling, there is a popular spot in front of the Beacon Isle Hotel known as **Deep Blinders**; behind the reef is a sandy area where you might see stingrays.
Pro-Dive, in the **Beacon Island Hotel**, T044-533 1158, www.prodive.co.za. PADI dive centre, runs daily diving and snorkelling trips and rents out equipment.

Golf
Goose Valley Golf Estate, Goose Valley Rd, off the N2 east of Plett, T044-533 5082, www.goosevalley.net. A challenging par 72, 6000-m, 18-hole golf course on the banks of Keurbooms Lagoon designed by Gary Player with good ocean views.
Plettenberg Bay Country Club, Piesang Valley Rd, T044-533 2132, www.plettgolf.co.za. Lush 18-hole course in the middle of a private nature reserve, Piesang Valley. The Knysna loerie and woodpeckers are often seen on the course. Priority bookings for members Dec-Jan, visitors welcome the rest of the year.

Skydiving
SkyDive Plett, at Plettenberg Airport, off Robberg Rd, T082-905 7440, www.skydive plett.com. Tandem skydives with stunning coastal views, and if lucky, you may spot whales and dolphins from the air. After a briefing, flights over Plettenberg Bay take 20 mins, and the drop is from 10,000 ft with a 35-sec freefall; R1800, R400 for a DVD.

Surfing
Garden Route Surf Academy, T082-436 5410, www.gardenroutesurfacademy.com. 2-hr lessons from Plett's beaches, R450 including board and wetsuit.

Whale and dolphin watching
Several companies organize whale-watching trips in season (Jun-Nov), about 2 hrs and cost around R650, children (under 12) R350. Both the companies below are permitted to get within 50 m of the whales. Out of season there are cheaper (R400, children under 12, R200) trips to see seals, dolphins and marine birds.
Ocean Blue Adventures, T044-533 5083, www.oceanadventures.co.za. Can also organize sea-kayaking.
Ocean Safaris, T044-533 4963, www.ocean safaris.co.za. One of the vessels is called *Fat Boy*, the local nickname for a southern right whale.

East of Plettenberg Bay *p155*
Boat trip
Keurbooms River Ferry, the ferry departs from the jetty on the east side of the Keurbooms River Bridge on the N2, 7 km from Plett, T083-254 3551. 2½-hr boat trip plus walk and swim, 1100, 1400 and 1700, R140, children (3-12) R70, under 3 free, picnic baskets can be organized in advance (or bring your own) and there's a cash bar. This is a relaxing way to be introduced to the plants, sights and sounds of the Keurbooms Nature Reserve, and the ferry goes upstream through a spectacular gorge. At the furthest point there is an optional 30-min guided walk; make sure you are wearing sturdy footwear. The company also rents out self-drive motor boats for R220 for 2 hrs; they carry 4 and you get a lesson on how to use them.

Bungee jumping
Bloukrans Bungee Jump, see page 157 for details.

Garden Route National Park (Tsitikamma Section) *p157*
Untouched Adventures, office at the Storms River Mouth Rest Camp, T078-871 1952, www.untouchedadventures.com. Can organize a number of activities in

the park including snorkelling among the rocks in front of the restaurant, from R100, scuba diving including wetsuits, etc, from R450, and 2- to 3-hr combo trips for R400 of kayaking and kloofing which involves kayaking from the suspension bridge at Storms River Mouth as far as it's possible before alighting for a scramble over the rocks in the gorge.

Storms River Village *p160*
Tour operators
Blackwater Tubing, Tube 'n Axe Backpackers, see Where to stay, page 168, T042-281 1757, www.blackwatertubing.net. This starts with a briefing at Tube 'n Axe, before a short a drive through the Tsitsikamma forest, then a steep descent by rope ladder to the Storms River gorge followed by a float on a giant inner tube to the suspension bridge within the Garden Route National Park (Tsitsikamma Section). The 'blackwater' refers to a stretch of river where you float under 2 overhangs of rock so close together, it's like floating through a cave. The excursion takes around 4 hrs and costs R550 per person.

Tsitikamma Canopy Tour, the office is on Darnell St in the middle of the village, T042-281 1836, www.canopytour.co.za. This is the original canopy tour, although there are several others around South Africa. It is a fantastic way to see the forest from a different angle, which involves climbing up into the giant yellowwood trees and gliding between 10 different 30-m-high platforms on a steel rope, the longest of which is 100 m. Excellent for birdwatching, and the Knysna loerie may be spotted. Suitable for all ages from 7 years old. Departures are every 45 mins Sep-May 0700-1600, Jun-Aug 0800-1530, the excursion lasts around 3 hrs, costs R450 and includes light refreshments. DVDs and photos available.

⊖ Transport

Swellendam *p133*
It's 240 km to **Cape Town**, 225 km to **George**, 560 km to **Port Elizabeth**, 270 km to **Knysna**.

Bus
Buses stop at the Swellengrebal Hotel on Voortrek St. **Greyhound, Intercape** and **Translux** all stop here daily on the Cape Town–Durban route. **Cape Town** (2 hrs), **Port Elizabeth** (9 hrs), **Durban** (24 hrs).

Towards **Cape Town** the Baz Bus arrives in Swellendam 1800-1815, towards **Port Elizabeth**, 1200-1215, allowing plenty of time to see the sights in the afternoon, and drops off at Swellendam Backpackers.

For more information, see Getting around, page 132.

Mossel Bay *p137, map p137*
It's 394 km to **Cape Town**, 55 km to **George**, 116 km to **Knysna**, 80 km to **Oudtshoorn**, 206 km to **Tsitsikamma**, 375 km to **Port Elizabeth**. The N2 bypasses Mossel Bay, almost halfway between Cape Town and Port Elizabeth.

Bus
Buses stop at the Shell Truckport at Voorbaai on the N2, 7 km from Mossel Bay. Arrange a taxi with your hotel, but remember that some buses pass through in the early hours. **Greyhound, Intercape** and **Translux** all stop here daily on the Cape Town–Durban route. **Cape Town** (6 hrs), **Durban** (19 hrs) via **Port Elizabeth** and **East London** (13 hrs). **Intercape** and **Translux** also have a daily service between Mossel Bay and **Johannesburg** and **Tshwane** (**Pretoria**) (16 hrs).

Towards **Cape Town** the Baz Bus arrives in Mossel Bay 1530-1545, towards **Port Elizabeth**, 1345-1415. It drops and picks up at all the hostels.

For more information, see Getting around, page 132.

George and around *p138*
It's 420 km to **Cape Town**, 320 km to **Port Elizabeth**, 61 km to **Knysna**, 55 km to **Mossel Bay**, 93 km to **Plettenberg Bay**, 151 km to **Tsitsikamma**, 60 km to **Oudtshoorn**.

Air
George Airport is 10 km from the town centre, T044-876 9310, www.acsa.co.za. You'll need to pre-arrange a shuttle with your hotel or take a taxi, **Eden Taxis**, T044-587 8490. The main car rental companies have desks in the terminal building (see below).

SAA have daily flights between George and **Cape Town** (1 hr), and **Johannesburg** (1 hr 45 mins). Kulula and Mango have daily flights between George and **Johannesburg** (1 hr 45 mins).

Airline offices All air tickets can be booked online at www.computicket.com. Kulula, www.kulula.com. Mango, www.fly mango.com. **South African Airways** (SAA), www.flysaa.com. For further details, see page 7.

Bus
All buses stop at the old railway station at the east end of Market St. Greyhound, Intercape and Translux run daily to **Cape Town** (6 hrs) and **Durban** (18 hrs) via **Knysna** (1 hr), **East London** (9 hrs) and **Port Elizabeth** (4 hrs). Translux and Intercape also have a daily service between George and **Johannesburg** (14 hrs) and **Tshwane (Pretoria)** (16 hrs) via **Bloemfontein** (9 hrs).

Towards **Cape Town** the Baz Bus arrives in George 1430-1445; towards **Port Elizabeth**, 1515-1525; and drops off at Outeniqua Backpackers (page163).

For more information, see Getting around, page 132.

Car hire
The car hire companies all have desks at the airport. Avis, T044-876 9314, www.avis.co.za; Budget, T044-876 9204, www.budget.co.za; Hertz, T044-801 4700, www.hertz.co.za; Tempest, T044-876 9250, www.tempestcarhire.co.za.

Oudtshoorn *p140, map p137*
510 km to **Cape Town**, 55 km to **George**, 245 km to **Montagu**, 93 km to **Mossel Bay**.

Wilderness and around *p144*
Bus
Translux, Greyhound and Intercape stop at the Caltex garage in Wilderness, 20 mins before or after **George**. Towards **Cape Town** the Baz Bus arrives in Wilderness 1330-1400; towards **Port Elizabeth**, 1545-1600, and drops off at Fairy Knowe Backpackers (page 164). For more information, see page 132.

Sedgefield and around *p146*
Bus
Greyhound, Intercape and Translux services stop at the Shell garage, 15 mins before or after **Knysna** (see below). The Baz Bus stops in Sedgefield on request.

Knysna and around
p146, maps p147 and p149
It's 932 km to **Bloemfontein**, 500 km to **Cape Town**, 61 km to **George**, 1350 km to **Johannesburg**, 100 km to **Mossel Bay**, 120 km to **Oudtshoorn**, 32 km to **Plettenberg Bay**, 244 km to **Port Elizabeth**, 90 km to **Tsitsikamma**.

Bus
All buses stop outside the old railway station near the Knysna Quays. Greyhound, Intercape and Translux run daily to **Cape Town** (8 hrs), **Port Elizabeth** (3½ hrs), and **Durban** (18 hrs). Intercape and Translux also have a daily service between Knysna and **Tshwane (Pretoria)** and **Johannesburg** (14 hrs), via **Bloemfontein** (11 hrs).

Heading towards Cape Town the Baz Bus stops 1245-1300; towards Port Elizabeth 1630-1700. It drops and picks up at all the hostels.

For more information, see Getting around, page 132.

Plettenberg Bay *p152 map p153*

It's 525 km to **Cape Town**, 93 km to **George**, 32 km to **Knysna**, 171 km to **Mossel Bay**, 236 km to **Port Elizabeth**, 55 km to **Tsitsikamma**.

Bus

Mainline buses depart from the Shell Ultra City on the N2 out of town. Arrange a taxi with your hotel, but remember that some buses pass through in the early hours.

Greyhound, Intercape and Translux all stop here daily on the Cape Town–Durban route. **Cape Town** (8½ hrs) daily, **Durban** (17½ hrs) daily via **Port Elizabeth** (3½ hrs).

Intercape has a service between Plettenberg Bay and **Tshwane** (**Pretoria**) and **Johannesburg** (14 hrs) daily via **Oudtshoorn** (2 hrs), and **Bloemfontein** (11 hrs).

Baz Bus has a service towards Cape Town, expect to be picked up 1200-1215, and towards Port Elizabeth, 1745-1800.

For more information, see Getting around, page 132.

⊙ Directory

Swellendam *p133*
Medical services Swellendam Hospital, Drostdy St, T028-514 1140.

Mossel Bay *p137, map p137*
Medical services Bayview Private Hospital, Alhof St, T044-691 3718.

George and around *p138*
Medical services George Medi-Clinic, corner Gloucester and York streets, T044-803 2000, www.mediclinic.co.za.

Oudtshoorn *p140, map p141*
Medical services Klein Karoo MediClinic, 185 Church St, T044-272 0111, www.mediclinic.co.za.

Knysna and around
p146 maps p147 and 149
Medical services Knysna Private Hospital, Hunters Drive, T044-384 1083.

Plettenberg Bay *p152 map p153*
Medical services Plettenberg Bay Medi-Clinic, Muller St, T044-501 5100, www.mediclinic.co.za.

Contents

Footnotes

Index

Titles available in the Footprint *Focus* range

Latin America	UK RRP	US RRP
Bahia & Salvador	£7.99	$11.95
Brazilian Amazon	£7.99	$11.95
Brazilian Pantanal	£6.99	$9.95
Buenos Aires & Pampas	£7.99	$11.95
Cartagena & Caribbean Coast	£7.99	$11.95
Costa Rica	£8.99	$12.95
Cuzco, La Paz & Lake Titicaca	£8.99	$12.95
El Salvador	£5.99	$8.95
Guadalajara & Pacific Coast	£6.99	$9.95
Guatemala	£8.99	$12.95
Guyana, Guyane & Suriname	£5.99	$8.95
Havana	£6.99	$9.95
Honduras	£7.99	$11.95
Nicaragua	£7.99	$11.95
Northeast Argentina & Uruguay	£8.99	$12.95
Paraguay	£5.99	$8.95
Quito & Galápagos Islands	£7.99	$11.95
Recife & Northeast Brazil	£7.99	$11.95
Rio de Janeiro	£8.99	$12.95
São Paulo	£5.99	$8.95
Uruguay	£6.99	$9.95
Venezuela	£8.99	$12.95
Yucatán Peninsula	£6.99	$9.95

Asia	UK RRP	US RRP
Angkor Wat	£5.99	$8.95
Bali & Lombok	£8.99	$12.95
Chennai & Tamil Nadu	£8.99	$12.95
Chiang Mai & Northern Thailand	£7.99	$11.95
Goa	£6.99	$9.95
Gulf of Thailand	£8.99	$12.95
Hanoi & Northern Vietnam	£8.99	$12.95
Ho Chi Minh City & Mekong Delta	£7.99	$11.95
Java	£7.99	$11.95
Kerala	£7.99	$11.95
Kolkata & West Bengal	£5.99	$8.95
Mumbai & Gujarat	£8.99	$12.95

Africa & Middle East	UK RRP	US RRP
Beirut	£6.99	$9.95
Cairo & Nile Delta	£8.99	$12.95
Damascus	£5.99	$8.95
Durban & KwaZulu Natal	£8.99	$12.95
Fès & Northern Morocco	£8.99	$12.95
Jerusalem	£8.99	$12.95
Johannesburg & Kruger National Park	£7.99	$11.95
Kenya's Beaches	£8.99	$12.95
Kilimanjaro & Northern Tanzania	£8.99	$12.95
Luxor to Aswan	£8.99	$12.95
Nairobi & Rift Valley	£7.99	$11.95
Red Sea & Sinai	£7.99	$11.95
Zanzibar & Pemba	£7.99	$11.95

Europe	UK RRP	US RRP
Bilbao & Basque Region	£6.99	$9.95
Brittany West Coast	£7.99	$11.95
Cádiz & Costa de la Luz	£6.99	$9.95
Granada & Sierra Nevada	£6.99	$9.95
Languedoc: Carcassonne to Montpellier	£7.99	$11.95
Málaga	£5.99	$8.95
Marseille & Western Provence	£7.99	$11.95
Orkney & Shetland Islands	£5.99	$8.95
Santander & Picos de Europa	£7.99	$11.95
Sardinia: Alghero & the North	£7.99	$11.95
Sardinia: Cagliari & the South	£7.99	$11.95
Seville	£5.99	$8.95
Sicily: Palermo & the Northwest	£7.99	$11.95
Sicily: Catania & the Southeast	£7.99	$11.95
Siena & Southern Tuscany	£7.99	$11.95
Sorrento, Capri & Amalfi Coast	£6.99	$9.95
Skye & Outer Hebrides	£6.99	$9.95
Verona & Lake Garda	£7.99	$11.95

North America	UK RRP	US RRP
Vancouver & Rockies	£8.99	$12.95

Australasia	UK RRP	US RRP
Brisbane & Queensland	£8.99	$12.95
Perth	£7.99	$11.95

For the latest books, e-books and a wealth of travel information, visit us at:
www.footprinttravelguides.com.

footprinttravelguides.com

Join us on facebook for the latest travel news, product releases, offers and amazing competitions:
www.facebook.com/footprintbooks